"What would it mean for the work of diversity, equity, and inclusion not just to be effective and sustainable but also regenerative? Patrick Reyes offers a critical contribution to how we can enact the redemptive liberation we crave and desperately need as a broken society. Academic, theological, and human, Patrick persuasively narrates the cost of systemic inequality. With poignant reflection questions, *The Purpose Gap* offers a guide for dismembering the coloniality that is stealing our children's futures and marring their souls, and Reyes holds us each to account for doing more than just our best."

—Shaya Gregory Poku, Dean for Equity,
Social Justice, and Community Impact,
Wheaton College Massachusetts

"Patrick Reyes writes with fierce love and haunting hope, challenging readers to collectively build a new world, a world in which the margins become center: a world in which systems, structures, theologies, and practices are intentionally designed to prioritize the sacredness of all children, to close the purpose gap.

'I see your violence, and I will raise you hope and love,' he writes. Reyes offers a book that is both profoundly painful and stunningly beautiful, a song of survival and struggle, a journey through grief and violence, a story of abundant joy, life-giving love, and thick dreams.

This book is required reading for all who listen in the streets, who walk heavy with grief, for those who stand on tiptoe searching for hope and dance when liberation takes on flesh; it is a book for those who long for a world in which all children thrive, a world in which the communal knowledge and wisdom of field workers and grandmas, uncles caught in cages, and 'Brown, beautiful, bald' cousins redefine our institutions and organizations, systems and structures, pedagogies and theologies, our world-building and daily living."

—Janet Wolf, Director of Public Theology
and Nonviolent Organizing,
Children's Defense Fund

"For every academic library and educator's toolkit, *The Purpose Gap* articulates the liminality between what we have, what we could have, and what we wish we had as Brown image-bearers. Demystifying the hero's myth to reclaim the responsibility given to us by our ancestors, Reyes draws on the spiritual and intellectual well-springs of our *antepasados* with abolitionist teachings. Our children need to be free to imagine! As Brown folks all too familiar with trauma tourism, Reyes calls our institutions to name the gap between purpose and opportunity by drawing on cultural community wealth and our stories of our *sobrevivencia*. 'We are constellations, not single stars.' Reyes masterfully weaves storytelling, imagination, and critical consciousness to give us *The Purpose Gap*. Our communities deserve our cocreative narratives, our God-given gifts to not just survive but thrive in every facet of our lives, including the academy. *Adelante!*"

—Carolina Hinojosa-Cisneros,
author of *Becoming Coztōtōtl*

The Purpose Gap

The Purpose Gap

*Empowering Communities of Color
to Find Meaning and Thrive*

PATRICK B. REYES

WJK WESTMINSTER
JOHN KNOX PRESS
LOUISVILLE · KENTUCKY

© 2021 Patrick B. Reyes

First edition
Published by Westminster John Knox Press
Louisville, Kentucky

21 22 23 24 25 26 27 28 29 30—10 9 8 7 6 5 4 3 2 1

Book design by Sharon Adams
Cover design by designpointinc.com

Library of Congress Cataloging-in-Publication Data is on file
at the Library of Congress, Washington, D.C.

ISBN: 9780664266707 (pbk.)
ISBN: 9781646981915 (ebook)

Most Westminster John Knox Press books are available at special quantity discounts when purchased in bulk by corporations, organizations, and special-interest groups. For more information, please e-mail SpecialSales@wjkbooks.com.

For the teachers and elders who are closing the gap

Contents

Foreword

Americans will remember the year 2020 for many reasons. A global health pandemic. An economic downturn and shelter-in-place orders. A summer of racial justice uprisings. A critical national census. A presidential election with the highest turnout in history. The centennial of the women's suffrage movement. Essential to our self-understanding, yet missed by most in this litany, is a demographic benchmark reached in the middle of this year.

According to U.S. Census Bureau projections, it is the first year in the nation's history that most of the population under the age of eighteen is nonwhite. This Brown and Black majority disproportionately lives in poverty without access to health care yet more likely to have contact with the child welfare and juvenile justice systems. These children of color are more likely to be nurtured by an unemployed parent and wrestle with food insecurity, even though their mothers are essential workers exposed to the novel coronavirus to keep the rest of us safe.

More than 153 million citizens voted in the presidential race to impact the country's future. But the 74 million children huddled in their homes for virtual schooling changed the face of the nation. Their well-being and ability to thrive will be the best indicator of our health beyond the pandemic.

That's why I'm grateful to God for Dr. Patrick Reyes and grateful to Patrick for this book. In it, he shares glimpses of his personal story and professional sojourn as a marginalized member of America's rising majority. From afternoon walks with his daughter, Carmelita, to conversations to comfort his son, Asher, he models a life of purpose focused on the flourishing of future generations. The modeling doesn't end in personal testimony.

Patrick writes with the love of a parent and cross-sector curiosity of a child, inviting faith, leading philanthropic and social sector institutions into the journey of child-centered vocational discernment. He draws on design thinking, liberative theologies, poetry, and network analysis to offer approaches to closing the purpose gap. Then he summons each of us into the "daily grind" of closing that gap for children and communities through practical steps integrating this mission into our lives.

I get to work with Patrick through my volunteer work with the Forum for Theological Exploration. I have also enjoyed being his student as he in turn volunteers with the Children's Defense Fund's (CDF) Dale Andrews Freedom Seminary and Proctor Institute for Child Advocacy Ministry. In lifting models that show promise for closing the purpose gap, he is generous in his references to CDF's work. His own life invokes for me the "Beat the Odds" Program. This effort honors outstanding high school students who have excelled academically and served as leaders in their communities despite facing difficult circumstances. Their stories of resilience, courage, determination, and hope inform CDF's efforts to change the odds for all children.

Dr. Reyes is one who has beaten the odds for academic, professional, and vocational success for Black and Brown people in America. But he has done so to remind all of us that our collective purpose is to change those odds. Beating the odds requires us to build bridges (programs, networks, institutions) to overcome the wide chasm of well-being. Changing the odds by creating conditions, rearranging the context, and shifting the narratives that impact children and youth makes these bridges obsolete.

As a person of faith, I appreciate that Patrick is clear that the purpose gap is more than socioeconomic disparities. Healing, soul work, and spiritual wholeness are at stake. Our faith communities and nonprofit organizations keep sending children of color into the world to overcome obstacles by dressing them in Saul's armor: leadership books, Western theologies, youth development programs, vocational literature, and Christian education curricula crafted by and for the purveyors of the very systems they must resist. We haven't listened when they quote a young David in our hearing, "'I cannot walk with these; for I am not used to them'" (1 Sam. 17:39). In this work, Patrick, though thoroughly credentialed with facility in these systems, takes off Saul's clothes. He takes his staff in his hand, chooses five smooth stones from his Grandma Carmen, and draws near to the Philistine.

He shows us that in order to conquer the purpose gap we will need a new orientation to vocation, renewed networks, indigenous knowledge, and reframed theologies. We must practice different ways of knowing to advance the journeys of individual and institutional discernment. Our children's thriving calls us to strategies and tactics for pursuing purpose other than those formed from and within mainstreamed communities.

With this great call before us and stakes this high, we are blessed that God has graced us with a guide. I invite you to read with head and heart open to *mi primo* and teacher, Patrick, and the children of our community, whom his purpose serves.

Rev. Dr. Starsky Wilson
President and CEO
Children's Defense Fund

Acknowledgments

The purpose gap exists when people do not have access to the resources and opportunities to fulfill their purposes in life. We begin with acknowledgments because gratitude is good for the soul and because the many voices and spirits of our lives form and shape our purpose. They are the reason the purpose gap closes for some and is widened for others. In many ways, every thank-you expresses a relationship that turned the creative act of love and appreciation into the book you now read. In truth, acknowledgment is where the work of closing the purpose gap begins.

Family

I want to first apologize to my family. I have missed family reunions and funerals in pursuit of what I thought my purpose was. When my Uncle Rene passed away, I was working as an assistant dean and faculty member at an institution that would not survive regardless of my or any of my colleagues' and friends' efforts to keep it open. My uncle and I shared a special relationship. When I lived with my grandparents, he would come over after all my other aunts, uncles, and cousins had left. He wasted no time taking a turn massaging the feet of my grandpa, who was suffering and dying from diabetes. These evenings taking turns trying to bring life and circulation back into my grandpa's feet formed much of my thinking in this book. I wanted to honor Uncle Rene's life by acting out his sense of love and care for people, but at the time of his passing, all my energy was being poured into a dying institution. Unlike my family, which loved unconditionally, the institution was not designed to love or care for people of color, for a Chicano like me. I should have been with family. I should have been at the funeral. I should have said yes to offering words and love to my family.

The same goes for my cousin Bro. His death hit me harder than any other I experienced in my life. The thought of his "What's going on, little Pat? You still reading books?" and that cheesy grin, with his classic Chicano bald head and mustache, fills my heart with happiness. I am grateful for those angels I was able to spend many evenings with—Grandma Carmen, whose rosary I carry with me always, and Grandpa Julio, and my Great Aunt Carrie and Uncle Sal—whose loving spirits fill every page of this book.

There is a pain that comes from losing one's family, from losing the connection to the land and the people. I want nothing more than to return to their love, to close the gap between my Uncle Rene, my cousin, my grandparents, their siblings, and the generations that have gone before. I wish nothing more than to see the butterflies and hummingbirds of the plains and deserts of California. To pursue my purpose, life has taken me a long way from home, and I am homesick. It is, I know, an odd place to start acknowledgments. Everyday life as well as the connection to the above and beyond are essential if we are to thrive and close the purpose gap. I am grateful for the wisdom and love my family gave me. Without their love, I would not be here. They were the people who taught me about the divine, about the above and beyond, who showed me how to practice love in all its abundance. I am grateful for my father, who closed the purpose gap for me. He made and makes all things possible. For Jennie "Grandma" Reyes, your love and reading with our kids expands their imagination. Thank you to my in-laws, Barry and Elizabeth, for their love and support. To my brothers and sister, Kevin, Jason, Kane, and Katya: you all are the most inspiring humans I know. You all have overcome incredible obstacles and are inspiring new generations to find their best selves.

As you will read, my family are my spiritual teachers, who close the purpose gap even for me today. My children, Asher and Carmelita, fill my life. They connect to the spiritual plane in ways to which I aspire. Asher's practices of compassion and presence to the spirits in this world have reminded me to slow down and pay attention, to have a conversation with my ancestors, and to tell their stories. Carmelita is the namesake of at least five generations, carrying forward their spirit and fire of survival. Her attention to the natural world, to experiencing life in its fullest, inspires our whole house. The divine exists in the flowers, the roses, the desert plants on our walks, and the little wonders like the hummingbirds and butterflies that celebrate her presence and life. I am grateful to Carmelita for these reminders. To my wife and their mother, Carrie: you are the conversation partner I looked for my whole life. You bring meaning to the words I write, for without you I would have no purpose. You saved my life. My family connects me to my purpose: to create the conditions for the next generation to thrive. I do everything for all of you.

Those Who Inspire

My life is full of inspiring people who are closing the purpose gap for their communities. Part of my work is awarding grants and fellowships. At no point did I think that I would be able to influence the way philanthropy and foundation dollars go to provide a balm for those communities wounded by the legacies and violence of colonization and marginalization. To create and administer the resources that help close the purpose gap and to help others find purpose with my team is truly a gift. Beyond the team's resource design and delivery, they are also some of the most inspirational people I have ever met. As a field, philanthropy does not look like or bring the perspective of women or people of color. We are but single-digit percentages within this work. My thanks to Elsie Barnhart, whose work and family have made all things possible at the Forum for Theological Exploration, and whose guidance grounds our work. Like the people holding the Macy's Thanksgiving Day Parade balloons to keep them from crashing into buildings, she has kept our work front and center, never forgetting those for whom we do it. I also thank Heather Wallace for the wisdom shared through the act of tamale making and the many cultures, practices, and traditions that inform our work. We are a maize-based people. This team makes a difference in the work we do and, on behalf of future generations, reimagines those for whom we do this work. If we can live fully into our vocations, there is no reason that we cannot close the purpose gap.

Spiritual guides are among those with whom I have the privilege of working daily. I first began many of the conversations you now read in this book with the president of the Interdenominational Theological Center, Matthew Wesley Williams. Teasing out the edges of how to work on behalf of our people, you guide by beginning with the love of the whole human and by committing to the success and imagination of the people with whom we work. You inspire many of the words in these pages. I love you. I am grateful for you, your wisdom, and your life. You are the only person I know who can just look at the bibliography and know what the argument is and where it is going.

Kimberly Daniel coaches and guides me, providing strong insight about how to reexamine the questions I ask and the answers I seek.

Besides being an incredible communications specialist, you are my coach of coaches, friend of friends, and questioner of questioners. To our president, Stephen Lewis, the ultimate dreamer, imagineer, and innovator: you are always a few hundred years ahead of the field. You lead while drawing on a few hundred years of ancestral wisdom, so that we may design a future where all will thrive. The three of you inspire and push me to work a little harder, to go a little deeper, and not to fear those spaces that the majority culture has cast aside. You have challenged me to find freedom in the world and in myself. Thank you.

I encourage every reader to find experienced designers and leaders who inspire you and stick with them. To my prima Christina Repoley, with whom I share a wall in our office, I am grateful for the leadership and wisdom you have brought to my life and, more important, for your friendship. It is an honor to learn to lead with you in times of complexity and challenge. I am grateful for Rev. Darlene Hutto. Your gift of presence and your ability to call on the divine is unparalleled. I aspire to your creativity. I admire your ability to gather and hold a community and am grateful you have included me in your circle. To the rest of the FTE team—Melissa Scott, Allison Arsenault, Angela Giles, Diva Morgan Hicks, Chris Tina Mason, Traci Wright, Paul Bois, and Ted Boone— there is no doubt that the purpose gap would be wider without your work and care for the communities we serve. To Lakisha Lockhart and Jodi Porter, who stitch our Campus Ministries and High School Youth initiatives together, thank you. To Lakisha, who has spent all those years serving on boards and trying to make changes in the academy, let me say that we have many more ahead of us to get these rooms to dance and play differently! To our senior fellow, Dori Baker, I am grateful for your continued vocation to support the next generation of Christian leaders. Without the support of the program officers at the Lilly Endowment— Chris Coble, Jessicah Duckworth, Chanon Ross, Brian Williams, and the late John Wimmer—this work would not be possible. Thank you for having the imagination and gifts to create the conditions for future generations of Christian leaders to thrive. Thank you for your support for our work and the love you pour into your work.

In my first year at FTE, I started making lists of the many people who have inspired me alongside whom it has been my pleasure to work. For the many doctoral fellows who have come through FTE's programs, you represent the dreams of Charles Shelby Rooks and Benjamin Elijah Mays, who knew in 1968 that the work of scholars of color could save our society and, for some of us, write our communities back into the record, combatting erasure and violence. The fellowship was one way they sought to close the purpose gap. No more inspiring group of people is to be found than the faculty that I have had the privilege to work with over the years. If FTE had an educational institution, I am convinced that no one would go anywhere else. To Andrea Smith, Shanell Smith, Stephen Ray, Helen Kim, Jonathan Calvillo, Derek Hicks, Pamela Lightsey, Keri Day, Teresa Delgado, Karen Crozier, Shively Smith, Adam Bond, and Elías Ortega-Aponte, my thanks to you all for supporting fellows. Boyung Lee, your leadership in affecting change in institutions in transition and membership organizations with integrity is inspiring.

I am particularly grateful for Kimberly Russaw for making sure every fellow feels connected to the broader FTE family and guided by a good mentor. I need to thank Brian Bantum for keeping the faculty together and for inspiring us all with the words you place on paper. Chris Hong has been guiding my work since our doctoral program. You are my educator of educators, and I look up to you and your work. For Anne Joh, the most courageous scholar I know, not just for leading the next generation of teachers and writers but for being authentically human with every person you come across, I am grateful. You have literally and figuratively journeyed not just with FTE, but with all the organizations supporting decolonized and freedom work. Thank you. I need to share a special gratitude for Marsha Foster Boyd for coaching and leading me on my journey at FTE. Yohana Junker might be the most creative and talented scholar and artist I know. There is no doubt you are redefining the practice of education. I am grateful for the way you teach us to pay attention to how trauma and stress show up in our bodies and to how we people of color in these systems need to heal. Thank you for leading that healing work.

I am especially grateful for the writing check-in crew from the last couple of years. A special thanks to AnneMarie Mingo, Ekaputra Tupamahu, Lucila Crena, Angela Sims, Tamisha Tyler, Stanley Tyrone Talbert, Malene Minor Johnson, Lis Valle, Lydia Hernández, Catherine Williams, Vanessa Lovelace, Jessica Chapman, Pamela Lightsey, Angie Allen, Whitney Bond, Seth Gaiters, Lenora Knowles, Sheng Ping Guo, Prisca Dorcas Mojica Rodríguez, Tiffany Trent, Leah Nakon, and the many folks who joined the call from time to time.

Before anyone took a chance on me in the academy, Cristian De La Rosa and Joanne Rodriguez made space for me. I am grateful for you both and for the Hispanic Theological Initiative crew, Angela Schoepf, and Suzette Aloyo, for all that you do to support the next generation of Latinx, Latin American, and Chicano/Xicanx scholars. I am grateful for those mentors like Carmen Nanko-Fernandez, who continue to write and support even the most loco work from my generation. You are also the only one in our entire field whom my dad will listen to or read, and I am grateful for your family, like Alyssa, who is changing the world. We cannot survive the storms without family. I am grateful for those scholars who pulled me aside in San Francisco to say there was something from my community that mattered: Neomi DeAnda, Jeremy Cruz, Néstor Medina, Orlando Espín, and Jaqueline Hidalgo. Accepting a paper on a panel is one thing, but when you look after the next generation like each of you have and do, it makes a difference.

I am grateful for leaders like Edwin Aponte of the Louisville Institute, who paved the way for our vocation in an industry; for the first reader of my research, Martha Barceñas-Mooridian, who was also present for major milestones in my family's life; and for my advisor of advisors and mentor of mentors, Sheryl Kujawa Holbrook. Sheryl took a chance on me as a doctoral student and has modeled a powerful example of how to be in the world. I aspire not simply to be like you but to be you! Frank Rogers, thank you for showing me how to calm the madness in myself and others, for pointing me to listen to the various voices and parts that have kept me alive, and for "guiding my feet," reminding me that every word is written on the run. Finally, to my mentor and decolonial scholar of choice, Santiago Slabodsky: though I will never quite get to the radical decolonial hopes of your work, I am grateful that you continue to push the edge of that work and pull me toward a more liberative future!

Freedom Fighters

I am grateful to the late Dale Andrews and his family. You came into my life when I was just a seminary student, pissed off about the distance from both my community and the curriculum. You heard me complaining in the hallways and took me across the river to join a picket line, affirming where I felt called and needed to be. Your booming voice saying, "The people united will never be defeated," cast a long shadow in which I could take shade from the heat of the academy, reminding me that the distance between freedom fighter and scholar can be but the distance between a person's heart and their soul. I am grateful for the single most inspiring and collaborative group of scholar activists I know, the Dale Andrews Freedom Seminary at the Samuel Dewitt Proctor Institute for Child Advocacy Ministry. This group continues to bless me with love and support, as we collectively build for a brighter future for our children.

To borrow from Ched Meyers and Elaine Enns, the freedom seminary is where the seminary meets the sanctuary, soil, and streets. The faculty members of this collaborative are committed to the next generation in ways no other group of people I work with are. My deepest gratitude to Reginald Blount and Virginia Lee for continuing to hold us all together. A special gratitude to Charlene Sinclair for consistently facilitating and focusing faculty, which is never easy. To Victor Anderson, whose scholarship and work have shaped the seminary track, thank you.

I am grateful for the team of inspiration, Janet Wolf and Shannon Daley Harris. I remember that when I first met Janet I had never been to Nashville before. She gave me the single-best tour of the town and the people who are changing the landscape. She introduced me to the ever-powerful and inspirational Rahim Buford, whom I had met in a virtual class. You have introduced my family to the most inspirational artists and activists I have ever known. Shannon, you courageously march toward freedom with the mission of the Proctor family written in your bones, and you live the complexities of life: I have learned so much under your guidance and leadership. I am grateful for both of you—for your love and personal commitment to seeing the Alex Haley Farm thrive and your constant support of me and my work, even when I believe there is no way I can put one foot in front of the other. Thanks also to the inspirational leadership of Starsky Wilson and Greg Ellison. You animate every room and lead even when the spotlight is not on you. If you want to find good humans, who have integrity and love in every fiber of their being, look no further.

I am grateful to my Duke Leadership colleagues. I am grateful for the leadership of Dave Odom and Gretchen Ziegenhals, who bring together some truly inspiring people, including re-connecting me to my former boss and theological executive genius, Michael Delashmutt, the only leader I have ever seen talk about thriving institutions using math. Guess what, current and future executives of institutions? Math has everything to do with creating the conditions for future generations to thrive. I remain grateful for the friends from that cohort who are great authors, scholars, and leaders and now friends and colleagues. For those who lead courageously in their respective institutions, like Eric Barreto, Aaron Kuecker, Jennifer Ayres (who once moderated a panel and had to watch out for the safety of participants when I passed around a foot-long field knife), Nannette Banks, Hardy Kim, Mihee Kim-Kort, Andrew Kort, Christian Peele, Kermit Moss, Robert Saler, Fernando Rodriguez, Trey Wince, Kat Banakis, Jill Duffield, Dustin Benac, Emily Hull McGee, Bernadette Hickman-Maynard, Amanda Drury, Sarah Schreiber, and

Nathan Stucky. Let me express a special gratitude for Mindy McGarrah Sharp, my co–justice seeker here in Decatur, for the many coffees and strategy sessions to change stubborn systems. I am likewise especially grateful to Erin Weber-Johnson, who did not just support me but supported my community and my closest friends.

Artists and Spirit Seekers

We all know the feeling when we see a performance or a visual art piece or hear something that strikes a nerve or breaks open our hearts. We say, "That was powerful," because those who work on that artistic plane have the power to connect to the divine and the ancestors in ways to which many of us aspire. I was privileged to serve on the board of ARC (Arts/ Religion/Culture) and am grateful for the many people I met through that endeavor, including Callid Keefe-Perry, who has been one of my longest-standing friends on this side of the adult life. You are *familia*. My thanks to Yara González Justiniano, who is both scholar and children's author. Ashley Theuring continues to teach me about the connection between trauma and faith. I would not have survived 2020 without your work. For Erling Hope, I am grateful for your attention to lifting beauty as central to the expression of the divine. I wish I had one ounce of your talent. Kate Common, thank you for designing futures we all wish to live into. I am especially grateful for Oluwatomisin Oredein, whom I first met as a fellow. Poetry best expresses the ideas we hold most dear in the academy. Your writing breathes life into my spirit. And anyone who has not read the work of Carolina Hinojosa-Cisneros, you should. Her poetry has filled our home and the spirits of my children. Thanks to *As the Crow Flies Design* group and its leader Kate Morales, who supplies the most incredible visual facilitation, embodied art, and collective organizing for a more beautiful future. Your work lines my walls. Thanks also to the graffiti artists back home, before I knew what art was or is, who spray-painted the holy on empty concrete canvases across my hometown.

Thanks to the everyday friends who orchestrate change in our neighborhoods. I am also grateful for the friends I now have met in Atlanta, who, through the art of facilitating and teaching our tradition, showed me that we can change hearts and minds. Thank you, Rabbis Lydia Medwin and David Spinrad. I am also grateful for those facilitators and parents who continue to write every day to challenge our way of thinking. To Gilly Segal and Erica Ramirez for the most inspiring writing I have picked up in some time in remarkably different genres. I am especially grateful for my *primas* and *primos* back home who are shaping the spaces that formed me, such as bel Reyes at Innovation Bridge in Sacramento, Juan Gomez at MILPA Collective in Salinas, and my friend Raul Rico, who is changing the space that formed us both. You are the most inspiring humans I know! To all those friends who have picked me up off the floor and inspired me in this world, I am grateful. Thank you to friends like Altagracia Perez Bullard, Lemec Thomas, Alex Froom, Blake Huggins, and Stephanie Edwards. I do not pick up the phone often enough to talk to each of you. For the leadership team at Clairemont Elementary School, my local church and faith leaders, and my neighbors, thank you.

Editors

I am eternally grateful for my editors, Robert Ratcliff and Frances Ellen Purifoy, who worked their editorial magic on several versions of this manuscript. To the Westminster John Knox Press team, I am so grateful for the patience with the language and tone and the edits and rewrites. I am even more grateful for the ideas, not just mine, that you bring into the world that are so desperately needed right now. I also want to thank you for being good humans and carrying some of the most generative spirits into the world. It is what makes a difference in the world.

I am overwhelmed with the love and support of my community. There are so many more people I could thank. I did not leave you out intentionally. I love you. You have made a difference in my life and for my children. I would not have a purpose outside of you, outside of community. I am grateful for every one of you. Thank you for saving and calling me to life.

Introduction

The phone rang. "Your cousin passed away." It hit like a ton of bricks. The last time I talked to him was a few years back. He was smiling, dancing, being silly as I had always remembered him.

As I sat with my grief and pain, I struggled with how my cousin would be remembered. Like many in this country, he experienced incarceration for use of controlled substances. Dying from addiction, diabetes, and lack of necessary love and support, he left this planet entirely too early.

What a contrast to the life I was living and what I stood for as a faith leader. When I got the news, I was preparing to talk to a group of college students about how to create conditions for thriving while my family back home was preparing a funeral. My cousin's death, more than any other loss, challenged my notion of what it means to thrive. It brought into focus the fact that, for so many people, the move from surviving to thriving is not just some inward journey, exploration of purpose, or "aha" moment. When the conditions are so dire, life-threatening, and oppressive, thriving may feel like nothing more than trite expressions, like "Living the American dream," "You can be whatever you want to be if you work hard," or "Follow your dreams." These sayings only apply to those with privilege who do not have to face the threat of extinction.

I wrote about my relationship to this cousin in my first book. When I moved into my grandma's house, she made it clear that I was sleeping in his bed, a bed dedicated to any person in the family who needed it. I still remember Grandma Carmen saying, "We are glad you are here, *mijo*, but that bed and room are not just yours."

My grandparents surrounded me with love and care, yet I was sleeping in my cousin's bed. My cousin, who left behind four siblings, dozens of cousins, and four children, was no longer here. I couldn't help but feel it was all because I took his bed. But, of course, there was so much more to our stories than a simple piece of furniture. As I started to track his life and my own, it became clear why he was now in the above and beyond while I was traveling across the country working and speaking about creating conditions for life.

Whenever violence overwhelmed and consumed my life, my grandma and a whole host of witnesses cast a different narrative for me. That list of supporters is long, including family members, teachers, pastors, friends, *primos/as*, homies, teammates, classmates, and so on. People told me throughout my life they saw something in me that I did not see in myself.

My cousin and I were similar in many ways. We both had the classic Reyes Chicano look: bald, Brown, and beautiful. Yet, unlike in my life, there were very few conditions present for him to thrive. The narrative around the less-than-positive aspects of his life were not the results of a bad break, a few bad choices, or a couple of rough friends, the sort of things people reminded me of when I messed up. Society assigned painful moments as part of his narrative as if he chose that life. Our community would say there was something wrong with him—that his character was the problem. He was a "bad kid." No one wanted to take care of him—not just in young adulthood but also when he was a child. How do you thrive when the world sees you as a problem? How can you find purpose when the world has written you off?

Here, however, is the painful truth: None of these narratives accounted for the conditions, the context, the love, or the lack thereof that surrounded my cousin.

He suffered a major injury when he was younger. A car accident sent him flying through the middle seat, and the rearview-mirror stem pierced his head. He had to have part of his brain removed, spent over a year in the hospital, and needed services and care for the rest of his life. He was not a bad child. He was a Brown child who suffered a traumatic brain injury and waited for the rest of us to pick him up, to support his life, and to say, "We see something in you that you do not see in yourself." We had a responsibility to do this because the accident made it so that he was not able to dream a different narrative for himself. He was a Chicano young man living in America. The world casts us as "Gangster no. 1" instead of seeing our God-given potential. The police follow us. The education system expels us. Job opportunities are exceedingly rare, especially for those who must check the box for those who were formerly caged on an application form. People design these oppressive conditions. They represent a history of trauma and neglect against my Xicanx, Chicana/o, Indigenous, and broader Latinx community.[1]

What you are going to find in this book are stories, studies, and dreams about care for the conditions of our lives, of our communities, and of our bodies. For one to thrive, understanding the conditions that already surround us (and others) is the first step. For so many of us, purpose is defined, stolen, or withheld before we even enter the world. The question now is "How do we understand and influence these conditions?"

This book attempts to do this work; it bends toward the positive. Written into my bones and my flesh are the markers of trauma and abuse that my people have suffered. These scars live alongside the tattoos outlining the traditions, practices, and wisdom of how to survive and thrive in this world. I have lived and worked my entire life in marginalized and oppressed communities and know that too often books and studies addressing conditions in these communities can be overwhelmingly revolutionary or post-apocalyptic (understandable given the contexts in which the oppressed find themselves). This book acknowledges that violent and oppressive conditions exist while making the point that for those just trying to survive, moving toward thriving is not beyond your reach. Where the headlines are filled only with ill tidings, I try to provide some good news.

"What about those who are taken too young?" you might ask. "What about those locked in cages? Children separated from their families at the border? What about the stolen lives of the young people I mourn? What was their purpose in life? To die?"

I have worked with hundreds of leaders who are searching for meaning and purpose in the face of such questions. They include young adults discerning a call to ministry, scholars of color, higher-education executives, nonprofit leaders, private industry boards and executive teams, survivors of abuse and trauma, those whose lives were stolen as they lived in cages, former gang members, and essential workers, such as fieldworkers who make sure you can eat. I serve on boards of local nonprofits and universities and serve my community in my children's school system. I have facilitated hundreds of hours with leaders from various walks of life as they seek answers to questions like "What is the meaning and purpose of life?" For those on the "underside of history," for those forgotten or, worse yet, considered a problem before they even got a shot, these questions weigh on the soul. They point to something missing—a gap—in how we as scholars discuss meaning and purpose. We steal lives of meaning and purpose from young people when we deny them access to resources, people, networks, and even the imagination. The *purpose gap* is about more than just economics or wealth. It is more than the housing gap or the education gap. It is the compounding effect of all these gaps on the next generation.

Before young people can find a firm grounding in their purpose, we first need to close the gap. Like the education, housing, opportunity, and wealth gaps, the purpose gap exists where people cannot achieve what they were born to do. It exists when people are not able to fulfill their calling, resulting in lives of meaning and purpose stolen from future generations. The purpose gap exists because of the war on our children's future.

The literature on vocation, meaning, and purpose designs a narrative for a specific person: white, middle socioeconomic level, and professional class. I ask you, What about Brown, working-class people? To put a finer point on it, I wonder about all the people—mostly Black and Brown—left out, left behind, and left for dead. Did God not call us as well? I ask about all those children locked in cages at the border in 2017–2018. I wonder about those young people who took to the streets in 2020, asking along with author Kimberly Jones, "How can we win when we are up against the legacies of slavery? What about the income and wealth gap generated from the enslavement, theft, and violence against Black and Brown lives? How can children of color of this generation win?"[2]

I wonder what resources we must design to direct our own lives? I write this as the COVID-19 pandemic rages in the United States and around the world. The question of purpose confronts us as we decide whose labor is essential among workers whose lives are considered unimportant. Like during an earthquake, I have witnessed with the rest of the world what happens when the tectonic plates of our society, burdened by unsustainable pressure, finally slip and grind against one another, shaking the very foundations of our world.

As a Chicano, Christian author, writer, thinker, and human who is raising two wonderful children with my Jewish wife, I write, in many ways, from just outside the purpose gap. Tragedy and violence, however, drove the writing of this book. First, we mourned the deaths of the victims of the Tree of Life Synagogue shooting in Pittsburgh on October 27, 2018. We remember that day when an anti-Semitic shooter murdered eleven innocent people. Then we witnessed the July 28, 2019, shootings at the Gilroy Garlic Festival just miles from my dad's home. We have tried ever since to make sense of the fact that family and friends who had survived the violence in our streets could not escape the senseless violence of hate. Stephen Romero (age six), Keyla Salazar (thirteen), and Trevor Deon Irby (twenty-five) had full lives ahead of them that were cut short by a single human with hate in his heart for them and all the members of *mi familia*. We lost three innocent lives that day. In less than a week, the violence returned in an El Paso Walmart on August 3, 2019. Twenty-three people were murdered in cold blood, and another twenty-three were injured. It was one of the deadliest hate crimes against the Latino/a community in modern history. Those lost were remembered on both sides of the border, as Ciudad Juarez and El Paso held services to mourn the loss of life. As the country mourned this explicit attack on Brown life, the very next day a shooter killed nine people in Dayton, Ohio. Each attack was by white men upon people of color. Like many others I responded to these incidents by calling those who were organizing vigils, checking in on family, and holding conversations with my children about the violence against our community.

I watched on the news as political extremism took hold, leading to the abandonment of my *primos/as* on Puerto Rico after Hurricane Maria and other natural disasters. I watched with the rest of the world as our government separated families at the border and placed children in cages. To date children continue to die behind bars at the U.S. southern border, children whose families came seeking a better life. Their stories have been cut short, never to be told outside fleeting mentions in local news reports.[3] I completed this book while watching protests and violence erupt following the deaths of Breonna Taylor in her own home,[4] the modern-day lynching of Ahmaud Arbery while jogging,[5] and the death of George Floyd[6] as a police officer crushed his neck. I wrote the final words as Bay Area police killed Sean Monterossa, who was on his knees when police opened fire. I was mourning the death of eighteen-year-old Andres Guardado,[7] who was working security when police gunned him down. I turned in my final manuscript just a week after twenty-seven-year-old Rayshard Brooks[8] was killed by Atlanta police in the drive-thru of a Wendy's. Brooks's eight-year-old daughter had her dress on and was waiting for her dad to come pick her up to go skating, and that Wendy's burned to the ground as the city erupted in a collective cry for justice. As I wrapped up my work on the manuscript, I mourned with the nation the loss of Carlos Ingram Lopez, who died while in police custody, crying out for water and his *abuela*.[9] The report of his death was released a month later—a reminder that they can take our lives in a moment, yet it takes much longer to acknowledge the violence against our people. All these tragic deaths, all this violence, is now. It is not some distant past. It is right now.

The systems that govern and dictate our lives do not include our thriving. This truth extends to the literature on vocation, meaning, and purpose. In their present state, these writings do not apply to those who cannot see or imagine tomorrow. Those of us who know that these stories of violence and death could have easily been our own stories must ask what it will take to imagine a better future. We tell our children that they can be anything they want to be. But we don't tell them the world will never grant them the time, space, or grace to live lives of meaning and purpose.[10] Do utterances like "Find your life's meaning" or "Hear the call of God" not apply to our essential workers who toil in the fields?

What Is the Purpose Gap?

I can see the purpose gap plainly. This book is an attempt to articulate what that gap is, why it exists, and how to find freedom in spite of it. I hope to provide just a few guideposts for people to see what thriving looks like when the purpose gap has been closed. My argument is not complicated, so I want to start with a brief illustration to show what I mean by the term "purpose gap."

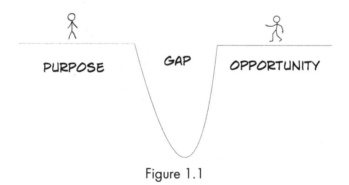

Figure 1.1

For those on the side of the gap who have discerned their purpose, the opportunities to turn that purpose into a sustainable life are not always clear. The road is unpaved, and the gap is wide. Their elders are on the same side of the gap with them, so there is no way to the other side except the extraction of the best and brightest. For example, a scholarship for a young person of color to attend an elite university is an exception, not the rule. It extracts a single individual from the community, leaving the rest of their peers behind. This gap is so unsurmountable that it takes extraordinary circumstances to get the person to realize their purpose through this sort of opportunity.

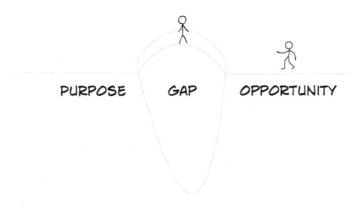

PURPOSE   GAP   OPPORTUNITY

Figure 1.2

A few of us have discerned our purpose *and* have received access to a bridge built typically by someone from our community who has already found a way to the other side. To be clear, not everyone in the community has access to the bridge. The bridge supplies access to resources and opportunities but does not guarantee them. Gatekeepers guard both sides of the bridge. Those in the community who are afraid of people realizing their purpose strive to keep the gate closed. Some on that side of the bridge will use words like *traitor* (in my case, *pocho*) to those who seek to cross. These gatekeepers aim to say that to rise above one's station, one's assigned place in society, is a violation to the community. However, there are also gatekeepers who help push the gates open. These champions will not only walk you across the bridge but celebrate your arrival on the other side. Like Moses standing on Mount Nebo, they believe in you and your purpose. For me, this was my grandma. She was with me every step of my vocational journey, every step of my education. I remember her smile when, as a first-generation graduate student, representing the less than 1 percent of Latinos/as to get a graduate degree in any field, I told her on Sunday that I was beginning my PhD studies the following week. She died a few days later during my orientation. As written in Deuteronomy 34:4–5: "The Lord said to him, 'This is the land of which I swore to Abraham, to Isaac, and to Jacob, saying, "I will give it to your descendants"; I have let you see it with your eyes, but you shall not cross over there.' Then Moses, the servant of the Lord, died there in the land of Moab, at the Lord's command." My grandma did not have access to the same opportunities I did. She was a brilliant woman, as you will come to see in this book. It is not just about how she overcame and sacrificed so that future generations might thrive. It honors her gifts, wisdom, and knowledge as equal to anything I received in my education, and it acknowledges the creation of opportunities to cross the bridge and honors those whose knowledge and wisdom never required leaving our community.

Once you cross the bridge, there is no guarantee of success. Guarding the other end of the bridge are the trolls from the land of opportunity. These are the inheritors of wealth who were born on this side. They "belong" on this side of the purpose gap and see anyone entering their land as a threat. We see this play out in xenophobic conversations in industries that imagine they are meritocracies, like education. Some of these trolls may have experienced obstacles to achieving their position, but the question was never *if* they would succeed but simply *when*. They had the choice to stay in this space or to go. Once someone has crossed the bridge, they are in a land that is completely foreign with no real help or guidance. This is best evidenced in first-generation college students of color who are navigating systems of education not designed for us and must mirror dominant cultural definitions of success.

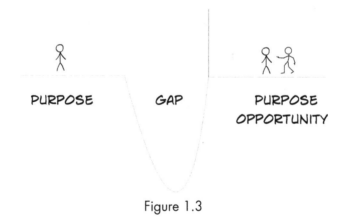

Figure 1.3

In Figure 1.3, we see the land of opportunity. Everything here works to the advantage of those individuals born on this side of the gap. The privileged descendants of power and privilege inherit a world built and designed for them. The conditions are perfect for them to thrive. Here the purpose gap is all in the mind. For those born into privilege and opportunity, the only obstacles are internal. The gap exists to keep those resources and opportunities for themselves and future generations. Their barriers blind them to the lives of purpose of those on the other side of the gap. A wall separates and maintains their power and dominance.

This is not to downplay the internal purpose gap, which is real. People face internal gaps in each of these illustrations. In Figure 1.1 the internal gap might be internalized racism and oppression, where people have come to believe the lie that they deserve the gap that exists between themselves and their purpose. Internalized oppression suggests that there is always some deficiency to overcome: "If only I had another degree, better skills, technical ability, or the like, I would deserve to fulfill my purpose." In Figure 1.2, it may be imposter syndrome in the land of opportunity. Because they do not recognize their surroundings, have no guides, and are figuring out how to navigate new opportunities on their own, the gap widens to make accomplishing their goals difficult to impossible. The internal gap could be navigating best options and opportunities and seeking credentials. The gap here is the challenge between having enough resources to pursue vocational pathways. If I have discerned that my purpose is to heal, do I have the test scores and money to go to med school? The internal gap has to do with *having enough* and not *being "good" enough*. People in this image find the support and encouragement they need to pursue their purpose.

In Figure 1.3, the internal resistance manifests itself in words like *happiness, joy,* and *satisfaction*. The question is not whether one will be comfortable; it is whether a sense of fulfillment will accompany that comfort. And for those in this picture, even if they personally do not have the resources, the barriers to gaining them are minimal. If you are guaranteed an education and the connections that will lead to a well-paying career, the purpose gap you face is whether you will live up to your own expectations and those of your family and friends. Saint Francis is a notable example of someone who willingly set aside his privilege, turning his back on his father's money while choosing to serve the poor by becoming one of them.

I authored this book for people in the first two scenarios: for those whose purpose gap is so insurmountable that a book such as this might find itself in a public library where they can pick it up and see a little hope. As a regular patron of public libraries, I know that they are a true gift to the communities they serve. In fact, if you want to know more about how to close the purpose gap through books, look at Yuyi Morales's *Dreamers*. It is an exploration from the Latino/a community that humanizes our immigration narratives, fills the pages with images from our community, and celebrates the library as a place where people from our communities can find freedom.[11] I am writing particularly for our communities and the children of our communities. I want to help parents, teachers, social workers, friends, neighbors, and elders see that to create conditions for people on the margins to thrive is not just central to our purpose, but it is the very heart of our tradition. *The Purpose Gap* looks to create opportunity within our own communities, making the "gap" more than just surmountable. This book hopes to reframe the entire design of the conditions that created the purpose gap and our responses to them in the first place.

We will no longer settle for gaining access to the systems of oppression that created the purpose gap as achieving our purpose. If we choose to cross the gap, it will be on our terms. If we choose to build in our own spaces, it will be on our terms. We will close the purpose gap by any and all means necessary so that generations from now our descendants will have access to the resources, knowledge, and practices to dream big dreams and achieve their many purposes.

My secondary audience is for those in that second picture, who build, manage, guard, and cross the bridge from purpose to opportunity. It reflects my own experience, so much of what I write is from this perspective. Without my father going first across the bridge in education, when a poor Brown student was a novelty in every classroom, I would not have a bridge to education myself. While I had to navigate much of academia on my own, learning to code-switch, translate, and operate in different spaces to survive, I had my father's example to lead me and my grandma's love to get me to where I am today. It was the community that supported, fueled, held, and loved me. Many of the stories and illustrations in this book come from this perspective.

My purpose is to close the gap so that every human will have access to the people, processes, and resources needed to achieve their purpose—to build a bridge from purpose to opportunity. We can do this work no matter our circumstance, but we need to be realistic with our starting place. The myth of the American dream plagues too many of our imaginations about purpose.[12] This myth is not just economic, though economics certainly matter. As Robert Putnam showed, "As income inequality expands, kids from more privileged backgrounds start and probably finish further and further ahead of their less privileged peers."[13] The ever-widening gap between the haves and the have-nots, between the modern-day Egyptian elites and marginalized Hebrews, wreaks havoc on our communities. More troubling is the impact of this violence on the imagination of the children from these communities. Closing the purpose gap means not turning away from reality by escaping into the false idealism of the American dream. To close the purpose gap, we must draw on our own spiritual and intellectual wellsprings.

We must take command of the story we tell about our communities and reject the lie that we are not excellent enough to achieve our life's many purposes. But it is not simply about "pulling ourselves up by our bootstraps." For me, this book is not about being the first in my family from the barrio to achieve some standard. Rather, it celebrates the "firsts" who made sure they were not the "lasts." I wish to reframe the narrative about what we are capable of if we collectively reframe who, how, and what we do to close the purpose gap for those most marginalized.

Jonah Sachs writes in *Winning the Story Wars: Why Those Who Tell (and Live) the Best Stories Will Rule the Future* about a similar phenomenon: the meaning gap.[14] He explains how stories and myths make and shape meaning in our lives. He says that "myths are the glue that holds society together, providing an indispensable, meaning-making function . . . when myths are functioning properly, they bring us together and get us to act by using a specific formula that appears to be universal across cultures."[15] The core features, such as symbolic thinking, story, explanation, and ritual, have tethered groups of people together for all of human existence. Origin stories, family histories, institutional stories, and extraordinary narratives of the fantastical and impossible supply the imaginary stitches of our communal blanket. Sachs also points to a myth gap. What happens, he wonders, when we give up the power of our own mythmaking, meaning making, and storytelling? He challenges us to say that a myth gap starts to arise when our communal stories are no longer strong enough to hold people together.

In an age of technological and societal disruption, there are forces that are actively trying to disrupt our communal mythmaking. The storytellers define the myth gap; they determine what stories are worth telling and who listens. Sachs writes, "A myth gap arises when reality changes dramatically and our myths are not resilient enough to continue working in the face of that change."[16] He argues that we need to find a new generation of creators, storytellers, mythmakers, and meaning makers to address the gap. These storytellers, as you will read, are you. By the end of this book, you will be able to close the purpose gap.

For colonized people, the myth gap has always been clear. For those here in the West, there is a documented record from 1492 onward of the destruction of an entire continent's myths and stories. In the transatlantic slave trade, lives, stories, and spiritualities were tossed into the sea. Human history reveals the myth gap—borrowing, stealing, suppressing, and expressing the stories that give our communities meaning. From the Greeks to the Romans, from the Toltecs to the Aztecs, people have borrowed, appropriated, and reimagined myths of conquerors and conquered alike. The gap continues to widen between dominant culture and the colonized, co-opted, and destroyed lives, narratives, theologies, and histories.

In the following pages, we will explore the purpose gap, help close it, and leave you, the reader, with a sense of purpose. This is no small order. For those left out of the literature on "finding one's meaning," please know that this book is for you. If you resonate with the works of Ibram X. Kendi, if you have been marked or "stamped" for death by a culture that wants to keep you from achieving your purpose,[17] then this book is for you. If you are not one of the oppressed, damned, marginalized, or those left behind and left out, you are still welcome. Know that you are reading over our shoulders. You are not the center here. But by your very presence in the conversation, we are implicating you in the necessary task of closing the purpose gap for all those who do not have access to the resources, networks, and opportunities you have. Returning to Kendi, if you are going to be here, you have to be committed to a "potential future: an antiracist world in all its imperfect beauty. It can become real if we focus on power instead of people, if we focus on changing policy instead of groups of people."[18] It is an opportunity for you to examine your own power, privilege, and complicity in the ever-widening purpose gap.

This book is about helping you find your purpose, but more importantly, it is about closing that purpose gap for our communities. To close the purpose gap, we must acknowledge that it exists. We must dive deeply into what that means for our spiritual and intellectual inner lives and what it means to survive in the midst of this reality. We must also explore ways to discern our many purposes when there are systemic structures at play to keep us from them. We must design solutions that are free from oppression and that provide access to opportunities for the next generation to thrive. Can we build thriving communities without having to gain access to systems of domination? Can we build on our own terms? Can dominant society support our building without getting in the way or claiming ownership? This communal and networked work requires an organized effort from all of us who care about humanity.

Closing the purpose gap means creating the conditions for future generations to achieve meaningful and purpose-filled lives. It means removing the barriers, generating the resources, building the power, and imagining the future where those who are most marginalized thrive. It is spirit work. Closing the purpose gap is the realization of Jesus' Beatitudes in the

Sermon on the Mount: Blessed are the poor in spirit, those who mourn, the meek, those who hunger for righteousness, the merciful, the pure in heart, the peacemakers, the persecuted, the insulted. Closing the purpose gap is realizing the promise of the Beatitudes: "'For theirs is the kingdom of heaven'" (Matt. 5:10). We are building a world in the purpose gap that imagines and realizes this vision.

Framing

I want to leave you with a word about the style and tone of this book. Like any good facilitator and animator, I want to set proper expectations. Regarding time, I have set out to design and draft a four-hour book. It is just long enough to read in two to three sittings. Have a cup of coffee (or four or five if you are like me), get up and walk, reflect on your own purpose using the guiding questions, or see them as discussion points for your leadership teams. My hope is that this book will create a dialogue with your life and help you create the conditions in your institutions and communities for the least of those within them to thrive.

Regarding audience, I wrote a book in love with and on behalf of my people. I write for our children. I write to my beautiful Brown children. For those familiar with my writing, I tend to bear the full weight of the oppression, violence, and injustice in every letter on the page. The focus here is the thing that is central to closing the purpose gap: love. The purpose gap exists because we have made choices as a society about whom we do and do not love. As people of faith, we have sometimes expressed this love violently by excluding people we do not recognize as belonging. It has occurred in the church even though Jesus, whom we follow, was an exemplar of radically inclusive love.

I have a powerful sense of calling and purpose, and I identify with the biblical story of Ishmael (Gen. 17:20). On the one hand, elders told me that I was born to live a purposeful and meaningful life. Cast into a desert, God finds us there. The text has named us, Ishmael, *God hears* or *God will hear*.[19] In my journey from being chosen by God to standing on the brink of survival, I have heard God calling me to call others to life, but I have also met people who have not felt that love. They are still by the water, discarded by society and family. My work has taken me to prisons, to fields where people are surviving the day-to-day, back-breaking work of putting food on the table, and to the halls of higher education. It has led me to work with young adults pursuing their call, many of whom experience a seemingly insurmountable purpose gap, given institutional bias against LGBTQIA+, Black, Indigenous, people of color, immigrants, marginalized bodies, and our beloved in the disabled community. In writing for all these family and friends, I realize that the least I can do is offer a book out of love. I hope these pages reflect my love and my hope for us.

When I began working on the book, the fundamental question I held before me was "What if I wrote as though I loved the reader? Could a book about purpose, written that way, heal our community?" I am sensitive to the cultural gaslighting that often takes over vocational literature. Those from marginalized communities are not in these texts, nor were they written for us. The purpose gap is real. The obstacles people face or succumb to are both historical and contemporary facts. I wanted to acknowledge this reality and to say to you, the reader, I love you with all my being. Marian Wright Edelman, founder of the Children's Defense Fund, writes in her masterpiece *The Measure of Our Success* that it "is the responsibility of every adult—especially parents, educators, and religious leaders—to make sure that children hear what we have learned from the lessons of life and to hear over and over that we love them and that they are not alone."[20] This message is a fundamental truth of the work that God is calling us all to pursue. For many of us that purpose will be primarily to call others to life, to create the conditions for them to thrive.

Structure

Part 1: Why the Purpose Gap?

Part 1 teases out the purpose gap and answers why we need to address it. It explores why creating conditions for people to thrive requires our collective effort. Chapters 1 through 4 make plain the case for why we need to close the purpose gap. In chapter 1, we will look closely at the historic conditions of the purpose gap. We will challenge the myth that we all have equal opportunities to find our purpose and passion.

In chapter 2 we begin to challenge the story of purpose. Theologians, historians, and artists alike have all bought into the linear storytelling of meaning and purpose, otherwise known as the hero's journey. We challenge that notion if we really look at our lives and the stories that inspire those who are overcoming the purpose gap, for they reflect non-linear notions of space storytelling. When we do so on our own terms, we reframe the narrative arc and design of our everyday lives. In chapter 3, we examine the cultural commute of people of color in this country and how these commutes—both literally and figuratively—intentionally create distance between people and their purpose.

In chapter 4, we look at ways that communities and institutions have vocations. We challenge the mission and purpose of organizations and ask if they close the purpose gap for the people they serve. These chapters together lay the framework for the "conditions" of our lives. The history, the stories, the design, and the communities and institutions that govern our lives can define, expand, or close the purpose gap. Through understanding how they work in concert, out of our singular control, we can begin to see the purpose gap a little more clearly and build a foundation for strategizing to change the conditions of our lives.

Part 2: How Do We Close the Purpose Gap?

Chapters 5 through 7 aim to answer the question "How do we close the purpose gap?" How do we create, design, and build systems, structures, contexts, ecologies, and communities that support the thriving of the next generation? We have discovered that to close the purpose gap the work is communal because the desired outcome is for a thriving community. This is not a self-help book to help individuals achieve their purpose. Rather, we challenge that myth in chapter 5, suggesting that instead of creating conditions for stars to shine, we should turn our attention to building constellations. Chapter 6 explores this theory a little more explicitly, examining the roles of networks in creating conditions for all its members to thrive. Chapter 7 turns toward home. Here we look at how difficult it is to build networks and celebrative collectives. Home is often the hardest place to close the purpose gap, both because home is difficult to define and change and because, at the same time, it has a definition and is always changing. We wrestle with this paradox and what it means for our own leadership in our institutions and the communities we serve.

Part 3: What Is My Purpose?

The book concludes with the following question: "What does thriving look like if people are able to live into their purpose?" It explores the traditions, skills, and practices needed to cultivate and support leaders who can close the purpose gap. In chapter 8, we turn to inspiring stories of impossible feats. Here I make the claim that everyone in the community has a role to play in closing the purpose gap. Chapter 8 reexamines our notion of education, one of the principal vehicles for social transformation, as out there or tethered only to the classroom and curriculum. If we are going to help the next generation find meaning and purpose, we must reclaim and value the knowledge and wisdom from our communities. Education happens everywhere, healing and transforming.

Closing the purpose gap must be part of our everyday lives. Chapter 9 concludes part 3 by reframing this daily living around the notion of a "good day," where we actively lift one another up, support one another, and create the conditions for future generations to achieve meaning and purpose. We imagine together how to have a good day.

I have a purpose: to help future generations know that they are the embodiments of the love, wisdom, and traditions of their ancestors. I did not *find* my purpose. My purpose found me in the form of my community. We can close the purpose gap together.

PURPOSE

Part 1

Why the Purpose Gap?

Razor wire covers the horizon
I can see the wire cutters
To find a way through
A journey said to be impossible
I would need to bleed.
To get to the other side

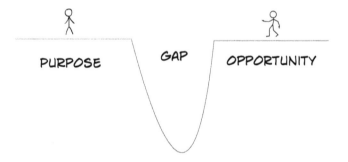

PURPOSE   GAP   OPPORTUNITY

Cut the wire
Hold open the small hole
To help others pass without incident
To collectively remove the horizon
Returning a landscape
Removing artificial barriers
To its natural wonder
And finding freedom.

Chapter 1

Conditions

Daring to Dream

In 2018, between May and the end of June, more than 2,300 children were separated from their families at the U.S. border.[1] Family separation was not the act of a few bad politicians. It was an explicit U.S. strategy described as deterrence—the same strategy the military uses, where the punishment of certain actions will be so severe that people choose not to engage in them. The message is clear: *If you come here with your family, we will break your family, break your spirit, break your will to find meaning and purpose in this country*. Children have been held behind chain-link fences and, in one case, under a bridge,[2] sleeping on concrete floors away from their families. All of this is punishment for wanting a better life and daring to seek it out. The purpose of these families' journey, of bringing these innocent children on it, was to find a better life among us, their neighbors. And in response we stole their lives and purpose. Brown Latinx/o/a and Latin American children, like my family, have been denied a life of flourishing. In fact, we are collectively and actively deterring them from pursuing their purpose.

I watched the news like the rest of the country, witnessing pastors and faith leaders, many of them my friends and colleagues, go to play, pray, worship, and break bread with those on both sides of the border. Not one of those nights did I sleep with dry eyes. Their sacrifice, their faith, and their love for their children were not unlike my own. Gilberto Ramos, a fifteen-year-old boy, travelled to the United States to get his mother's epilepsy medicine and find a better life. He was found dead in the Texas desert, recognizable by the white rosary that his mother draped around his neck and a phone number written on his belt.[3] What separated these young people from my own family's experience was the distance of just a few generations on this side of the border.

When I was in seminary, I spent time offering spiritual care visiting adults who were awaiting deportation, often separated from their families, and even more tragically, whose families did not know their location. When I arrived at the facility, I would sit in the parking lot, praying to God for strength because I felt personally responsible for stealing their many purposes. I gripped my own rosary, a gift from my grandma that I still carry with me. These were my friends who had hopes and dreams for themselves and their children, who came here to close the purpose gap for their own children. Their children's view of the world would be shaped by this harrowing violence.

There is a program in my hometown of Salinas, California, where a local pastor and priest take children to federal prisons all over the state to visit their incarcerated parents. These children get to "play" with their parents under armed guard and in view of razor-wire fences. How can these young people imagine their purpose in life? For Black and Brown children across this country, we have stolen the purpose of the next generation. The children look lovingly at their parents. Happiness overflows when these young people reunite with their family members. Accompanying this meeting is a guard with a shotgun in hand, ugly physical barriers, and the volunteer who was their sole means of seeing their loved one. Can anyone doubt that this scene will forever shape that child's imagination about what is possible? American adults have declared war on America's children, committing violence over the question of who has a purpose and who does not. The denial of the sacredness of every child is a sin we have committed collectively. To close the purpose gap for all children and people on this planet requires that we repent and undo the systems that judge some lives worthy of freedom and others not.

Those who do not see their connection to these young people caged like animals are blind to the oppression and violence committed against Black and Brown children. Those who say, "They are not my children," "It is not my problem," or "My community has our own problems," are traumatizing their own children as well. It is a moral injury that will last for generations. Those who choose to break the cycles of violence will look back at this generation and say, "I can't believe my family let that happen."

Others of us can neither ignore nor explain away this trauma because we live it. We inherit this generational trauma. We feel in our bones and our skin the attempted genocide of indigenous people on this continent and Jewish people on another, the violence of apartheid and slavery, the lasting effects of Jim Crow, and the abuse and murder of generations of Black bodies through policing and mass incarceration. They are the sum of our history, which creates horizons within which there is no imagining a better world, only surviving this one.

When our children are not free to imagine, they live in fear of the future. There is no celebration of their potential. On a drive home from an extracurricular activity, my son said to me, "I wish I wasn't Latino because then I would be safe." Parents, educators, social workers, and pastors alike remind children that we love them, not just because it is the right thing to do, but because the world sends these innocent children the opposite message. We have to be realistic about the ways our children of color behave in a certain way around police, to explain the violence against other children who look like them, and to prepare them for a world that has tried to eradicate or enslave them. Closing the purpose gap is about these conversations. These are conversations about purpose and meaning. What does it mean to discern purpose as a person of color? Does God call us to live a life of meaning and purpose? Does God allow us to imagine lives beyond the cages designed to capture our dreams, to snatch our lives' many purposes, to incarcerate our imagination about our own self-worth? This is what we mean by the term "purpose gap." There is a deep chasm between the children who get to dream freely and the children whose purpose must be shaped within a nightmare, between Pharaoh and Pilate on the one hand, and Moses and Jesus on the other, tattooed by death even before coming into this world.

There are truths that our collective bodies know and hold. A pain expressed in a word, a shout, a whisper, a hand gesture, or a look that does not need translation. Closing the purpose gap is about working through and exploring the wisdom and practices from our communities that might give the next generation a chance to dream with less fear and to dream of the realization of freedom. For example, I work at home with my children using a mixture of practices that deepen their sense of self. This work is accompanied by the ancestors, the community, and, of course, their parents, who love them beyond all things. I teach my children how to perform rituals, say prayers, and practice traditions that have been handed down over generations to ensure their survival and connect them to the above and beyond.

As I outlined in the introduction, intimate moments with our own communities and in spaces designed for our thriving do exist. They include neighborhood playgrounds, fields, worship spaces, historically Black colleges and universities, Hispanic-serving institutions, tribal colleges, and the like. Yet with these exceptions, we largely spend our time responding to dominant white, Anglo, Protestant, patriarchal, cis-gendered, able-bodied, neuro-homogenous, heteronormative, and anthropocentric categories of existence. A gap exists between the dominant culture's ability to create meaning and purpose and my own. A misperception confronts us, saying that the only knowledge creators are the descendants of the dominating, colonizing, and violent forces. To assert our wisdom and knowledge, especially to say that our lives are divine and equal, is to demand life in the face of death. There will be resistance. If we are to liberate ourselves, we must demand our freedom and the right to dream, the right to have a purpose in this lifetime.

We have constructed and designed worlds around this myth of white supremacy and Western superiority. It is as though our society is part of a science fiction novel in which the author created a world reflective solely of his own white, male experience. Not a single day goes by in which whiteness, patriarchy, and colonization do not affect my life. In the grocery store, labels in the produce section provide a helpful reminder that people like me plant and harvest the food while privileged white families reap the benefits. From the dishes, to the coffee, to the clothes, the cars, the roads, the buildings, the systems and structures, rules and regulations, laws and legal structures—within all of these I will, at some point in my day, encounter whiteness as it subjugates, oppresses, and celebrates its victory. There is no denying it exists, because it surrounds us.

On the other hand, *we* exist everywhere too. The wisdom of my ancestors guides me and leads me. The love of our *tías*, mothers, and *abuelas* guides us to lives of meaning and purpose. Their example proves why I need to author this book in a hue, a tone, and a color that reflects the love of the divine. Next time someone of my hue or tone, or our brothers and sisters, *primos* and *primas*, look for literature to help find meaning and purpose, they will have in this book something that reflects both their reality and their beauty. If, as I have argued elsewhere,[4] vocation is the call to life, then I claim here that external conditions have as much to do with one finding one's purpose as does one's internal discernment. To understand the purpose gap, one need only the vocational literature, the theology of vocation, and the self-help genre to see it was not intended for us.

Those from marginalized and minoritized communities must begin with our material reality. White, upper-middle-class scholars typically author works in the fields of vocation, meaning, purpose, and related disciplines in self-help and psychological well-being. That is not to say that the writing coming from my colleagues Dorothy Bass,[5] David Cunning-ham,[6] Kathleen Cahalan,[7] Dori Baker and Joyce Mercer,[8] Diana Butler Bass,[9] Parker Palmer,[10] and David Brooks,[11] or the great collection William Placher[12] pulled together in exploring the vocational writings of Martin Luther, George Fox, Walter Rauschenbusch, Søren Kierkegaard, and the like, are necessarily wrong or bad. It does not mean that we cannot go back to definitions as set forth by Thomas Merton,[13] Dorothy Day,[14] or the like. It is not to dismiss Rick Warren's popular *The Purpose Driven Life*, because there is deep value in knowing that our purpose exists beyond our own desires. However, when Warren writes, "You were made of God, not vice versa, and life is about letting God use you for his purposes, not your using him for your own purpose," I cringe.[15] For young children of color who are locked up against their will, whose lives are cut short, who never have a shot, this was not God's nor should be society's plan for the innocent. They should not be used and abused. Suffering children are not in God's plan, and if it is, that is not a God worth believing in.

White authors write from a particular place that could not be farther from the fields in which I grew up, a fact none of them would argue, for the backgrounds and cultural vantage points of white authors often go unaccounted. In a slightly comical story, I was set to present with several scholars on the topic of meaning. One of them, a preeminent scholar and middle-aged white woman, asked me what I was going to talk about. I told her about my work on meaning and purpose. She asked if I knew her work and the work of one of her friends, emphasizing that they are both well known. I responded, "Of course. In my research, I make sure to look at people doing similar work." And after a slight pause I added, "Do you think you and your friend know my work?"

Without hesitation her response was "No." However, she knew the work of all the other presenters that night, two white scholars who did nothing in our shared field of study. I am not saying that everyone must know my work, but the assumption of power was clear. I was supposed to know her and her friend's work, but they do not have to be curious or even think twice about what is appearing in their own discipline from my community. Their work is the standard, and mine is only a niche, a particularity, a margin to the center.

Even in the best-case scenario, authors from majority cultures qualify their writings with a level of awareness, saying something like, "I want to recognize my privilege. My white, cis-gendered, middle-class, hetero-normative, and educated background informs how I write and think."

Sometimes they will add something like, ". . . who writes from stolen land and recognizing that I benefit from years of oppression to communities of color." Without missing a beat, they all seem to go on to re-create the same power dynamics in their writing that they had set out to dismantle with their recognition of power and privilege. As Jennifer Harvey writes in *Raising White Kids*, it is not just about acknowledging difference; it is about being race-conscious enough to undo and dismantle the very systems that create the purpose gap between white children and everyone else.[16] If you have the power to acknowledge white privilege, you have the power to dismantle white supremacy. The distance between the two is closer than people think.

I want to acknowledge some especially important work that I think drives this point home. I love Brené Brown. I am a better person because of her writing, which has calmed some of my inner doubts and rage. It has influenced my thinking and has challenged me in ways that have made me a better person, scholar, parent, and human. However, I want to address an assumption she makes that has become a famous Internet meme. In *Rising Strong*, she tells a tender story about parenting and wanting our children to know that we love them: "'All I know is that my life is better when I assume that people are doing their best. It keeps me out of judgment and lets me focus on what is, and not what should or could be.'"[17] In her book *Rising Strong*, she quotes her therapist, who told her, "'People are doing the best they can'"[18] (which became the Internet meme). Brown argues that by assuming people are doing their best and appealing to their better nature, we will be whole and happy. We could live a better life.

On this single point, I disagree with Brené Brown with every fiber of my being. Though she is writing to discuss how to make sure people feel loved, just as I have set out to do, we have remarkably different starting places.[19] People are *not* doing their best. Her social location may give her that viewpoint, but it does not provide the full picture, not even close. The purpose gap is real, because, in fact, her people have not always had the best intentions. Even though it is easy and pleasant to assume people are at their core altruistic and working for the freedom of those around them, the facts suggest otherwise. Even well-meaning people are not doing their best to create conditions for others to thrive.

To close the purpose gap, parents of color must teach our children they are loved despite a world that is not doing its best. In a very embodied way, I teach my son how to survive this world that has set out to destroy his people more than once in recent history. As a Latino Jew with indigenous roots, there have been multiple attempts to annihilate his peoples.

Those who were doing their best watched as it happened, over and over. I must teach my son, and my daughter, about these histories, precisely because people are not doing their best.

Basic activities like jogging through a white neighborhood are not safe for some of us. Working is not safe for some of us. To call the police is certainly not safe for us. To demand an equitable education is not safe for us. To believe that people are doing their best is to tell yourself a lie with a strong historic precedent for marginalized and communities of color. The propagation of the idea that people are doing their best is a truth that is part of a long line of self-justifying, colonialist ideas that are rotten at their core: colonial piety.[20] You may want it to be true because it helps you feel better. But if we are going to create conditions for future generations to thrive, we start from our material and historical reality. The truth is that the history and legacy of colonization, the ramifications of slavery, the continued incarceration of our families, and the exploitation of our people and our labor all point to a different set of facts, a different set of conditions that create and exacerbate the purpose gap. The purpose gap is best expressed when someone in Brené Brown's target demographic— middle-class, educated, white women—read her work and know that it was written for them, and someone like me knows that it was written for them too. I must translate her work to make it applicable to readers of color, a task that all students and people of color must do constantly within dominant culture. My people are not even an afterthought. And at the same time, I recognize Brown's writing is as close as it comes to helping someone like me find my inner freedom.

Let's look at a few more pieces of evidence to show how the belief that everyone is a "good Samaritan" is wrong and dangerous. "Sixty million and more" is the dedication in the late Toni Morrison's *Beloved*, signifying all those lives lost to the transatlantic slavery system that empowered those of white, European ancestry and robbed Black and African American people of their history, culture, wealth, health, and homeland.[21] The ramifications of the transatlantic slave trade on the vocational outcomes of African Americans in this country go well beyond Thomas Craemer's modest reparations estimate of $14 trillion.[22] The impact of generational trauma, the stripping of generations of wealth, health, and the sacred, the lost stories and ancestors, and the loss of being treated as beloved by God ripples across generations. The journey still haunts the collective imagination of what is possible: that freedom and purpose were stolen. Consider Zora Neale Hurston's *Barracoon*, a work drawing on her interview with Cudjo Lewis, who survived that journey as a child. She conducted the interviews in 1927 and 1931, but the book was not released until 2018.[23] What does it mean to discern your purpose when you have a living memory of the transatlantic slave trade? Angela Sims's incredible work *Lynched: The Power of Memory in a Culture of Terror*, grounds the history of lynching in the oral histories and memories of African Americans today. What does it mean to have living memories of these heinous acts informing your imagination of the possible?[24] The question of purpose is central in Octavia Butler's *Kindred*.[25] Her main character, Dana, finds herself transported between two realities: her life in the twenty-first century as an accomplished professional and a life enslaved in the antebellum South. The violence against Black life and Black lives, and the relative silence about that violence in my colleagues' work on vocation, meaning, and purpose on the matter, casts a deep shadow over that work.

Elie Wiesel writes, "For the survivor who chooses to testify, it is clear: his duty is to bear witness for the dead and for the living. He has no right to deprive future generations of a past that belongs to our collective memory. To forget would be not only dangerous but offensive; to forget the dead would be akin to killing them a second time."[26] While at Boston University, I had the privilege of sitting with Elie Wiesel for coffee. Throughout his career Wiesel honored the more than six million Jews murdered during the Shoah, the Holocaust. He was clear that it was not enough to just remember those who were lost. It was important to remember that *the world watched* as the Jewish people were targeted and executed for simply existing. People were not doing their best. To turn away, to write about something else, would be to betray the memory, the unfulfilled lives and purposes not pursued of the Jewish children in the concentration camps, of our human brethren. Though his philosophy was different from Wiesel's, Viktor Frankl's reflections on life on the inside of a concentration camp, *Man's Search for Meaning*, explores similarly the question of how one finds meaning in such harrowing circumstances. He writes that although the world may want to strip a person of their humanity, each human is unique. He claims that "this uniqueness and singleness which distinguishes each individual and gives a meaning to his existence has a bearing on creative work as much as it does on human love."[27] His vision of life, meaning, and purpose is cast from inside the concentration camp. It is from that place that purpose is discerned.

David Treuer writes, "In 1890, the U.S. Census Bureau tabulated that there are fewer than two hundred thousand Indians left alive, of populations that had likely numbered over twenty million."[28] The sustained genocide of multiple indigenous peoples in North America has been carried out over generations. When people and cultures are wiped out, we do not have the luxury to assume people are doing their best. In *The Heartbeat of Wounded Knee: Native America from 1890 to the Present,* Treuer carefully lays out the ways indigenous peoples have been targeted for genocide and how some found the means to survive. If you are an indigenous person or descended from those who survived this intentional genocide, how do you discern purpose from this space? How do we assume everyone is doing their best, when history, and the current reality, has proven the exact opposite?

These atrocities and genocides, all perpetrated on an international scale and all tethered to the white, European quest to dominate the globe, prevent me from buying into any line that suggests, "People are doing their best." Worse yet would be to say that these practices of domination no longer exist, hence ignoring current conditions and dismissing the deep-rooted and persistent effects of colonialism. *Coloniality* is a term used in academic circles to describe the lasting impacts of colonialism and supremacy.[29] One example of this lasting impact is that on any given day in the United States, nearly 48,000 children are incarcerated. According to the Prison Policy Initiative, at least 10 percent of those youth are incarcerated in adult facilities.[30] Nearly 5,000 children are locked in with adults, most of them Black and Brown. We have sealed their futures as a society. We are not doing our best. How does any one of those young people discern their purpose in a cell? How do their families discern purpose knowing their loved ones, their children, are treated like animals?

How do my people dream or imagine their purpose when immigration enforcement raids their places of work? How do we reflect on our place in the world when white individuals can place our lives in peril by summoning the police to answer false threats to their privilege? How do we find our purpose when military-style police squads can burst into our homes and kill us simply because they got the wrong address? How do we take time for ourselves to discern our calling when we can be lynched simply for jogging along the street? How do we trust those sworn to serve and protect when police can casually choke the very life from our bodies? How do we slow down to discern our many purposes when we have those images and more always before us? How do we live into our call when the world riots and burns in response to that hate?

In 2020, while George Floyd lay dying from a police officer kneeling on his neck, he called for his mother. This was the same cry on the lips of those whose lives were stolen and brought to these lands. That cry for Mama reverberates on the border as children traverse the desert for a better life, only to be separated from their parents and locked in cages. It is the call of neglected Puerto Ricans after natural and political disasters. It is the same cry when indigenous children were pulled from their families and forced to go first to religious schools and missions and later to government boarding and residential schools. This theft of life and purpose stretches across generations. What does it mean to be human in systems of domination such as these?

How do we imagine people are doing their best when Eric Garner, John Crawford, Michael Brown, Ezell Ford, Dante Parker, Tanisha Anderson, Tamir Rice (a twelve-year-old child with a toy in his hand shot dead by police), Rumain Brisbon, Freddie Gray, Sandra Bland, and Vanessa Guillén, a US Army soldier murdered inside Fort Hood, are constant reminders of the opposite being true? How do we discern our purpose when we live in a country that separates children from their families? How do we discern our purpose when 2,654 children are removed from their families, many being placed in cages?[31] How do we discern life when detained children die because of their immigration status, considered not to belong to us? Darlyn Cristabel Cordova-Valle (age ten), Jakelin Caal Maquín (seven), Felipe Gomez Alonzo (eight), Juan de León Gutiérrez (sixteen), Wilmer Josué Ramírez Vásquez (two), and Carlos Hernandez Vásquez (sixteen) passed away while being detained for seeking a better life.[32] These young people made it to the border, but what of all those who did not? The journey has killed so many others, like Gilberto Francisco Ramos Juarez (fourteen), the young man mentioned above whose mother gave him a rosary and wrote a phone number on his belt.[33] These are children who speak multiple languages yet experience a poverty rate far higher than most other groups. These are my people, pursuing their purpose, creating a better life for the next generation through back-breaking labor, performing tasks considered as "essential," even as their lives are not. Seventy-five percent of Latinos/as/xs work in the construction, agriculture, or hospitality industries. Without unions, the conditions in the fields would lack bathrooms, shade, and water. These rights had to be fought for using arguments that animals had better protections in the fields. People are not doing their best when basics like water and bathrooms need to be part of an organizing campaign.

Why do we think that people are doing their best as, in the wake of the COVID-19 pandemic, racism, prejudice, and hate crimes against Asian and Pacific Islander persons skyrocketed to a hundred per day?[34] A reminder is found in the heartbreaking graphic memoir *The Best We Could Do*, by Thi Bui.[35] Bui traces her family's attempt to create a better life, despite the death-dealing and traumatizing narratives caused by the conflict in Viet Nam in the 1970s. People are not doing their best. And for some of us, discerning life's meaning and purpose comes with this backdrop. These are the conditions we live and breathe.

This book is written with this historic and contemporary backdrop of violence and oppression. We will discern purpose within this backdrop, never letting it escape our gaze because the pain never escapes our flesh.

Reflections

Where is your starting place? What histories and names are you remembering? What are your stories that demonstrate this world was not built for you? What did your ancestors have to survive for you to draw breath?

Chapter 2

Retelling the Story of Purpose

In one of my first academic jobs, I was supposed to help college students find spiritual wellness and purpose. The workplace was hostile and exploitive. Not only were people of color paid fifty cents on the dollar compared to our white colleagues, the environment was extractive. The administrative burden rested on my colleagues' and my shoulders. However, anytime the cameras came out, the invitation was always to tell my story, to put my wounds on display, a Chicano novelty. After one engagement telling my story and facilitating some "theatre of the oppressed" exercises for about two hundred students, faculty, and administrators, I heard a white colleague say, "I discovered him." Columbus in the flesh. Like an animal at the circus, I was paraded around campus to perform tricks. I was not invited to share my expertise or my research but to perform my pain on stage. I was part of an act, stories from over there, the stories these students, faculty, and administrators would not get in the main curriculum. By the end of my time there, I was often given directions on what and how to tell my stories for stakeholders. I worked hard to get this job. I wanted to belong, especially since Latinos/as are still some of the least-represented groups in higher education. I wanted my education to count. I wanted to make it. My purpose was to show that education can transform lives, but it was serving everyone but my community. This job was killing me.

The institution had underground tunnels connecting some of the buildings. A few months into this job, I got a phone call. "Can you meet me under the building?" A friend and colleague witnessed what damage had been done to my soul. When we first met, it was an exchange of stories, an exchange of tears. We both wanted to be here. We wanted to show that we could make it. The trauma, the exploitation, the manipulation, and

31

the emotional violence were overwhelming. The only way that we were going to make it, however, was by working together, checking in, and supporting each other through this time in our lives. We had to rewrite our stories of purpose. It was no longer about getting into the academy, being the firsts. Our purpose was about creating conditions so that we were not the lasts. We committed to creating conditions for people of color to generate knowledge authentically by, for, and with our communities. That work is always done in community. We had to support one another. Divided, we lost. United, we could never be defeated.

There is hope for the oppressed to discern their many purposes, for which Howard Thurman offers wisdom:

> Always moving in upon a man's life is the friend whose existence he did not know, whose coming and going is not his to determine. The journeyings take many forms—sometimes it is in the vista that opens before his mind because of lines written long before in an age he did not know; sometimes it is in a simple encounter along the way when before his eyes the unknown stranger becomes the sharer of tidings that could be borne only by a friend. Sometimes a deep racial memory throws into focus an ancient wisdom that steadies the hand and stabilizes the heart. Always moving in upon a man's life is the friend whose existence he did not know, whose coming and going is not his to determine. At last, a man's life is his very own *and* a man's life is never his, alone.[1]

We are not alone. We who are oppressed, dispossessed, and descended from those who survived slavery and colonization can discern purpose by sharing experiences and friendship with one another. It comes from our seeing one another, sharing the nod, and recognizing our humanity, and from that ancestral wisdom that exists in the stories we tell our children and our children's children. Our inner lives are never ours, alone. We do not close the purpose gap for ourselves. We bridge it or build alternatives for future generations so that they may thrive.

Survival is not a complete solution for closing the purpose gap, but it is a "balm in Gilead" to be placed upon our wounds so that we may do more than survive another day. Simply drawing that breath is what God calls some of us to do. Having found our breath, we are free to listen to that deep and ancient wisdom that exists below our skin. We can ground ourselves in the love of our community and begin to imagine how to close the gap for our children. We do this by acknowledging that we can let go of some stories we have been taught while holding fast and repeating others. Let us start with one story we can leave behind.

Hero's Journey So White

The stories told in much of the literature about finding one's purpose employ a familiar narrative arc, with a clear beginning, middle, and end. Frequently they set the context for this arc in highly idealized terms, not unlike those found in J. R. R. Tolkien's fantasy trilogy *The Lord of the Rings*. The first book in the trilogy, *The Fellowship of the Ring*, begins with a description of the Shire, the peaceful home of the Hobbits, where inheritances, birthdays, fireworks, and a generally slow pace of life fill the first pages of this epic adventure. Readers are pulled into the simple life, only to find themselves thrust, like the trilogy's hero, Frodo, out of the simple Shire and into foreign lands with elves, orcs, wizards, goblins, trolls, and indestructible ring wraiths whose sole purpose is to recover and possess the ring of power Frodo has been chosen to destroy.

Frodo's journey would not have been so extraordinary if Tolkien had not written such humble beginnings for his young protagonist and hero. A hobbit, the smallest and most content of creatures in the universe, now had the weight of all existence on his shoulders. Frodo crosses forests, mountains, and swamps with dead souls and fights trolls and giant spiders. The weight that comes with living into his chosen vocation gradually eats away at him. It is not inconsequential either that Tolkien writes in the aftermath of World War I, penning words in the trenches, reflecting on the destructive nature of power.

Frodo's story arc is not unique. Many scholars have explored this arc in what Joseph Campbell famously named the hero's journey.[2] The hero's journey fits a particularly linear narrative: birth, life, and death, as we are told in Genesis 3:19, "'You are dust and to dust you shall return.'" Similarly, the ministry of Jesus in John's Gospel is cyclical to and from Jerusalem. The hero's journey defines this process of self-discovery, illuminated in works like Paulo Coelho's *The Alchemist*[3] or by authors like J. D. Salinger,[4] Herman Melville,[5] or Charlotte Bronte.[6]

But what about those who are never called to some great journey by the universe or those who were left behind? What about those whose journey feels like a perpetual middle, a constant quest to overcome obstacles toward no clear end? What if they find themselves, as I did, hiding in hallways underneath buildings trying to support and care for others who thought they had been called to this work?

The hero's journey is a myth and not a universal process for discovering and actualizing one's purpose. Heroines from communities on our side of the gap do not receive the call to adventure and never have a choice to refuse the call if they do. They receive no supernatural aid and are often unable to travel beyond their communal bounds. Therefore, they never have trials and temptations, gain new skills and knowledge, and have no need to return to a home they never left. Prior to even beginning the journey, many people today have been left out. It is determined before their birth that they are not worthy of the journey at all. The conditions are such that their imagination about what is possible is never activated. We are not all hobbits going about our lives, living serenely in an ideal home, not wanting the call to adventure. There is no road out of the Shire, and those who do leave never return.

Drawing on this vision of the hero's journey to discern vocation, David Brooks writes that at some point in each person's life there is an annunciation of purpose. He says that "the best thing about the annunciation moment is that it gives you an early hint of where your purpose lies. The next best thing is it rules out a bunch of other things."[7] The annunciation for many people of color occurs when we are born, stamped from the beginning, inheriting the violence of generations. The annunciation is when we draw our first breath and all the limitations of the world are actualized. Or worse, the annunciation is the whisper of opportunity that we might survive and overcome these many obstacles to achieve a life that we did not want. The purpose gap is best expressed in what is not said in Tolkien's books or that white framework of storytelling. To overcome the purpose gap, Tolkien would have had to focus on the rest of the Shire and how all the people of that place were activated and achieved purpose. Frodo and the ring of power would not be the central figures in the book, with the rest of the characters only serving to help him achieve his purpose. To draft a new story of purpose would be to insist that there are no side characters.[8] Other humans and creatures are not just the supporting cast in my journey. Closing the purpose gap is about the community, not the individual. It is a fundamental reorientation to how we discern and pursue purpose.

The hero's journey also reflects a particularly misleading linear life trajectory. The dominant culture's vocational literature completely disregards place and community. Finding and pursuing purpose is not a linear or spatially inconsequential endeavor. Our tradition and sacred texts are good at displaying the many dimensions of the nonlinear arc, not just those of the headliners. Miriam and Mary are two examples. Miriam is constantly calling her people to life. She helps Moses survive by sending him in the basket, and when Pharaoh's daughter finds him, she suggests to the daughter that Moses' mother should care for him. Miriam danced in front of the people as they escaped from the Egyptians. When she challenged her brothers and was stricken with disease by God, those she cared for and loved stood by her side until she was healed. These events in the story take place in the context of Egyptian slavery and the wilderness—in sites of social abandonment, as liberation theologians have rightly named it.[9]

I think of Mary, a Brown teenage girl, called by God to bring a child into the world, to ensure his freedom and safety, and ultimately to watch the boy of promise crucified before her very eyes and mourn with his friends and followers. She not only took on a pregnancy that was taboo in her community, but because of the decree of Herod, she also ensured the survival of her Brown son by fleeing to a foreign land. Mary survived in all these spaces, but she also went to where Jesus performed miracles and was crucified, as seen in such iconic works of art as Michelangelo's *Pietà*. A Hebrew sister dancing life into her people; a Brown mother cradling her crucified, tortured, and dead son: bravery does not describe the strength of these two women. They are people who were called to extraordinary acts but who were challenged to survive, live, and exhibit leadership in the community as it grieved and experienced trauma.

As a Chicano educator, I am attuned to many such nonlinear, antiindividualistic stories of mythmaking and purpose. They are spatially and culturally attentive. From foundational creation myths of the Mayans and Aztecs to narratives of modern imagination, I am constantly reminded that the stories we tell ourselves are not linear and need not be redemptive. I love to tell animal stories to my children, whether about the hummingbirds of our mythologies or the *Coyotl*, coyote, the clever savior or sibling figure in so many of our stories. Coyote stories are my favorite narratives. *Prima* Coyote does everything, from saving humanity to warding off winter or going with leaders across the land, doing so as neither hero nor villain. These stories sometimes have lessons and are sometimes stories of wonder and awe. The most important feature is that Coyote, a survivor, a recognizable symbol on this land, challenges our notion that humans are the center to the story here on earth. We are not the sole beings with a purpose. Coyote serves as a reminder that our purposes cannot be discerned apart from the world we inhabit.

Meaning is discerned at the intersection of the stories we tell ourselves and the worlds we build and inhabit. It is not just linear storytelling that is the problem; it is the redemptive arc we seem to require of stories about meaning and purpose. We want to go from broken to whole—from being in need of redemption to receiving redemption—from "good to great."[10] We want to go from not knowing our purpose to pursuing our purpose with the fire of generations past. We want to learn the skills necessary to overcome obstacles and better pursue our purpose so that we are not a generation lost in the desert. More tragically, many of us do not want to imagine a life without purpose or think that we have stolen purpose from others.

What if our stories are not linear or redemptive? Can they still be purpose filled? A foundational story I learned very early, one that operates at the intersection of identity and the hero's myth, is *The Life and Adventures of Joaquín Murieta: The Celebrated California Bandit* by John Rollin Ridge.[11] The narrative centers around a Mexican American hero similar to Zorro (imagine Antonio Banderas, who portrayed Zorro in the 1998 film). Joaquín's home is raided by white, American settlers, who murder his family and steal his property. In response, he creates a group of more than two thousand freedom fighters who take revenge by stealing back land and property and robbing miners. Joaquín eventually loses his way, going from freedom fighter to violent bandit, and loses the sympathy of the public. John Rollin Ridge, a member of the Cherokee Nation, is often considered one of the first published Native American writers in the United States, and Joaquín is the first Mexican American hero in literature. Following the publication of the book, Joaquín's life may have inspired a similar figure in California history, Tiburcio Vasquez, a California *bandido* in the late 1800s. The book, flawed like the author, displays a sort of racial hierarchy reflecting Ridge's own complex relationship with his Cherokee identity, superiority he felt over California indigenous peoples, and his sympathies for nations who signed treaties with the American government and whose property and rights were not respected. Like the ambiguity of Joaquín's own position, Ridge as a "first" is challenged for his limitations and prejudices. To close the purpose gap is to see these complexities, acknowledge the impact of their existence, and name their limitations.

My favorite world-building narratives are from the writer Octavia Butler. In *Parable of the Sower*, she introduces, "God is change." Butler's parable trilogy and *Kindred, Bloodchild,* and *Dawn*, create worlds beyond worlds.[12] They spoke to the deepest parts of my soul and reflect the complex reality of history. *Kindred* presents a powerful reminder that slavery will always be with us. We are never so far removed from the time when African lives were stolen, when human children were bought and sold. No human's purpose is to be enslaved or owned. Rudolfo Anaya's *Bless Me, Ultima* also occupies this space between worlds.[13] It certainly could be a coming-of-age story, but one occupying a particular space and incorporating a spirituality that does not recognize time in the same way. It begins as a series of stories in the Southwest where complex characters struggle with belonging and survival, as opposed to travel and adventure. Butler, Anaya, and others show us that the redemptive arc of the hero's journey as seen in *The Lord of the Rings* is not the only way to tell a coherent story.

When I talk about these complex stories and histories with those whom I am helping discern their calling, they often react with a challenge. This complexity does not fit with the redemptive, individualistic, and linear story they often tell themselves. "You don't know my story" is the phrase I hear most often, especially from white liberals sharing the room with people of color. Whenever diversity, equity, inclusion, and access come up during our discernment gatherings, and especially when focusing on those who have been marked for death and left out of the majority culture's definitions of who is human, people always want to move to celebrating difference as quickly as possible. Curiously, white participants often want to differentiate their histories from larger white colonial narratives; they are individuals, unique, and set apart. For example, I am often told long histories about "my poor immigrant Irish, Italian, German, Scandinavian, British" ancestors who came "to this country with nothing." Especially in settings where people of color occupy the most seats, this sort of "I am not just a generic white person" narrative is a knee-jerk reaction that often goes unexamined by white allies. To say that everyone in the room must share their stories equally is not inclusion. To require those from marginalized, colonized, and disenfranchised communities to share the narrative platform with every white, colonial story someone wants to spin is to dishonor the purpose of a preferential option for those voices that have been silenced or forgotten. To be blunt, those white stories have been told. They are mainstream. We need stories like the ones Butler and Anaya tell, stories authentic to our experiences. Even in the way we tell our personal narratives, there is a myth gap about what stories are celebrated, taught, and valued.

The reason exploring the diversity of white stories does not get us closer to closing the purpose gap is simple. I, along with anyone educated in the United States, am uniquely qualified and proficient in the diversities of white storytelling. In fact, I have an elementary, high school, bachelor's, master's, and doctoral education in what amounts to white storytelling and meaning making. I know these histories and their diversities. If Malcolm Gladwell is right about people becoming experts after dedicating ten thousand hours to a particular thing, then I am beyond an expert in white narratives.[14] Regardless of one's color, race, or ethnicity, in the United States we receive these stories as core curriculum. American history, for example, is taught from a white, European-descendant perspective. The country was started on the east coast and moved west. It began with white, Anglo-Saxon Protestants who were trying to find a better life. Then came the others. The move into the "wild west" was considered manifest destiny. We are taught a watered-down version of the stories of Spaniards, Russians, and Americans who came all the way to California's Pacific Coast occupying land, murdering, stealing, and then forcing people who had lived there for millennia to work on land that used to be their own. The people who pushed their way onto this land had assumed purposes that did not recognize the rights or humanity of those who already lived here.

In school, we learned the "classics," including narratives of the birth of civilization in the Mediterranean. We learned about the troubles in Europe and any contact they had with the East. For language classes, English is core curriculum. And even other languages now taught in elementary schools are usually limited to European languages like Spanish, Latin, French, and Italian. Schools are gradually offering Mandarin, Japanese, and Korean, but indigenous languages, spoken on this continent prior to the arrival of all Europeans, are disappearing faster than we can count. It pains me to no end to learn about the number of white liberals who speak Spanish, claiming some proximity to Brown people, while failing to recognize the neocolonialist interests that underlie their reasons for learning the language. Learning Spanish checked a box for them: it allowed them to work in the Christian mission field, perform service projects on the other side of the tracks, add another line to their C.V., or simply feel good about themselves. All the while *la lengua* was being taken from us, cut from our very mouths.

Those of us on the other side of the purpose gap, who have often been the subjects of this "trauma tourism," were actively attacked and colonized, language being one of those first things that colonizers acquire to infiltrate cultures and communities. The gradual erasure of our indigenous languages is another tactic of colonial domination. We face assimilation or annihilation. It is as if my colleagues are unaware that Spanish was thrust on us in the first place, as if Brown people on this land always spoke in that tongue. In 1531, the Spanish were under orders to place my native ancestors in *reducciones*, to reduce them to mission and congregation centers. This resulted in the *Camino Real*, a chain of missions in California that every California fourth grader learns about in social studies. The explicit mission was for the Franciscans, under the leadership of Fr. Junipero Serra, to teach the more than a hundred groups of indigenous people to learn Spanish and vocational skills and to convert them to Christianity. Alta California adopted and inherited these cultural markers of colonial power. Even today, some Catholics still celebrate Fr. Serra, California's ecclesial conquistador. When my well-meaning friends speak English and Spanish, they don't feel the pain these colonial tongues cause, but I do, my people do, my ancestors do, and my descendants will.

The Treaty of Guadalupe Hidalgo in 1848 that ended the war between the United States and Mexico gave much of what is now the American Southwest over to the U.S., ensuring that English and white, U.S. culture would be imposed on the people of those territories. My white, Spanish-speaking colleagues do not know that like so many treaties signed in the United States, the first results of this one were the reduction, assimilation, or extermination of my people and culture. Then, as always, Brown people had to keep fighting.

My white friends do not feel or experience the pain of 1947, when a young Sylvia Mendez and her family had to fight for equal rights. Her struggle for access to education was decided in the courts nearly seven years before Supreme Court Justice and former California governor Earl Warren issued his now-famous statement, "In the field of public education the doctrine of 'separate but equal' has no place."[15] The Mendez family fought for equal rights not just because Mexican and Mexican-descended children were split into separate schools in California but because those schools created conditions for the continued discrimination and colonization of Mexicans, Mexican Americans, and Chicanos/as in California. In the landmark ruling, the U.S. District Court judge ruled,

> The equal protection of the laws pertaining to the public-school system in California is not provided by furnishing in separate schools the same technical facilities, textbooks and courses of instruction to children of Mexican ancestry that are available to the other public school children regardless of their ancestry. A paramount requisite in the American system of public education is social equality.

The ruling goes on to say,

> The evidence clearly shows that Spanish-speaking children are retarded in learning English by lack of exposure to its use because of segregation, and that commingling of the entire student body instills and develops a common cultural attitude among the school children which is imperative for the perpetuation of American institutions and ideals. It is also established by the record that the methods of segregation prevalent in the defendant school districts foster antagonisms in the children and suggest inferiority among them where none exists.[16]

Even in this liberal ruling on behalf of our people, one colonial language is replaced by another to espouse progressive ideals. Our opportunities must come at the expense of the erasure of our culture and language and assimilation into the values of the new, pious colonizers. Our purpose and the conditions necessary to achieve it are still being defined by someone else's standards.

My father tells the story of his own school experience in the 1960s, just after this legal decision was reached. Anti-Mexican bias thread its way through his years of attending school in Bakersfield, California. Rocks were thrown at his school bus, and my grandma had to race to school to pick him up because his life was under threat.

My colleagues and friends romanticize the work of César Chávez, Dolores Huerta, and the United Farm Workers in leading the now infamous strikes for farmworker justice. They tell me how Chávez nearly died from a hunger strike for his people, for my people. They miss the part where my family and community, who were already on the brink of survival, put their lives on the line to fight for a fair wage. "*¡Ya Basta! Huelga!*" were not just a bunch of signs to hold at a protest. These words came with empty stomachs, crying children, and the physical pain of back-breaking labor (when it was even available). More importantly, these words emerged from a demand for equal opportunity for future generations. These words live in our bodies, written in our flesh as we toiled in the fields. My friends learned this history from a professor, a book, a film, or someone like me. I have been forced to learn it from the moment I appeared in this world, targeted for either assimilation or extermination.

In the 1990s, this animus toward us returned. In 1994, California Proposition 187, also known as "Save Our State," was placed on the ballot. Its intent was to establish a state-sponsored screening process to bar non-U.S. citizens—like those who work in the fields that feed our nation—from receiving public services, most notably public education. California voters passed it by 58 percent. Even though it was ruled unconstitutional by the courts, the fear it created in people like my father was unimaginable. Though California had always been home, now there was another explicit target on our back, even though we were citizens. Proposition 187 fueled hatred toward all people of Mexican descent. In 1998, California Proposition 227, or the "English in Public Schools" Initiative was approved by 61 percent of the vote. It required that students with "limited English proficiency" be taught in separate classes, effectively returning us all the way to the days prior to the Mendez decision! A study released prior to the proposition said it would affect almost 25 percent of students in K–12. It was not repealed until Proposition 58 passed in 2016. These are but a few ways that anti-Hispanic, -Latinx, and -Xicanx bias and the quest to dominate and assimilate shows up in our history. We can count the ways in which oppression manifests itself. We can take inventory of the ways the purpose gap not only exists but is made worse every day.

All this to say that if you look to me to provide equal attention to the European and colonial histories that we have inherited, I will certainly disappoint you. It is not that those stories are not meaningful or worthy of being taught. Yet if this work is to break new ground in the literature on meaning and purpose and the field of vocation, it needs to honor the stories that are authentic to those communities that are often overlooked, marginalized, and forgotten. If the literature on meaning and purpose does not expand our imagination about our place in the world, then it has failed to do its job. The book you are holding was written in the shadow of the acts of cultural attack and erasure described above. Written in English, it draws on training and education that were driven by colonial narratives. While that training has credentialed me to write this book, I know that I must now do my best to unlearn it. I know that my Chicano identity, like the identities of many persons of color, is intricately tied to being both the colonizer and the colonized.[17] Rather than try to physically, spiritually, socially, intellectually, or economically split myself in half between these two sides of the dichotomy, I, like most readers, have to live into a tension of a both/and. I have a responsibility to decolonize knowledge, and to do so, I may have to undo the very education I received, to write otherwise, and to privilege different stories. I acknowledge the role my ancestors have survived so that I might recover their stories and a sense of purpose for my life.

My hope is that as you journey through this book, you will write your own purpose, drawing on the wisdom of your ancestors and the freedom they want so desperately for you to find.

Reflections

This reflection is not a set of questions but the practice promised in the opening story. Read it through all the way or go to thepurposegap.com to experience the guided meditation.

- Take a moment to get comfortable. Pay attention to your breath.
- Breathe in (one, two, three, four); hold (one, two, three, four, five, six, seven); and breathe out (one, two, three, four, five, six, seven, eight). Breathe like this a few more times until you find yourself present to this moment.
- Now that you are present, imagine the face of someone who loves you more than anything. See in your imagination this person who calls you beloved.
- Call to greater focus their face. See the color and texture of their hair.
- Scan their face. Pay attention to the wrinkles in their forehead.
- See the shape of their eyes. See the color of their eyes, starting from the whites all the way to the pupil.
- Scan down past the shape of their nose, and see them smiling back at you.
- Sit with this person who calls you beloved. See them gazing at you with love.
- In your mind's eye, hear them (or see them sign) the words you need to hear right now.
- What are the words only they can say to you that you need to hear in this moment?
- This person offers those words of love and generosity that you so desperately need to survive, to thrive.
- Sit with their words. Let them wash over you. Know that you are loved.
- See yourself express gratitude for these words. You can see in your imagination giving them a hug, holding their hands, or just simply smiling back.
- Sit with this moment of exchange of love and gratitude.

- Be present to love for just a moment longer. Take as long as you need.
- As you say good-bye to this person who loved you into being, know that you can return to this moment. This good-bye is not forever. It is just for this moment. Let the feeling of gratitude and love wash over you for this time with someone who loves you.
- Say a final good-bye.

Know that you can return to these moments whenever you want. Take inventory of this experience. Who loved you into being? What words did they tell you that only they could say? What was it that you needed to hear?

This meditation was taught to me by my grandma, whom I often see when I do it. It is a practice I do with my son on most nights. If you are a parent, it is wonderful to discover when you lead your children in this reflection that often the person they see is you. I have brought this meditation inside prisons and classrooms and have used it with my friends and staff. The most important thing we can do to close the purpose gap is to remind ourselves that we are loved. We are given this gift by at least one person who knows that we were destined for some great purpose, and, at the very least, that purpose is to know that we are loved into being. Come to this reflection often. When someone else has given us the gift of love, and we likewise lead others to know that they are loved, we close the purpose gap in our souls, those inner worlds that are full of doubts, trauma, pain, and fear. It does not mean that those things go away, but it is a reminder that someone saw all of that and loved us fully.

The practice is simple and allows you to see a loved one, to see how a loved one's cheeks turn upward when they smile at you, to see the way their eyes hold depth, not just in color but in the way the individual rings and colors within those eyes stare back at you like a Frida Kahlo painting, a journey in self-reflection. It reminds us that when the world marks us for dead, someone spoke or is speaking into our life. When I facilitate the practice in groups, I am often overwhelmed by the love and presence of our ancestors that overcomes the room following the exercise, the tears that flow. The collective imagination of any group of people knowing they are fully loved generates the energy capable of closing the purpose gap.

Chapter 3

Designing Purpose

"I am writing because they told me to never start a sentence with *because*. But I wasn't trying to make a sentence—I was trying to break free. Because freedom, I am told, is nothing but the distance between the hunter and its prey."

Ocean Vuong, *On Earth We're Briefly Gorgeous*[1]

My freedom to find my own vocation occurs only when I can give a gift of life, my life, my time, my breath. It is the freedom to choose to give. In chapter 1, we explored the history behind the purpose gap. In chapter 2, we looked at the conditions that create a different starting place for the oppressed. The purpose gap is not an accident. It is designed. In chapter 3, we will explore how this design has impacted oppressed communities and individuals.

When I write, I do so with both pain and rage from the limitations of my freedom to give a gift without expectation. Writing a book, for example, is certainly one way to express that love. But to create the conditions for us to be free, we need community. I am not talking about the beloved community or a dream where freedom is inextricably bound up in the oppressor's goodwill.[2] Rather, I write and design for something far more radical. I am writing about the freedom to choose my purpose or many purposes in life. To live fully into this freedom is the gift I want to give the world. When people have discerned their purpose and are fully alive, the world benefits. If you say that my liberation, my freedom, is bound up in your solidarity, I am no longer free to give you the gift of my presence as an equal.

In conversations of meaning and purpose, in movements for freedom, sentiments often emerge, like, "We will need everyone to make real change." This puts the burden not just on the oppressor to change; it also asserts that the oppressed need to change before they can reach that freedom. The inheritors of a system built on oppression want even our definitions of freedom to be defined with and by them. They want us to acknowledge inherited, unjust power. They want us to recognize that we have no power without them, when their power over us was designed for them to have power over us. Drawing on the work of Frantz Fanon, Nelson Maldonado-Torres makes the case that we cannot achieve freedom until we are free to give a gift without obligation or expectation.[3] When the demand of solidarity is made, it maintains the logic of *power over*. To colonize multiple continents, Europeans stole freedom and purpose. For their descendants to demand participation in the undoing of the system from which they continue to benefit is a remnant of a colonial logic of power that says they are still necessary for the purpose of Black and Brown bodies. It is, however, only in our complete freedom, on our terms, and the gift of our love on our terms, that freedom exists. The oppressed, in achieving freedom, will not do what was done to us to others. We will offer the gift, but we must be free to give it. We must be able to define liberation on our terms, reclaiming the purposes that were stolen from our ancestors.

The power of our ancestors still flows in underground rivers and spiritual wellsprings from which I drink. I am not of this world. I am of God and beloved by God. For those who have been dispossessed, who face annihilation, our liberation and our freedom can only be tied to this body, to this community. When we meet the world fully liberated, then we will know our survival, our lives, our vocations will be a gift to this world. Until this world recognizes us as equals, I reserve my vocation, my life, and my purpose for my community. For my community first called me to life when the world tried to take it.

Cultural Commutes

I left for seminary on a long arduous journey, for I was the first to venture east and first in my family and community to go to graduate school. I sold my motorcycle in Sacramento, California, a yellow Suzuki SV650, to get a little cash before the journey. Two friends, Dante and Lisa, moved with me, or, rather, I went with them. I had a stack of books and a pile of clothes. In our moving van, I occupied the back 1/31st, if that's a number representing cargo size.

I had started the application for seminary but hadn't completed it. Instead of enrolling right away, I went to work. I worked for Home Depot in Sacramento, so I transferred to one of their New England stores: the Saugus Home Depot, located on the side of Route 1, a six-lane highway north of Boston. This treacherous and exposed road became my daily four-mile commute, a difficult one in winter. Have I mentioned I had never lived anywhere with snow?

It was the most terrifying commute of my life. There was no bus route that would take me to work. The closest stop was around a twenty-five-minute walk away, and again, back along this dangerous highway. Dante and Lisa would give me rides on the days they didn't need the car to get to work; thank God for them. For the days they couldn't give me a ride, I bought a small BMX bike, built for tweens. I would ride on the side of the highway in the late afternoon at the same time that angry, hurried, and distracted parents drove on Route 1 to pick up their children from school, usually yelling at the backseat or the radio rather than paying attention to the road.

One day after work as I pedaled this bike, for which I weighed about a hundred pounds too much, a minivan came tearing through the parking lot. I could see that it was heading directly for me. I couldn't get out of the way in time, so I just ditched the bike. As I jumped off, the van came to a screeching halt, barely bumping into the bike that now was on its side in the driveway to the parking lot. The driver got out and looked at me, coffee in hand. "I am having the worst day ever! Are you okay? Do you understand me?" My reaction to the racial undertones of the woman's suggestion that I didn't speak English came rushing to my face. Considering that she was having her "worst day ever," my reaction will bar me from ever being considered for beatification.

This four-mile commute in New England was the hardest commute I have ever had, including the two-trains-and-a-bus, ninety-minute commute from Salem, Massachusetts, to my job at Northeastern University in downtown Boston that I would endure a few years later. It was often cold—especially in autumn. It was not even doable during the winter, so I had to quit my job, though I still find it funny that I was invited back to work the Christmas tree lot. Can you imagine this bald, Chicano, sun-kissed, olive-colored-skinned man, who did not even own a winter coat at the time, selling Christmas trees while attending seminary in New England?

When I was younger, I remember my dad working a lot. It is where I get my work ethic. Every day, he would drive over an hour to make it to his work in his little white, two-door, hatchback Daihatsu Charade. These cars, which stopped U.S. sales and production in 1992, sported a three-cylinder, motorcycle engine that produced 53 horsepower. For reference, most of the small electric or hybrid vehicles today are at least twice as powerful. He would drive this little death machine to a microchip plant, one of the only Latinos in his division. He did this commute to give us a better life. More importantly, I never remember him missing school functions, baseball games, or musical recitals. He was always present. According to Daniel Siegel and Tina Payne Bryson, the most important thing a parent can do is show up.[4]

My ride to the Home Depot on that BMX bike and my father's daily commute both represent the commute people of color and marginalized groups must do to survive every day, not just physically but also socially, psychologically, spiritually, and intellectually. This commute is not relegated to the road. People of color are often provided insufficient resources, such as my BMX bike or my dad's clown car. We do these commutes not just to get to work but to advance our lives and the lives of our children. The late Clayton Christensen, renowned innovator, educator, and business professional specializing in innovation, says that one of the key ways to understand how to derive value is to understand the "job-to-be-done."[5] His insights about innovation are invaluable for those who have the capacity to innovate. For many of us, we are trying to survive our daily commute. The job-to-be-done is to find our daily bread, put enough food on the table, pay our rent, and get enough sleep to wake up and do it all over again.

Commutes are designed. Whether by bike, car, bus, train, plane, or walking, how we get from one place to another was designed. The roads, rail lines, walking and bike paths, and sidewalks are literal representations that allow people to achieve their purpose, to get from one place to the next, from work to home, from community center to church, from school function to athletic events, from backyard cookouts to the park. There are values placed on how we design our transportation systems. If you commute via public transit, you know exactly how many stops there are before your destination. If you are poor, you know that most public transportation is intentionally designed to limit your accessibility. If a train is the preferred way of travel, as it was for me in Boston, the poor must take busses just to get to the train. This is by design.

If your commute is on the freeways, highways, and interstates, you know all the land-markers and junction points. You can see design in the roads we build. In Atlanta where I currently live, there is a junction between two major interstates, I-285 and I-85. Where these two meet is Tom Moreland Exchange, known informally as Spaghetti Junction. It is considered one of the worst truck logjams in the country. Not only is it a mess to drive through; it is an eyesore from any angle. A five-level or "five-stack" interchange, it connects 300,000 cars daily on its fourteen bridges. The design challenge is clear: to unclog traffic. Not only does the interchange *not* do that; the costs to build and maintain the exchange, both economic and social, are extravagant.

However, there is also a purpose cost. As reported in the *New York Times* by Kevin Kruse, the interchange system was designed to separate citizens. He writes,

> The Downtown Connector—a 12-to-14-lane mega-highway that in theory connects the city's north to its south—regularly has three-mile-long traffic jams that last four hours or more. Commuters might assume they're stuck there because some city planner made a mistake, but the heavy congestion actually stems from a great success. In Atlanta, as in dozens of cities across America, daily congestion is a direct consequence of a century-long effort to segregate the races.[6]

This interchange symbolizes the purpose gap. What it connects was designed to separate, to segregate. To make it through the interchange, drivers persist through miles of backup. If you live in Atlanta, you can feel the Black/white split, with the majority of Black and African American families living south or west of the exchange, and majority-white communities in the northern suburbs. However, gentrification is happening at an alarming rate in Atlanta, pushing many families even farther south of I-20 or west of I-85, south and west of Atlanta, respectively. Historically, Mayor Bill Hartsfield in the 1950s used the creation of I-20 for the explicit purpose of separating Black and white communities.

Such divisions are not unique to Atlanta. Sara McLafferty and Valerie Preston analyzed the commutes of New Yorkers and found that "Blacks, Asians, and Hispanic women and men are concentrated in jobs that have long commutes." At the same time, "the urban core has become a region of heightened advantage, as White men, and an increasing share of White women, commute short times to well-paid jobs."[7] My hometown of Salinas segregated Mexican Americans and white communities using Highway 101, literally splitting the town in half. Two distinct communities: East Salinas or Alisal (Latino), and Salinas or South Salinas to locals (white), even though these two parts of the city are under the authority of

Salinas. This historic divide can be seen in the discrepancies in income, education level, and access to long-term economic and social opportunities. Sociologist Jessica Trounstine writes,

> Segregation is *not* simply the result of individual choices about where to live. Neither racial antipathy nor economic inequality between groups is enough to create and perpetuate segregation. The maintenance of property values and the quality of public goods are collective endeavors. And like all collective endeavors, they require collective action for production and stability. Local governments provide this collective action. . . . At stake is the quality of life accessible to residents and markets available to commercial interests. The result has been *segregation by design.*[8]

In the city of Salinas, where the majority of the community is Latino/a, the average person has at least a 25-minute commute, usually to agricultural or service work. Alisal, a neighborhood within the Salinas city limits, is 97 percent Latina/o. Only 38 percent of those over the age of twenty-five have a high school diploma; 5 percent have a four-year college degree; and less than 1 percent have a graduate degree in any field. What residents are commuting to is manual labor and low-wage jobs, with no viable alternatives or industries. The community stays in poverty, displayed in the average adjusted gross income of only $28,710. There is no way for families to generate wealth or capital. More importantly, to afford the cost of living in the California town, where the average price of a home in Alisal is nearly $335,000, it is no wonder that the census bureau classifies it as having a "high" population density per capita at 6,678 people per square mile. People must live on top of one another. We can all agree, especially when field workers toiled in the soil throughout the global COVID-19 pandemic, it is essential work. The purpose gap exists due to the lack of options and choices. People in Alisal have few choices other than to provide the seasonal labor for the fields and packing sheds, and it is by design.

Compare Alisal to what is referred to as South Salinas, where the majority of white residents live and represent a small minority of just 12 percent of the total population in the broader city of Salinas. Residents in this part of town have an average income of $55,082. While the cost of their housing is not much better at $474,897, there are only 1,919 people per square mile, a third of the population density of Alisal. Not only do they own homes at higher rates than those in Alisal, but the social networks in South Salinas also represent management and ownership in agribusiness and the professional-services class. A conscious decision to design the two communities apart from one another has led to an oligarchical relationship that perpetuates the few getting rich, and it creates both physical and psychological barriers against Latino/a/x young people seeing their purposes beyond the fields they labor. As my dad tells me, "It's truly amazing that you got out of Salinas."

Cultural commutes are some of the greatest barriers to closing the purpose gap, and we are not just talking about a few extra minutes in traffic on the freeway or bus. Not only do the oppressed have to overcome historic injustices, but we must also contend with modern designs built on those histories. If we want future generations to thrive, many of us are traveling extremely far to the sources of power. The cultural commute is more than just the physical miles from Brown neighborhoods to white concentrations of power; it also includes the cultural travel: the code switching, translating, and learning to survive a game that is designed for us to lose. The few who can move to the other side of these commutes can shorten the commute of future generations. However, to truly close the purpose gap, it is not just about surviving the commutes. Our work is to challenge the existence of the commute, to challenge the very design of our worlds. If society was designed to marginalize and oppress us, closing the purpose gap means creating alternative worlds where the cultural commute does not exist, where people can live and thrive on their own terms and see themselves reflected in the design.

Reflections

Write about your cultural commute. What is the distance between your starting place and your destination? Was the commute designed to ease your work and life purpose? What is the distance between your culture and the dominant culture? What was the cultural commute of your ancestors?

How would you redesign your commute? How would you reimagine your cultural commute to serve you and the generation coming behind you?

Design and the Purpose Gap

The commutes and the roads that divide our communities are designed. To put it in biblical and theological terms, who was more likely to become an architect or artist under Egyptian or Roman rule? And knowing that the Torah and the New Testament are about finding freedom, is it desirable to achieve "success" under or within these empires? The design creates the conditions for individuals to achieve their purpose. It will be helpful to see the genesis of design and design thinking. Design thinking envisions the practices and processes to discern novel ideas and solutions to timeless problems. The term goes back to John E. Arnold and William J. Clancey's 1959 book *Creative Engineering*.[9] However, the practice of design goes back much further. The engineering of Teotihuacan, or the "Calendar Stone," epitomizes design that combines function and beauty from my culture. In recent years, design and design thinking have become their own disciplines in every industry. However, Liedtka and Ogilvie suggest that four principal questions define the overall discipline of design:

1. What is?
2. What if?
3. What wows?
4. What works?[10]

These four questions provide the cornerstone for designers, who are committed to designing solutions to real-world and human problems. The standards—musical pun intended—we can gather from these four principles of design thinking come from Liedtka and Ogilvie.[11] They argue that design can be used to create social good, to create conditions for all to thrive.

Looking at these four principles within the narrative above, I find myself answering the four questions in relation to the purpose gap:

1. *What is?* People are intentionally segregated and, for my people, provided little escape from poverty, violence, and abuse. There is a gap between access to the tools and resources for Black and Brown children achieving their dreams and for white children.
2. *What if?* What if there were opportunities to find meaning and purpose without the fear of poverty, violence, and abuse? What would it look like for a Latinx child in the United States to have the same opportunities as their white, middle-class counterparts? Or what if Black and Brown children, who are more likely to get locked up in this country, had the opportunity to find freedom in education instead of incarceration in cages?
3. *What wows?* For decades, freedom schools have been spaces and places closing the education gap through literacy for Black and

Brown youth. More importantly, those children are growing up to expand that imagination, like Mayor Michael Tubbs of Stockton, California. In 2016 and at the ripe age of twenty-six, he was elected mayor of Stockton. He has experimented with a program of guaranteed income of $500 a month for selected citizens for an eighteen-month trial period. "What wows" is an African American young adult running for mayor of a major U.S. city and having a vision bold enough to try something new and then re-budgeting to actualize that dream, closing the opportunity gap for others behind and beside him.[12]

4. *What works?* What works is young adults and people of color not waiting for well-meaning people to do the right thing but taking power and agency and creating conditions for our communities to thrive. If you do not come from a minoritized community and if the implications of that sentence make you anxious, be assured that when the community looks out for those most marginalized, the entire society is better for it.

As we ask these four questions about the implications design has for our lives, we must be aware that design is all around us. People are making decisions about the way we structure our lives that have implications for how we discern our purpose. To think that the same design thinking that has widened the purpose gap has produced the tools to close it would be foolish. Prior to critiquing its value, though, let me provide two examples where design was particularly powerful for challenging the cultural divides and creating beauty on our own terms. Both examples are not from engineering but from the arts.

At the same time that design thinking came to define systemic innovation in the late 1950s and 1960s, Rod Serling's *The Twilight Zone* premiered, and Miles Davis dropped *Kind of Blue*. Why does this matter? Serling's *The Twilight Zone*, recently revamped by Jordan Peele in 2019, provided social commentary of his era, namely, regarding civil rights and human nature. Serling did so through compelling storytelling on television. Viewers of all colors and creeds were mesmerized by the show, where story lines challenged popular notions of who belonged in our community. Beauty is in the eye of the beholder, for the rise of white supremacy in small-town America, or the lack of connection and deep sense of isolation people feel were all themes Serling addressed in his work. Every episode is a masterclass in design, as Serling attempts to story the very conditions people were experiencing in their everyday lives.

Both Serling and Davis expressed the human experience of their time. They designed prototypes—sketches in Serling's case and musical tracks in Davis's. These prototypes get formed and re-formed, iterated repeatedly to gain deeper insights and accomplish their purpose. Serling knew the limitations of a story thread, which he showed in "The Monster," an episode where an alien comes to a Mexican town across the border from Texas. People mistrust and kill the monster only to reveal that the mysterious being brought a gift containing a cure to cancer. It is a sorely needed commentary today as we lock children up at the border. The doctor who will cure cancer may be sitting in one of our cages. Serling knew his commentary on fear of the other did not just relate to immigration but also to race. He wrote "Eye of the Beholder" to show the limitations of our standards of beauty. "Monsters Are Due on Maple Street" explores the breakdown of relations in "Anywhere, U.S.A." The full breadth, captured in the seasons and the eventual remakes, were the products of design: conscious choices to world-build. It was a new art form, a story arc, that allowed commentary on the breakdown of our social relations into every home. Through his design, Serling provided a mirror to the prejudice and marginalization of his time, and he was able to deliver that message into every home through his popular show.

Miles Davis's *Kind of Blue* similarly brought a new art form into every home. Using modular jazz, *Kind of Blue*, aside from being the highest-selling jazz album of all time, grew its own legend. As the story goes, Davis recorded tracks in just one or two takes. Although not true of all the tracks on the album, the story around it continued to capture the imagination of listeners. Davis invited saxophonist John Coltrane, who I have to add is one of the all-time greats (I'm biased, as that is my instrument); Julian "Cannonball" Adderley; Bill Evans (and Wynton Kelly for one track) on keys; Paul Chambers on bass; and drummer Jimmy Cobb. The legend goes that Davis gave a set of scales for each performer to guide their improvisations, and after a warm-up, they started rolling the tape. Together, they orchestrated some of the most iconic tracks ever to be played.

Kind of Blue, in its totality, is a similar expression of social commentary. Drawing on various genres and forms, the album is an expression of what might be considered the greatest design sprint of all time.[13] Davis brought together a group of diverse players with expertise in a variety of domains (in this case instruments), provided some design parameters (in the form of scales), and they began their rapid prototyping. These experts played together, finding what worked, keeping what went well, getting rid of what did not serve the track or album's theme, and iterating until Davis had the feel he wanted. What I love about considering Davis's album as human-centered design is that it does not presume or jettison expertise. In much of the design-thinking literature and in the design sprints I have been a part of, we think that the diversity bonus or novel idea will come from random novices getting together in a room and seeing what emerges. Sometimes this produces innovative ideas, but to execute those ideas, we need people who are willing to work on the problem and master the skills and tools to the point they may create new tools and skills.

What I love about Serling and Davis as exemplars of design is that they provide an artistic twist to the mechanistic and engineering backdrop of design thinking's foundation. They provide an emotive, storied element to design that speaks to the purpose gap directly. Both Serling and Davis create art from the real world, from the complex problems and issues of their time. Many designers would analyze the individual components of their work. For example, how did Serling use human-centered design and design thinking to create a single episode of the *Twilight Zone?* How did Davis use design principles to create individual tracks for *Kind of Blue?* Serling and Davis, like many leaders in design today in the social sector, are not thinking about singular products but, instead, are concerned with the larger questions of the day. The human-centered design questions that they were asking were not how to make a better individual episode or track, though they certainly did that. Rather, they were asking, "How do we create something that provides the colors, hues, soundtrack, commentary, and emotion to the times in which we find ourselves? How do we change how people experience everyday life?" It is in the scope of work that they are designers.

Take my friend and legend Don Lewis, esteemed musician and electronic engineer. He created the Live Electronic Orchestra (LEO), an electronic system of multiple instruments, and later machines like the Roland TR-808 drum machine that allowed musicians to create their own drumbeats. Not only is Don Lewis one of the most gifted musicians of our time; many of the beats on the tracks you listen to are created on machines that trace their origins to his designs. If you are trying to create a new sound today, his expertise would be invaluable.

These examples are expressions of "What if?" What if design was leveraged to close the purpose gap? Can we create otherwise? Is there a way to leverage design to design our lives in ways that are equitable and just?

Reflections

What are you designing? Where do you have expertise? What room can you walk into and have instant expertise? What story are you telling? What music are you making?

Designing Purpose

Some very clever designers have been thinking about this relationship between design and finding purpose. The clearest examples are Bill Burnett and Dave Evans. Famous for one of the most attended classes in Stanford University history, Bill Burnett, executive director of the design program at Stanford, and Dave Evans, product designer, management consultant, and co-founder of Electronic Arts (EA for the gamers out there), applied the principles they used in industry to design the ideal life. Their book *Designing Your Life: How to Build a Well-Lived, Joyful Life* instantly became a *New York Times* bestseller.[14] Their process is simple and provides some clear advice. They emphasize curiosity, trying things, reframing problems, focusing on process, and asking for help.[15] They apply design principles to one's life, often expressed in our chosen vocations and personal lives. Design principles are leveraged to clarify, prioritize, and act on one's values. In their follow-up work, *Designing Your Work Life: How to Thrive and Change and Find Happiness at Work*, they focus their research on how one can leverage design for work.[16] They leverage the same process: Stay curious; try stuff; reframe problems; focus on process; ask for help; and tell the story. For those in college or exploring a new career path in a white-collar, professional setting, both books are incredibly helpful. The way that Burnett and Evans create the space to discern one's purpose using design is helpful and accessible—or is it?

One of their case studies includes their Bay Area neighbor, IDEO. IDEO, a design and consulting firm founded in the early 1990s, has also provided some of the most concrete definitions and practices of design thinking in the popular zeitgeist. Under the leadership of Tim Brown[17] and its founders David Kelley, Bill Moggridge, and Mike Nuttall, they have leveraged design thinking in industries such as education, film-making, furniture, and electronics, and, more recently in 2011, IDEO .org was established as the nonprofit wing to help the social sector bring design thinking into the world.

While reading their work and the countless number of writers who emulate their work, I had to ask myself, "How does one design for community?" How do we design for the thriving of those most marginalized? Specifically, would this approach to design still work for students outside a prestigious institution like Stanford? What if Burnett and Evans offered their course at the institution to which I went just 130 miles away, California State University, Sacramento (Sac State)? Stanford, with seven thousand students and an annual tuition and fees of $53,529 as of 2020, is consistently ranked in the top ten of institutions, often vying for the no. 1 university ranking spot depending on year and class. Professors are some of the most peer-reviewed in their fields. They have a near-perfect completion rate for students. Contrast Stanford with Sac State, with enrollment at around 23,450 and just over $7,000 annual tuition and fees. It is not ranked nationally. Only around half of their student body graduate in a six-year period. Both schools serve a shared purpose to educate the next generation, but for whom? And for what? What are they preparing students to do in the world?

I am not going to rehash the history of higher education or the purpose of private research universities versus public colleges and universities. Michael Wolf[18] and Kathleen Fitzpatrick[19] do an excellent job at providing that history and sketching out a purpose for higher education. Instead I ask, "What if this course were taught at my undergraduate institution?" because I am genuinely curious about the options available to students like me. What difference would it make in the lives those colleges students who are first-generation students of color? While Burnett and Evans can explore work and life with students at Stanford, the options, the vocational pathways, the many opportunities to find purpose and meaning are vastly different than those for the students of Sac State. That does not mean that the students are any less capable. In fact, one might argue given the student body, using measurements like those outlined in Angela Duckworth's *Grit: The Power of Passion and Perseverance*, that students at Sac State might actually fair better in facing adversity when searching out their purpose.[20] If we are going to take conditions seriously, we need to go back to "What is?" We need to start taking seriously how we are designing.

In *Design Justice: Community-Led Practices to Build Worlds We Need*, Sasha Costanza-Chock delivers a powerful challenge to individualist design principles noted by many of the industries above.[21] Costanza-Chock writes out of a community of designers committed to thinking about just, inclusive, accessible, and decolonial design. She makes the case that design, when redefined through the collective, will benefit the community and the individual. Thus, the questions are not simply about scale and simplicity, and the question of "good" shifts to include the community in the process. Does the design reflect the needs of all its members, not just a chosen few? Does the design lead to the liberation of the least of these? Does the design reflect the freedom people are trying to achieve in their daily lives? Questions like these radically redefine the project of the Stanford classroom. It does not just recognize the purpose gap, but it starts from that place.

Costanza-Chock writes,

> Design justice is a framework for analysis of how design distributes benefits and burdens between various groups of people. Design justice focuses explicitly on the ways that design reproduces and/or challenges the matrix of domination (white supremacy, heteropatriarchy, capitalism, ableism, settler colonialism, and other forms of structural inequality). Design justice is also a growing community of practice that aims to ensure a more equitable distribution of design's benefits and burdens; meaningful participation in design decisions; and recognition of community-based, Indigenous, and diasporic design traditions, knowledge, and practices.[22]

Costanza-Chock reminds us that these principles for "good" design come directly from the community. She shares the principles of design justice that were generated in the Design Justice Network community. The ten principles of this network, which we will return to in the chapter about networks, focus on healing, empowerment, and well-being for the community. They focus on sharing and not exploiting the community and amplify and rely on the voices who are most impacted by the design.[23] The focus of design is on building together the worlds and communities we want to inhabit. It is designing so there is not a purpose gap.

This is world building. Good design is taking responsibility for changing the conditions of one's material world. Anthropologist Arturo Escobar challenges our notions of design as a benevolent practice in and of itself.[24] In *Design for the Pluriverse: Radical Interdependence, Autonomy, and the Making of Worlds*, Escobar claims that design is about the ethical practice of community and world building. Escobar is not content with the idea that design is limited to or only produces products, buildings, and things to be consumed or used. Driven by a similar commitment to justice and decolonial alternatives in design, Escobar suggests that design is the process by which we order, define, and build worlds. This has profound implications for how we inhabit those worlds. It is more than just care for the environment; it is living with regenerative purpose, where what we design serves future generations. We return to this question of inhabitancy in our conversation about taking the work of closing the purpose gap home in a later chapter. But for now, I hope that you carry forward the idea that design provides a powerful set of tools for us to think generatively about how we think about the worlds we inhabit. It is not a complete tool kit, and, as Costanza-Chock and Escobar have pointed out, it needs to be rethought considering its modern bent toward colonial industrialization. Design, however, when imagined through our communities, can heal and close the purpose gap.

We need to design new systems and worlds that reflect our communities. We do that in our closing chapter when we draw on our past to design our future. What in our collective histories and traditions was forgotten, destroyed, or co-opted that we can recover or reimagine for our collective freedom? How do we build worlds that reflect a regenerative future for us collectively—worlds that create more life than they destroy? As Brazilian educator Paulo Freire affirms, the "people's vocation" is to humanization and life.[25]

Can the flourishing of the community be the stated purpose of design? Can we construct collective purpose? The answer is yes.

Chapter 4

Vocation of Communities and Institutions

Communal Vocation

I have a painting hanging in our home of the interior of the Everett Public Library. Libraries have always been special places for our family. When we were dating, my wife worked in a music library, and I would often find her sorting through the stacks of old manuscripts, soaking up their papery scent. Growing up, the library was a place of retreat and quiet where no one judged my eagerness for reading. When we lived in Everett, Washington, we lived in an apartment next door to the library. The library had a coffee shop attached to it that cloaked the whole block in the savory aroma of coffee beans. For a writer and someone who loves to read as much as I do, it was a dream come true. I loved this library not just because I could check out as many books as I wanted or that it was within walking distance of my home, but also because of the programs and services it provided for my son, Asher, who was two at the time we lived there. They had a children's section with rows and rows of books, puzzles, DVDs, and music. It was one of the places where we met other members of the local deaf and hard-of-hearing community for evening classes and play time with his friends. It was at the library where he learned that whenever he wanted books, we did not have to pay for them.

By being local, people trusted us fully to borrow and return our favorite titles that filled our lives with joy. It is the same space where Asher learned to talk to and be with those who are experiencing homelessness, as libraries are now one of the crucial sites for many social services. The library redefined who mattered and who belonged, and my son learned firsthand not only that he but even those most marginalized in the city mattered and belonged. It was a magical place. A place that when you walked in the doors, the spirit of love, welcome, and hospitality washed over you. When you opened the pages of the book or talked to the people who were both regulars and worked at the library, you walked away feeling loved and more connected than ever before. This library was a holy, sacred space. People came as they were, received what they needed, and left feeling connected to the broader community. It was fulfilling its mission to the fullest: "The Everett Public Library connects the community and all its members to resources and services that inform, educate, and entertain. We provide open access to lifelong learning. We embrace the future while preserving the past."[1]

Can institutions have a vocation? Can they have a principled orientation that guides their work, purpose, and reason for being? In all my work on meaning and purpose, community centers and libraries emerge as institutions living into this call of meaning and purpose. From field workers and ex-gang members to scholars and executives, these spaces have created the conditions for all members to thrive. These institutions are living out their call. They have a vocation. Our question thus needs to be, Do all institutions have a vocation or purpose? And can that vocation or purpose be to close the purpose gap?

The United States accepts the idea of "corporate personhood," which says corporations, differentiated from the people that make up an institution, have the same rights and responsibilities under the law as an individual person. Whether or not corporate personhood should be something that exists in U.S. legal battles, the idea that corporations, organizations, and institutions have similarities to people is not new for scholars. Since institutions create conditions or in some cases are themselves the conditions in which people find meaning and purpose, it is important for us to see how institutions frame or think about their purpose in the world. In the simplest of analogies to describe this importance, if you are training to be the next great musician, an institution like a library might help you understand the history of your vocation, but it is not the place to practice it. Knowing why institutions exist is important for us to understand how we might better work with and within them to activate and design our own purposes.

Walter Wink, in his well-read trilogy exploring the "Powers," suggests that institutions have spirits, angels, and, though he never goes so far as to say it, I would argue vocations and purposes as well. To illustrate this point, he asks of the dominant system,

Do these entities possess actual metaphysical being, or are they the "corporate personality" or ethos or gestalt of a group, having no independent existence apart from the group? I leave that for the reader to decide. My main objection to personalizing demons is that they then are regarded as having a "body" or form separate from the physical and historical institutions which, on my theory, they are the actual interiority. Therefore, I prefer to regard them as the impersonal spiritual realities at the center of institutional life.[2]

What Wink is clear about is that institutions, governments, organizations, churches, and large systems in general absolutely have a spirit. If we want to design conditions for people to thrive through our institutions, he says that it "requires a kind of spiritual discernment and praxis."[3] I will return to address the vocational literature on discernment shortly. First, it is crucial to see how Wink addresses this diagnosis of communities, institutions, organizations, and systems, which he affectionately names "Powers." Wink's diagnoses for systems and institutions is a theological model. He argues that we must recognize that Powers are good. And like humans, the Powers have fallen and because of that, they can be redeemed. His prescription is to redeem these fallen Powers by, as the title suggests, engaging them through nonviolence guided by the teachings of Jesus. As a linguist and biblical scholar, Wink weaves together how this prescription becomes the work of good people to redeem good institutions.

What is the role of religious leaders and the church regarding these Powers? Andy Crouch is clear to remind us that all institutions "create and distribute power" and have "the ability to make something of the world."[4] Crouch cleverly argues that "power is simply (and not so simply) the ability to participate in that stuff-making, sense-making process that is the most distinctive thing that human beings do."[5] In Crouch's definition, institutions have the power to design our society. The church not only has a call, vocation, and purpose. More importantly, it has the means and power to act on its purpose.

According to Wink, that purpose is to "practice a ministry of disclosing the spirituality of these Powers."[6] Wink goes as far as to say that the "church cannot discharge its divine calling."[7] The divine calling is to name the spirit of the Powers and to redeem them. In Wink's assessment, the church, in its best form, is not part of the Powers. It has a role to play to address the Powers, a vocation to hold the Powers accountable.

This is reflected in my own tradition, as Robert Chao Romero writes in his groundbreaking work *Brown Church*.[8] As a scholar of the Chicano/a movements, he reflects on *El Plan Espiritual de Aztlán* as a foundational artifact of the Chicano/a and civil rights movement, a document that affirms life. The focus of "*La Causa*," fighting for "labor rights for farmworkers, educational reform, and women's rights," found its genesis in the Brown Church.[9] The Brown Church, to which I feel very much indebted for my notions of freedom and liberation, finds its genesis in contested histories. Like the history traced in the previous chapter, Romero notes that the Indigenous people of this land were subject to the colonial Christian empire whose policy was to dominate in order to either convert the "savage" to Christianity or commit genocide against the people, "codified in *El Requerimiento* in 1513."[10] But this is not the only story. Another story of the Brown Church is a story of redemption that holds the colonial church accountable to the violence against Indigenous people and people of color.

Only a few decades after the *Requerimiento* of 1513, Romero recalls the writing of Bartolomé de Las Casas (1484–1566), "the central founder of the Brown Church and progenitor of Brown Theology in the Americas."[11] He recovers Las Casas's writing as a social justice witness, which combines theological, legal, and scientific evidence to advocate for those who had been dehumanized in the Americas. Romero notes that Las Casas's vision for shared humanity evolved over the course of his lifetime.[12] He argues that there is a historic thread from Las Casas until today with the Brown Church, one that believes in and advocates for the sacredness of every human being. This thread includes Sor Juana Inés de la Cruz (1648–1695), who was an interdisciplinary scholar and writer before the term existed. She drew on the sciences, poetry, theology, and the arts, writing on behalf of the Indigenous people in Mexico. She was fluent in colonial and ecclesial Latin, Spanish, and the local Nahuatl. If there ever was the patron saint of closing the purpose gap, it would be Sor Juana. As Theresa Yugar reminds us, she challenged the Powers:

> Her life and writings critiqued patriarchal ideologies and social structures that denied the full self-actualization of the people in her social location, Spaniard, non-Spaniard, man or woman. . . . The realization of the dream demanded that the narrative and the oral traditions of her ancestors, the Mesoamerican Nahua people, be heard and affirmed by all people in her post-conquest world. Their cosmic worldview and belief systems needed to be reclaimed. In Sor

Juana's her-story, the ancient wisdom of the Nahua people held the answer to harmony in her region and the epistemological question of what it meant to be human after the conquest.[13]

Sor Juana is recognized as the Latina feminist who attempted to bridge the gap between the descendants of those who were victims of the conquest and the Powers of her time. She was attempting to close the purpose gap hundreds of years ago.

Romero continues this history through the civil rights era, reflecting on the Chicano theology latent within the now iconic United Farmworkers Union founders César Chávez and Dolores Huerta. In the *dichos*, everyday philosophy and sayings, that Chávez learned from his family and that fueled his sense of nonviolence, God and Jesus were on the side of the poor. This spirituality kept alive a long history of Brown spiritual freedom fighters and was leveraged for political and social change on behalf of the most marginalized.[14] Their theology was rooted in both their faith in the gospel and their unique cultural context.[15] Romero claims that the Brown Church's role is to recognize and work to restore dignity to every human, to close the purpose gap for every living person. The Brown Church has long been the church that Wink hopes will redeem the Powers.

I offer no criticism against Wink's work in how to address the Powers, and he certainly addressed the spiritual and physical violence of the church's complicity in colonialism, violence, domination, patriarchy, and homophobia. However, while the Powers may need redeeming, this view of redemption can only come from a place of relative safety, a sense that the vocation of the Powers is redeemable. I can imagine Wink writing in the early 1990s, thinking about his audience: good, church-going people who support the Powers, even in less-than-holy activities.

The conditions in which he formulated this view of the system, the way he entered the text, was different from that of, say, Romero or the author James Baldwin. Baldwin, with whose experience I more closely align, famously claimed he had to flee the United States to write so that he could focus away from the racism that threatened his life. The Powers did not view Wink with such regard. He certainly challenged its vocation, and therefore was a threat, but he was not an outsider. He was an insider who was able to claim nonviolence without any violence afflicting his body. Or, at least, this was my first read of his work.

In the late 2000s, I was able to meet Wink and participate in one of his final lectures. I came ready to remind him of the conditions of the *barrio* and to persuade him that systems were not redeemable—that the only way to push back was to actively resist death. The vocation of these institutions was death. Not the celebratory death I had come to know, the death of poets like Octavio Paz and the death and connection to ancestors I practice in my home every year. I wanted to convince him that the Powers were out to annihilate us, to commit genocide. The purpose gap was too real. We had so few options to us. There was no way these Powers he wrote about were redeemable. But during Wink's lecture, he quoted a few biblical verses from Matthew 5:38–42. It is worth remembering the words here:

> [38] "You have heard that it was said, 'An eye for an eye and a tooth for a tooth.' [39] But I say to you, Do not resist an evildoer. But if anyone strikes you on the right cheek, turn the other also; [40] and if anyone wants to sue you and take your coat, give your cloak as well; [41] and if anyone forces you to go one mile, go also the second mile. [42] Give to everyone who begs from you, and do not refuse anyone who wants to borrow from you."

To explore these texts, he embodied them. He invited three actors to join him through each of the ideas in the text in a reverse performative order.

First, he looked at verse 41, about going an extra mile. He had a friend give his bag to him. He then walked around the room one time with it in hand. After completing one full lap around the room, Wink, as old and fragile as he was at the time, took off and scurried around the room a second time. The room immediately laughed. He suggested that Roman law allowed soldiers to force citizens to go one mile, but anything beyond that is a violation of the law. By forcing them to go an extra mile, the soldier now is placed in a predicament to be punished or plead with a citizen to give his pack back. Either way, he was not viewed as the strong, powerful Roman soldier. What we have here is Jesus "helping an oppressed people find a way to protest and neutralize an onerous practice despised throughout the empire. He is not giving a nonpolitical message of spiritual world-transcendence. He is formulating a worldly spirituality in which the people at the bottom of society or under the thumb of imperial power learn to recover their humanity."[16] Wink embodied this text in a humorous way, and in many cases, given his age, dramatized how to carry that weight an extra mile as a way of asserting his own humanity. This moved me, but it still did not mean that the Powers were redeemable.

If someone were to sue you, give them your cloak. Wink had a friend, in a staged act, strip down to his underwear. Like going the extra mile, he reflected that those in debt during this time were often driven into more debt. The system is very similar to the credit system we have currently. This continuation of forcing people to pay back more money, with interest, and more if they miss paying, perpetuates poverty. Standing before Wink, the young man appeared almost naked, just as in the verse. He says by the poor giving over their garments, "there stands the creditor, covered with shame, the poor debtor's outer garment in the one hand, and his undergarment in the other."[17] Not only is the creditor not going to win this case, but he is officially embarrassed in the process. Would the Powers be so heartless to take the very clothes off his back? If they did, it was shameful for them to look on a naked body. The act was to embarrass the Powers. It was an act of radical defiance.

Even today, people who are experiencing poverty are more likely to accrue debts that they simply cannot afford to pay off. Imagine the following radical act of defiance: imagine that during the housing crisis that accompanied the great recession that started in 2008, those who had their homes and lives stripped from them all showed up in court, turning over their undergarments? What if the big banks, who received tax dollars from these very same citizens, were confronted with the damage they caused to the nearly 10 million people who, while naked, lost their homes between 2004 and 2012?[18] As I write this, I wonder what would happen if in the period directly after COVID-19 in 2020, the world paid first the poor who were already in debt prior to the pandemic instead of the corporations? What if those who lost everything because of the economic recession approached the banking and finance industry without clothes? What else could they take? Certainly, humans would not take the "shirt off another's back."

As I watched these vignettes, I thought to myself there is no way he is going to convince me to turn the other cheek. We either run for our lives, or we stand and fight. Fight or flight. Survival in the streets taught me how to navigate the powerful striking my body. There was no third option. I read his text. I knew the argument. Turning the other cheek was a way of addressing inequalities of the day. A backhand was the strike of choice by the Powers toward all those who were inferior. To turn the other cheek would be to assert equality, to claim humanity, for the Powers to strike you as an equal. A nice argument for someone to make who had never been in fights like me or my community. We fought or ran for our lives. Wink asked for a volunteer. He could sense my energy in the back row, knee bopping up and down, ready to challenge the thinking. He invited me up to the front of the room. I stood in front of him. His eyes squinted. He read the passage briefly, and then pretended to back-hand me. He made a face where it was clear that he was not only going to strike me down like a Roman soldier, but he looked at me with disgust, as if I were less than human, as if I deserved it. I remember my face getting a little red. We were just pretending, but there was something very real in his eyes. A white man striking the Chicano young person in front of him. I had been here before.

Instantly, I was taken back to the fifth grade when I used to get in a fight with a particular classmate. Fist fights were a regular thing, usually at the end of recess as we had those "Next point wins" moments, trying to beat the bell. The Powers, who in this story are our elementary school teachers, allowed us to play tackle football, something that, thank God, has changed in elementary schools. At the end of one recess, I remember my classmate coming up and clocking me for tackling him too hard on his final play. We began to go at it, separated by our teacher by the necklines of our t-shirts. I am sure our teacher was overwhelmed and tired of the number of times this fighting took place. He brought us back to the class-room. "Today, we are going to learn about the justice system," he said. "I need some volunteers to be our jury." For the rest of that morning until lunch he held a mock trial with our class. The jury of our peers let the other kid off. They found me "guilty," and our teacher as the judge took the liberty to give me the "maximum" punishment, a phone call to my parents. It is worth noting here that I had one friend on the jury, Aimee, always my first pick in sports because she was not only a good friend but also the best teammate. She came up after to tell me she was the lone dissenting voice, because the teacher had made it clear he did not want to talk to the other parents, who were white, and he "could handle" my dad. A white teacher could handle one Brown dad.

Even in fifth grade, I had a sense of justice, so I refused. The maximum punishment, according to this ad hoc judicial process, was that I was to miss the rest of recess for the week, had to write these stupid one-pagers about character in cursive, and go to the principal's immediately to contact my parents. I was doing none of it, especially getting up from my seat to go to the principal's office. Remember that long commute my dad had? I was not making him drive all the way to the school to get me. I remember sitting there, stone-faced, and saying to the principal, "No." Had I read Albert Camus[19] or James Cone,[20] I would have known the power of this no. This no was my only recourse to assert my full humanity. I expected justice. I expected equality.

As I sat in defiance, the teacher became more and more enraged. He grabbed my desk and lifted me up in it and said he would take me out. I somehow managed to make myself weigh the desk down, throwing my weight into the ground like I was part of the carpet squares covering a concrete floor. He yelled and screamed for me to get up. I must have been smiling at this point because I knew I was winning based on how angry the teacher was. He was no more than an arm's length from my face when he spit directly into it. I remember being so overwhelmed that crying uncontrollably was all that I could do. I had refused the Powers, and the Powers spit in my face. From an early age I learned that my peers could not be counted on to provide support in the face of overwhelming power and that when push came to shove, the Powers viewed me as less than human.

Fast forward to this moment with Wink in graduate school. I knew the face that he was making. I knew that look in his eye. It was the face of my fifth-grade teacher. Disdain. Disgust. Supremacy. I was raised on fight or flight. There is no third way, and I would not allow another person to spit in my face. When professors and colleagues made that face when I would speak or ask questions "from my context," I was sure to fight or flight; no passivity here. It was the face that dominant-culture people make when they think you do not belong. I pretended to take the slap, but my body tensed, ready to respond. The body remembers the trauma of abuse and violence inflicted on it.[21] He said to the group, "We are only playing, but look at him. He did not make eye contact with me when he came up here, and he has not made eye contact with me since we started playing." Realizing that even in play, I had let the act change my behavior, even in the slightest, enraged me. There was no way I was going to let this stupid demonstration of a parable of Jesus be the source for these white educators to mock my Brownness, again. I was exposed. There were only two options: fight or flight.

I straightened up instantly, back straight, chest out. I was going to tell him about the weight of my family and my community. My neck puffed out. My chin went up. My eyes did not move from his. This little old man may have been playing, but I was not. He then said, "Now, I don't know you. But you look like you come from a long, proud family." The Reyes and Contreras families are not just strong; we are the embodiment of a strength in numbers, spirit, and blood. "If I backhanded you, it was because I thought you were less than me. Show me what would happen if you were back home?" I remember thinking, "This dude does not know what he is asking!" I was ready. This is what I came here for. I puffed out my chest a little more, lifted my chin, and stepped directly up to an incredibly wise and already grinning Walter Wink. With all the seriousness of someone who disrespected my family back home, I gave him the same look that made Danny Trejo a star.

The group erupted in laughter.

In this moment, I stood there and looked at him and knew exactly what he meant. Hearing the laughter triggered something. I felt disrespected even more. I was being backhanded by their laughter. When they disrespected me, they disrespected the community that still suffers under the weight of unjust systems back home. When they laughed at me, they laughed at the sacrifice of my ancestors to create the conditions to get me to where I am today. When they refused to recognize my people and my history, they took my very roots and ripped them out of the ground and planted their own in their place. My face only got meaner as I stared into Wink's eyes. He let us stand there for a moment, until he released the gaze and stepped back slightly. I had won.

He then looked at me and gave a smile. In the softest of tones, he said, "Now you understand 'turn the other cheek.'" He was right. I was immediately overwhelmed and filled with a sense of purpose. I understood it in my bones. I did not just cognitively have a change of mind about this Scripture passage being a pacifist excuse to take abuse or a warped version of nonviolence. My actions robbed the oppressor of the power to humiliate. They asserted and demanded that he and the room either fight me as equals or back up, because I was not going to let him or anyone else strike me as if I were not equal. I now saw the passage through my Brown lens, through the lens of the barrio, through the lens of the hood. Wink showed that if we got in a scrap, there was no winning for him. It was reminiscent of one of my heroes, César Chávez, who said in the height of the farmworkers, civil, and Mexican American rights movements, "Once social change begins, it cannot be reversed. You cannot un-educate the person who has learned to read. You cannot humiliate the person who feels pride. You cannot oppress the people who are not afraid anymore."[22] Chávez spoke those words in a speech to the Commonwealth of San Francisco in 1984, and they reflected his presence in Salinas, California, my hometown. It was Chávez witnessing the dehumanization and death of braceros and Mexican Americans. Wink had no idea how this moment resonated with the little Brown boy in me, how his words empowered that fifth grader, saw him, and acknowledged his life. In that moment, I felt a rush come over me. There was no doubt about it. Jesus was a homie.

Wink's point was that forcing him to hit me with his dominant hand would be to declare that we were equals. No more backhanding. The Powers are left with a challenge. In their quest to dominate, do they recognize the equality in this other person by fighting him, her, or them directly, or do they walk away in realization that backhanding as a tool to show dominance is no longer effective because we do not believe it? This person in front of the Powers is demanding equality.

The Powers cannot win in this situation. The rules and culture of the Powers create habits that try to render us less than human and, to play on Wink's work, powerless. When we recognize their rules, when we recognize their purpose, we can provide a powerful check on those institutions that define our lives. We can challenge the Powers' vocation and redeem them as Wink might have us do. When someone disrespects your humanity, respect your ancestors, community, and yourself enough to turn the other cheek. In that way, my personal vocation of survival meets the Powers' expressed purpose: domination, order, and hierarchy. It is to continue to show up and breathe. Turning the other cheek is about survival. It is about demanding the right to live. It challenges the very design of the system.

Reflections

Take some time to reflect on the Powers. List the Powers and how they affect your life. What Powers are active in your life? Are the Powers the government or society that is actively marginalizing groups of people based on their beliefs, color of their skin, how they self-identify, or whom they choose to love? Are they religious institutions that continue to limit the purposes of those who feel called by God but do not fit the white, cis-gendered, heteronormative leadership profiles? Are the Powers the education and health industries that limit the access certain people have to their services, or are they more personal? Are they our family systems and institutions that limit and define gender roles or lock us into family narratives that limit our potential? What Powers are holding you back from achieving your purpose? How might you reframe the context to gain your freedom, your humanity?

Defining Institutional Vocations

Returning to the idea that institutions have vocations, I have found a helpful definition of *vocation* in the work of colleagues Dori Baker, Stephen Lewis, and Matthew Wesley Williams. They claim in their book *Another Way* that vocation is "the long arc of a life spent searching for purpose and acting out call, and it applies to individuals as well as collectives."[23] Communities, institutions, organizations, and social structures have a vocation not just because they have a sense of call and a history but also because organizations often express and define their purpose in mission statements, allowing them to track how their vocations change over time. Mission statements are the clearest statements of purpose, and nearly every organization and institution has one. A mission statement is a big idea or broad understanding of an institution's work. Some are famous; others are less so. Below are just a few:

Faith Institutions:
- Catholic Charities U.S.A., service to and for the poor: "Catholic Charities is to provide service to people in need, to advocate for justice in social structures, and to call the entire church and other people of good will to do the same."[24]
- YMCA, recreational programs and services: "The Y is the leading nonprofit committed to strengthening community by connecting all people to their potential, purpose and each other. Working locally, we focus on empowering young people, improving health and well-being and inspiring action in and across communities."[25]
- The American Red Cross: "The American Red Cross prevents and alleviates human suffering in the face of emergencies by mobilizing the power of volunteers and the generosity of donors."[26]
- Homeboy Industries, founded by Father Gregory Boyle: "Homeboy Industries provides hope, training, and support to formerly gang-involved and previously incarcerated men and women allowing them to redirect their lives and become contributing members of our community."[27]
- Forum for Theological Exploration: "To cultivate diverse young adults to be faithful, wise and courageous leaders for the church and academy."[28]

From Broader Industry:
- Airbnb, a site that allows you to rent someone else's home: "Our mission is to live in the world where one day you can feel like

you're home anywhere and not in a home, but truly home, where you belong."[29]

- Google, a search engine and related application services: "To organize the world's information and make it universally accessible and useful."[30]
- The Walt Disney Company, entertainment: "To entertain, inform and inspire people around the globe through the power of unparalleled storytelling, reflecting the iconic brands, creative minds and innovative technologies that make ours the world's premier entertainment company."[31]

Mission statements are guides. Although they are incredibly simple, how an institution might live out its stated mission can take several directions. It is the "Why?" of an organization's existence. Wink's argument that that the Powers are good and need to be redeemed can be reflected in an institution's mission statement—they are all arguing for their best vocations.

From Catholic Charities alleviating suffering to Airbnb, which hopes to help you feel at home anywhere, we can see this benevolence in the mission-statement language. We can see how they live out their call in their services and products. Far more important than a platform for sharing beds and roofs, Airbnb's process for living out that call is equally as important as the feel-good mission statement. In other words, the ends need to justify the means in one's call, in one's purpose. How you live your professed call is as important as being able to name it. Airbnb does not redecorate or build homes for people, which could express their mission statement. Instead, they are a platform that connects travelers with people who have their own homes to rent. Vacation property rentals, bed and breakfasts, and the like have been around for some time. Moreover, communities like my own have been hosting family and friends on our couches for as far back as family memory serves. Airbnb's stated purpose is not that novel. Their mission statement provides an outward expression of how it wants to be seen in terms of vocation or purpose.

Disney, for example, started with theme parks and feature-length cartoons and now has streaming services, merchandise, and hospitality experiences. They create these services and products by first leveraging their "imagineers," who operate at the intersection of technology and art. To preview a conversation about design to come, they are engaged in "experience design," where they design and cultivate an experience of awe and wonder, whether someone is watching a movie or going into one of their parks. Disney provides an experience like no other. Take the now iconic "Main Street" that visitors walk through when they first enter Disneyland or Disney World. While it may feel like you're getting a piece of nostalgia, the purpose of Main Street when it was designed was to signal to visitors that it is the last remnant of what is familiar before they enter the Magical Kingdom. Once inside the park, the walls and fences are too tall to see beyond. For the 52 million annual visitors to Disney World, Disney is fully living into its vocation by providing inspiring and memory-making experiences for all who can afford to go.[32]

If organizations and institutions have vocations, how can they focus on the next generation? *Sesame Street*'s mission is to help children of all walks of life "grow smarter, stronger, kinder." It is a bold vision. When I watch the show with my children, I get to see their imaginations expanded and listen to songs written, performed, and celebrating kids like them. In one week in the 45th season, we saw Colombian musician Juanes and composer Lin-Manuel Miranda and heard the song "Color of Me." I don't think people understand what radical visions *Sesame Street* and *Mister Roger's Neighborhood* were for television. These shows had the unique challenge of providing content that was both engaging and nurturing. They wanted children to feel absolutely loved, to feel that they are special. As a reader you may be thinking, what is radical about that? *Sesame Street*, which first appeared on public broadcasting, reaches to the least of these. The vocation of public broadcasting is not to those who can afford it, like Disney. Its vocation is to reach the child who has limited access to other services, like preschool and, in some cases, basic needs and services. These pioneers set out to create conditions for poor children of color, for whom the world is not built and who are witnessing firsthand the oppression of their people and the hunger of their bodies, to make them feel loved.[33] Institutions like *Sesame Street* contain the "special sauce" as Andy Crouch might say: "The recipe for an institution, then, is four ingredients plus three generations: artifacts, arenas, rules and roles that are passed on to the founding generation's children's children . . . sustainable institutions are built on highly distinctive, meaningful and valuable artifacts that make something worthwhile of the world."[34] *Sesame Street* and *Mister Roger's Neighborhood* planted seeds in the minds, souls, and lives of children that eventually shape the imagination of adults who raise a new generation.

The conditions that determine whether people will thrive begin when children are young. Children have no control over or choice regarding such conditions as family structure, city, location, or date of birth, which have an enormous impact on what the child's future will be, more than we care to acknowledge. In a meritocracy and capitalistic society, where we think hard work equals better outcomes, we, as a society, do not want to acknowledge that a lot of our future is designed prior to our birth. We want success stories: "Rags to riches"; "We pulled ourselves up by our bootstraps"; "Everyone Is Self-made." We like *Hamilton*-style (the musical) stories, where we are not going to waste our shot! The fact remains, however, that most people in our society never get a shot in the first place. For the disbelievers, for the hopeful, or for those who do not want to see their success as part of the conditions that formed them, there is clear evidence that says the conditions matter a lot more than we care to acknowledge.

Brandeis University uses the Childhood Opportunity Index to track the opportunities children have in their lives. They look at things like education outcomes, access to job prospects, social mobility, and other factors that impact a child's life. They track data for major metropolitan areas in the United States. My dad and his family were raised in a space whose index reflects the least opportunity in the United States: Bakersfield, California, where I lived with my grandparents in my late teens and early twenties. What does it mean to be from the place that comes last on the Childhood Opportunity Index?

The impacts are clear. Life expectancy is shorter based on what neighborhood one lives in, with an average difference of seven years between those from very-low- and very-high-opportunity neighborhoods. There are also racial disparities. For example, the directors of the index suggest that where the typical white child is more likely to live in a Milwaukee neighborhood with an opportunity score of 85 (very high opportunity), the typical Black child is more likely to live in a Milwaukee neighborhood with a score of 6 (very low opportunity). To break it down further, the average white child lives in a neighborhood with an average opportunity score of 73, compared to Latinx and African American children, who live in neighborhoods with average scores of 33 and 24, respectively.[35]

It means that in order for me to write these pages to you, my father had to be extraordinary. My dad *is* extraordinary in many ways, defying the odds. For example, he had to navigate a lack of institutional support when he was growing up because his neighborhood had few institutions dedicated and designed to give him access to opportunities to explore his purpose. Although few in number, however, there are those institutions whose explicit purpose is to close the purpose gap in neighborhoods like the one my dad and I are from.

Freedom Schools

As part of the civil rights movement, Freedom Schools began to emerge in Mississippi in 1964 to address the opportunity and purpose gaps. As noted earlier, neither *Mendez v. Westminster* nor *Brown v. the Board of Education* (I, II, III) solved the education gap. In 1964, Mississippi, like many places still today, was spending disproportionate dollars on educating white students compared to Black students. In the early 1960s, the Student Nonviolent Coordinating Committee proposed Freedom Schools to close this education gap. In some places, like Prince Edward County, Virginia, districts had chosen to close schools rather than integrate them. Freedom Schools emerged as an alternative. All through the 1960s, students staged protests or attended Freedom Schools to address the unjust conditions they experienced. From Boston to Chicago to New York City, students of color and their communities were finding a new way to educate themselves. By 1964, and on the heels of the Freedom Summer project, Charles Cobb began to build the infrastructure for a network of schools, hosting a conference sponsored by the National Council of Churches. Literacy was the backbone of the curriculum, with academics, citizenship, and recreation being the larger categories.[36]

Freedom Schools closed the purpose and education gap, right? The answer for those scholars who attended those schools was "Yes!" Freedom Schools are more than necessary even today to close an ever-widening opportunity and purpose gap. The Children's Defense Fund (CDF), founded in 1973 by Marian Wright Edelman, still runs and maintains a large network of Freedom Schools. From their 2019 campaign, they served 12,138 scholars, trained 1,347 teachers, had 181 program sites and 108 sponsor organizations, and are in 97 cities across the country. The CDF Freedom School model aims at five essential components: 1) high-quality academic enrichment, 2) parent and family development, 3) civic engagement and social action, 4) intergenerational servant leadership development, and 5) nutrition, physical health, and mental health. The impact of these programs has been extraordinary. Their website states that "since 1995, more than 150,000 children (K–12) have had the CDF Freedom Schools® experience, and more than 17,000 young adults and child advocates have been trained on the delivery of the *CDF Freedom Schools* model."[37] Freedom Schools address the explicit education gap. If they could close that gap and meet all these goals, then access to education would no longer be a barrier to achieving one's purpose.

Freedom Schools emerged and continue to operate because of the failure of dominant society. Both conservatives and liberals alike have failed to create educational opportunities for students of color. The successes of Freedom Schools, embodied in the scholars they produced, are expressions of our work, our knowledge, and our love. The dominant society needs to see Freedom Schools as more than just summer literacy programs. White liberals, in particular, who often want to and do fund Freedom Schools, will have to ask themselves if they are truly committed to freedom. If they are, they will not just support the work of Freedom Schools; they will also rethink where and how they live and how schools are zoned and funded. They will have to think critically about the curriculum taught in academic programs and decide if they want equity in public schools, decentering their own white, colonial, and oppressive frameworks for the knowledge, wisdom, and education from our communities. In short, freedom is not just a program.

One example of an organization that has had an enormous impact in my home state is Homeboy Industries in Los Angeles. Founded in 1992 by Father Gregory Boyle, what began as a ministry to provide viable jobs to gang-affiliated youth has developed into a transformation hub, a place that is closing the purpose gap for thousands of young people each year. Over an eighteen-month program, formerly incarcerated or gang-affiliated youth and young adults are provided healing and work-readiness skills. The five main outcomes for which they strive are to 1) reduce recidivism, 2) reduce substance abuse, 3) improve social connectedness, 4) improve housing safety and stability, and 5) reunify families.[38] Each year, 10,000 former gang members go to Homeboy Industries seeking transformation. Their model achieves success in every area of their outcomes and has been replicated in hundreds of sites globally. Mixed into the "tortilla dough" is a spirituality that every human life should receive a chance to thrive. The purpose gap *can* be closed. As Father Greg reflects in his book *Tattoos on the Heart*:

> God's unwieldy love, which cannot be contained by our words, wants to accept all that we are and sees our humanity as the privileged place to encounter this magnanimous love. No part of our hardwiring or our messy selves is to be disparaged. Where we stand, in all our mistakes and our imperfection, is holy ground. It is where God

has chosen to be intimate with us and not in any way but this. . . . It is certainly true that you can't judge a book by its cover, nor can you judge a book by its first chapter—even if that chapter is twenty years long. When the vastness of God meets the restriction of our own humanity, words cannot hold it. The best we can do is find the moments that rhyme with this expansive heart of God.[39]

When we come to realize that there is human potential in every person and that some people have not been given a chance, when we reach out to close the purpose gap for those who are most marginalized, society as a whole benefits. Boyle doubles down on this notion, claiming "the call to the margins, led by those we find there, is exhilarating and life-giving and renews our nobility and purpose."[40] For those already on the margins, closing the purpose gap and working for the freedom of our people benefits us all. It helps inspire a new generation to close the meaning and purpose gap even more, to create the conditions for life abundant. To close the purpose gap, to claim the margins as center, is to realize the Beatitudes, to realize the purpose of Jesus. He was born a Brown boy, marked for death, to a Brown teenage mother who had to flee her homeland for his safety. He returned only to claim the margin as center. This is the work of the church. It is our work and our vocation.

Reflections

What communities or institutions have vocations that are making social change in your local, national, or global community? What is their stated purpose and mission? In what ways do they close the purpose gap? Are you included in their vision? Are those who are marginalized and left out both the designers and recipients of the value that organization brings to the world?

What communities and institutions do you need to create or join to help close the purpose gap? What communities and institutions have paved the way for you to achieve or help you achieve your purpose?

The Case for Creating Conditions for People to Thrive

My hope is that by now you understand the purpose gap. Its existence has led to a loss in lives that might have otherwise cured cancer, advanced exploration into space, helped people find meaning and process through spiritual and religious leadership, inspired a new generation of teachers, solved climate change, and the like. The purpose gap has left people out of not just realizing their own call but from benefiting the community. As Christians, it would be akin to saying nothing good could come from Nazareth. We all know how that worked out.

In part 2, we will address ways of closing the purpose gap. How do we create conditions for all people to thrive? While some of the stories in this chapter have given a glimpse of organizations and institutions that have had vocations to address this vocation gap, in the next chapter we will look at how they accomplish that work.

Part 2

How Do We Close the Purpose Gap?

My ancestors cry out from the above and beyond
I leave home to be with them
To learn from the masters
To build the constellations and networks
That will design our futures
From the fiestas and cookouts
In public parks, where we find life
To the home where we imagine our purpose.
Like Juan Diego
Tonantzín reveals herself
Implants herself on my heart
Freeing me to seek out the freedom of my people
My purpose.

PURPOSE   GAP   OPPORTUNITY

Chapter 5

From Stars to Constellations

Thank God for public parks. My favorite memories all take place in these sacred spaces held for the common good. From birthday parties to time spent down by the river and at public cookout spots, my family and friends would come together to share meals, dance, and create lasting memories. I remember the piñata hanging from trees and the dancing to the music from the family boom box. I also spent most afternoons at public parks, either as a place to hang out after school or to get in a quick pick-up game of basketball. I remember going to the local campgrounds at the lakes and forests, cooking and hanging outside with my closest friends. These public spaces are foundational for my imagination about what it means to be human and to be fully alive. For those on the other side of the purpose gap, they are often places to go for connection and for life. As part of my dissertation research with community members who worked in the fields, I asked what spaces were sacred and holy to them. They named playgrounds, soccer fields, and public parks as places that gave them a little distance from the day-to-day grind of daily survival.

When my parents split, my father moved into a small condominium. My brothers and I shared a bunk bed. Two on bottom, one on the top. The bed went from one wall to the other. Although the floor plan was tight, my dad knew how to make this room feel like the most expansive space we could ever live in. To this day, I don't think I've ever felt as much at home as I did during this time. My dad had a unique ability to inspire us and he knew the power of public spaces. He was able to shift our thinking from the small confines of our apartment on the literal and figurative margins of our town. He leveraged the natural world, which was mostly free, to help expand our imaginations about what was possible.

I remember going camping with him—sleeping on the dirt, with no television or phones, and eating only what could fit in the car. We played near rivers and waterfalls and roasted marshmallows by the fire. When the air was still, he knew these spaces took us away from the pains of our neighborhoods and the abuse we were facing at my mother's house. He knew that we would be inspired by the stars above our head. Those night skies that seemed to go on for eternity inspired me when I was just a boy, not sure I was going to make it to adulthood. It inspired me to know that I was a small part in an ever-expanding landscape. No solitary star above my head was the sole focus. The sky itself, as it seemed to move ever so slowly over the course of a few hours, captured my imagination. What a gift my father gave me, to show me that, when the world felt like it was shrinking in around me, I could open my mind to a beautiful and expansive universe. One of the most beautiful places he ever took me—on the cost of gas, hot dogs, and a $15 tent fee—was Yosemite National Park. That was the first night sky I saw unencumbered by light pollution. To this day, the night sky is the most inspiring thing I have ever seen. It is something I have enjoyed sharing with my son as, on clear nights, we take turns trying to find various planets through the hand-me-down telescope in his room.

To close the purpose gap, we must change our focus. The self-help industry wants us to believe that if we just work harder, spend more time trying to achieve inner peace, or clarify our purpose in life, we will all live happier and more fulfilling lives. When we pursue our purposes, others will recognize our power and clarity of vision. Everything from the prosperity gospel to some of my favorite pop songs tells us that we can have it all. If we just "lean in," we will achieve our purpose and goals.[1] I hope by now I have made it clear that while that may be the case for an exceptional few, for the community I come from, this "Pull yourself up by the bootstraps" mantra is simply not possible. The world stole our laces and our boots.

My grandma was leaning all the way in. She worked at the local high school, took care of the family, survived, but certainly did not have it all. She was poor, though if you ask her and every single person who lived in her home, they would say they never experienced poverty. She did not have access to resources that would allow her to redesign her life. Putting food on the table was far too important. The problem with the idea of "Just find your life's purpose," clear the clutter in your life,[2] and "set your intentions" to spark joy[3] and the "universe will conspire to help,"[4] is that notions like these limit someone like my grandma to nonexistence. The bar is not just set high, but it is as if these writers and thinkers never evaluated what their high bars were held up by. If they did, they would see that it is not the result of hard work but inheriting the wealth and property of systems that took wealth and property from others. These books are written for the few who can offload daily tasks to focus on their big picture. To whom do they think they offload those tasks? They never make it explicit, because they do not view us as human! We are simply a means to an end. The daily tasks they abhor or simply do not have time for, they suggest passing to people like my grandma, people from my community. We cook their meals, clean their homes and offices, take care of their children, and prop up the entire food supply chain from caring for the soil to getting the food to your plate, all so others can have it all. The focus of the self-help genre is focused on the wrong people! These are singular, often white, standouts who have discerned that the everyday stuff is beneath them. What if we stopped focusing on these "stars" and instead thought about us all as belonging to constellations in the universe?

I want us to begin to think about how to move us from this "exceptional" or "star" model to thinking about how to benefit the community, the common good.[5] We are building a constellation of stars, not celebrating the brightest star. Like our own sun, so many of us are attempting to be it—the only source of light. We want to be the one thing everyone pays attention to from sunup to sundown. We want people to share our social media posts and watch us rise and set with each day. We are constantly competing for attention, and our culture supports this behavior. In a TED Talk that has been viewed by 4.5 million people, actor Joseph Gordon-Levitt challenges us to move from getting attention to paying attention.[6] He reminds the viewer that social media platforms want you to shine. The more traffic you attract to your presence, the higher the revenue from advertisements.

Remember Icarus, son of the master craftsman, Daedalus? Daedalus created wax wings for the two of them to escape Crete. Daedalus warned Icarus not to fly too low or the sea would clog his wings. He also tells him not to fly too close to the sun because the sun would melt the wax wings. Icarus, excited and falsely assured by his new power, flies close to the sun, melts his wings, and falls into the ocean. We are but specks in this universe. Letting our ego get the best of us brings us crashing down to earth.

The challenge for us as creatives, as people pursuing our purpose, is to recognize that our star exists in a constellation of other stars, each burning bright. There have been days, certainly, when the sky has inspired me. I enjoy looking at the bright white clouds as they take on different shapes and the darkness that precedes a storm. But I must confess that I have never been overwhelmed with the beauty of the sun, probably because it is impossible to look at without losing your sight. The night sky, however, wows. Whenever I can get far enough away from light pollution, from our own artificial lights always seeking our attention, and stare at the night sky, I am never disappointed and always inspired. I am always taken back to my childhood and those nights with my dad in Yosemite Valley. What if constellations were our pursuit rather than single stars?

The focus on the individual star exacerbates the purpose gap. It features exceptions and does not build the capacity of the community. Returning to our opening illustrations in the introduction, the purpose gap exists because institutions find and extract the shining star in a community and leaves it without a star, also known as "the brain drain." Bloomberg has aggregated the data and developed the "Brain Concentration Index."[7] The index shows where workers in technical and specialized disciplines end up. While a "promising" student from Salinas, California, my hometown, might start there, they are more likely to end up in the Bay Area, Denver, or, in my case, Atlanta. Children from these places like my hometown have a low "brain concentration" and lack the constellation of stars to mentor, guide, and inspire a new generation because they are extracted from the community. The focus on exceptional stars has consequences for future constellations.

I want to invite you to consider the impact of the focus on stars. We have provided data above about the purpose gap. Another way to consider the gap is to look at the impact on young people who are discerning their purpose. I wrote the following piece, titled "My Walk with Steinbeck," when I was much younger, just after I left home for graduate school. John Steinbeck was the only author known to me from my hometown. He won the Nobel Prize in Literature, the Pulitzer Prize for Fiction, the Presidential Medal of Freedom, the National Book Award, and was a war correspondent and author of thirty-three books. People come from all over to see the Steinbeck Center and celebrate his legacy. Even then, I knew I wanted to be an author. The following reflection is intended to give you a glimpse of how important it is to be able to see yourself in the image of a mentor, elder, or exemplar, to see yourself as part of the constellation of stars.

My Walk with Steinbeck

I thought you were my only ancestor. You were the only one who could write my experience. You wrote seventy years before I came into the world, but you said the name of the space I called home. I walked with you all over the Salinas Valley. You accompanied me through grade school. I went to Steinbeck Elementary. Our mascot—or is it mascots?—were the Red Ponies, the name of one of your more famous short stories. I walked with you through junior high and high school. My love of literature, writing, of Salinas, all came from you.

You will not find the beauty of our landscape depicted so masterfully by any other writer. From your opening in *East of Eden*, to the hills in *The Long Valley*, or the sacred rolling hills of *To a God Unknown*, and the farmlands in *Of Mice and Men*, you gave voice to a broken land, to a broken people, to my broken soul.

I thought you were the only one who loved to write from our space. There was a grittiness to your stories. Somewhere between your experience and my own, there lived the truth of the valley. The sights and sounds were familiar, if they were, as you wrote them, only expressions of my dreams.

Who comes from Salinas? When I would introduce myself, your name always came up. Bringing a smile and a nod from those who were assigned your work in school. But that was it. A small group of people who caught a glimpse of the land, written more than a half century before I was even born, before I could taste the fog in the morning, endure the fields, to straddle the gap between the trauma and privilege of my childhood. No one said I was going to be the next Steinbeck. No one said I was going to be anything.

It was as if I were one of your characters. Was I Cal in *East of Eden*, bound by a land and marked for death? Am I Joseph Wayne, who in *To a God Unknown* is told by Juan to make a home on the land? Like Joseph, I have a special connection to the land, but it is dying and has taken everything from me. It took my childhood. It has taken my adulthood. It has taken my very life from me. To return would most certainly mean death.

Steinbeck, you are not my ancestor, but you visit me in dreams. *Travels with Charley*, is that our journal? You are a star, a dying star. When your light goes out, does it go out on Salinas? Does it go out on me?

Will I live up to your prose? Will I make you proud? Would you have cared about me at all? The answer is no to all these questions. But I write anyway.

I write for my life. I write for my people.

I recently workshopped this piece for young and emerging scholars coming out of the Salinas and Central Valleys. They were mostly community college students, with whom I wanted to share the limitations of my own imagination from our shared space. The head nods, affirmations, and tears that followed reflected how hard it was to dream in these education deserts. The crushed dreams, the aspirations challenged both by dominant society and our own families, and the memories of those who supported us though they did not even understand what we were talking about focused our conversation. It reflected that for so many of us, our highest aspiration is to follow and be like our stars, hoping in the very least to be the penumbra, the partially lit shadow of the star's light. The only alternative is to shine so brightly that we are extracted from our home communities.

The challenge we face is countercultural. Stars can be the focus of our attention, but creating a constellation is what changes the conditions for future generations. How do we get people to build constellations of stars, to create conditions where stars fill the sky, from our communities to others on the margins? How do we create the conditions where people are so inspired by our collective shine that they come from near and far to study with us, to learn from us, or, for those in our community, to stay with us? How do we create the conditions so that people see the constellation, acknowledge its power, learn from it, and be present to it without trying to colonize or claim it as their own?

Reflections

Who are the stars in your life? In whose shadow do you walk or on whose shoulders do you stand? Who showed you the stars?

Stargazing

In 2019, with the help of close colleagues and friends, FTE hosted a gathering of deans and directors of programs in higher education to think about how to create conditions for scholars of color to thrive. Our challenge was to show, not tell, these powerful individuals how to provide the gift of freedom to explore and be humbled by one's inspiring colleagues and surroundings. I wanted them to see our work as building the collective, not creating the conditions for the exceptions to the rule. I wanted them to experience that education could be healing. Industries like higher education use diversity, equity, and inclusion as code for finding the exception, the one or two people of color who can make it in their institutions. In the past, these meetings had always been about how to increase the number of students or faculty of color, and they always focused on recruitment and mentoring for the current system. Leaders of these systems are rarely ever concerned with closing the purpose gap through designing new systems or institutions. They are not trained in how to leverage power, wealth, and authority to create new ways of being together as a scholarly community. They are trained to maintain what is, a system set to re-create stars. We wanted them to reframe the challenge to closing the purpose gap and see it as a collective endeavor. We wanted them to see the constellations of stars.

The site I chose for our gathering was Yosemite National Park. I could not escape the memories of myself running in the park yelling things like "Wow! Can you believe this?" or "*Mira*, look at this!" Whether we drove into the park from the Southwest side, scaling up the Sierra Nevadas with the gorgeous vistas of the valley below, or came up and over from Nevada, passing Tuolumne Meadows and the exposed granite rocks overlooking pristine mountain lakes, I was in awe at the natural beauty of the park. When you enter the park itself and pull over for the "Tunnel View," you can see down the almost eight-mile-long Yosemite Valley, an overwhelming sight for any person who travels to the park. The view faces east, so the sun rising on the valley is one of the most awe-inspiring visions on this planet. On the left side, you can see El Capitan, scaling to the stars. Half Dome, a seemingly flat granite block, stares back at you from the back of the valley, standing 4,737 feet above the floor, more than 3.25 times as tall as the Empire State Building in New York. As if that's not enough, Bridal Veil Falls descends 600 feet to your right.

During the day, you can see wildlife like bobcats, deer, bear, raccoons, and all kinds of birds and smaller wildlife. And at sunset, as the day closes on the valley, the sun splashes in reds and yellows across the granite mountaintops of El Capitan and Half Dome, like a painting by God. The rock faces do not disappear. They only become more magical as the silver-speckled granite offers a glowing contrast to the night sky, a bluish-black backlighting with more stars than you can imagine.

When I think back on my childhood memories of Yosemite, I am reminded of that night sky. During the day, the sun provides enough heat for creatures to survive and thrive. At night, the sky becomes magical. It reminds us that our solar system is just one small part of an ever-expanding universe of other solar systems, each star reminding us of how small we are. The night sky can remind us that there are more than 200 billion stars in the Milky Way galaxy alone. There is great wisdom in focusing our attention on single stars, but when given the choice to stare at the sun or stare at the night sky, well, one burns your eyes and the other inspires.

This experience of wonder is what we wanted our group of deans and program directors to experience. In contrast to the individualist design principles challenged by Costanza-Chock, discussed in chapter 3, we knew "what is" for students and scholars of color, and our "what if" centered around how to create conditions for students and scholars of color to thrive. What is needed is not a tweak to the system that never valued humanity, our traditions, or our knowledge. We needed something that would wow, and we wanted to gather in a way that inspired. We wanted something that turns everyday life into something magical. During the "What wows" stage of design, "design thinkers take their prototypes to key stakeholders (and not just users) for feedback."[8] It is not enough to think you have a novel idea or an idea that will change the status quo, but you have to enact it and test it. We wanted to humbly reflect, to celebrate, to name next steps, and to be inspired together with our partners, and Yosemite was the perfect setting. With an agenda that framed the conversation, we would allow participants to take responsibility for the conversations they needed to have in order to lead institutional change back home.

We looked at the ways the gatherings had been done in the past—at institutions of higher education and in hotel ballrooms with an outside facilitator. We looked at alternative ways to host, at co-working spaces, facilitated by our organization's staff. While the practices were innovative and people walked away from these past gatherings, as one review said, "renewed and challenged to think differently about their work," no one walked away inspired to create something completely new. In the words of Ronald Heifetz, leaders were looking for technical solutions for their adaptive problems.[9] Our key stakeholders had already been through every type of training on diversity, equity, and inclusion. And while they certainly needed and desired growth to become anti-racist administrators, our purpose for gathering as a network was to help them imagine ways to create conditions for people to thrive at their institutions. Placing them in familiar settings, such as hotel meeting rooms, with a set agenda and expert speakers, would not inspire the least of them, especially not to change their practices. It is ironic that many times leaders demand or ask for change in behavior of others while enacting the very things we loathe. We needed something new.

A year prior to our meeting, I asked, "What if we did it in a National Park?" Drawing on my earliest memories of wonder, what about Yosemite? I had not been there since I was young, but the fact that I was still inspired all these years later meant that it created something magical. We added the park to our list of potential sites for several events in northern

California. I still remember driving down through the east end of the valley when we staked it out for the event. We spent a full day in the car to come down the valley. I was traveling with my colleague Elsie Barnhart, who struggled to keep up with all my crazy ideas and the 1,000-plus-mile tour of bad hotels and potential meeting spaces we had taken in the week leading up to Yosemite, our last stop. As we passed the Tuolumne Meadows on the way down into the valley, an unnerving silence filled the car. We had not spoken for an hour or so, and I was nervous. We could have both been on a plane that day had it not been for these final site visits in and around the park. Then Elsie let out, "This is stupid."

There we have it, I thought. I just lost one my favorite people to work with over a "what wows" pipedream. "Sorry," I said under my breath.

"It is ridiculous how beautiful this is."

When you hit what wows, the journey—the small moments of joy we experience along the way—becomes part of the destination, a slow crescendo to the moment you are cultivating. I've never left a party or celebration wishing that I hadn't spent time with the people I love. I've never finished a writing or running session and wished I hadn't started that lengthy process. By starting the process, by taking one's next most faithful step, we arrive at magical experiences.

Obviously, we chose Yosemite, but when the date for the gathering arrived and we took the bus drive up the winding journey to the park from Fresno Airport, we were met with rain, snow, and historically high winds. When we arrived at the park, the winds had died down, but as a preventative measure against wildfires, the gas company had shut the power off to two million people in northern California, including the Yosemite Valley. While the lodge had electricity and heat, the lodge hotel rooms did not. The temperature outside dwindled to the single digits overnight, and our leaders huddled under the extra blankets and flashlights provided by the lodge staff, who, I must say, are wonderful people and could not have been more professional throughout the whole endeavor. Unknowingly, I had asked very accomplished deans, directors, and professors of color, all of whom I consider friends, to brave the elements for this gathering in order to create conditions for students and scholars of color to thrive.

Can you imagine the stress we were all under, especially when half of the park staff evacuated because of nearby wildfires? As the convener of the event, I sat up late, covering myself with a blanket held up by the top of my head, using my little electric lamp for light, writing feverishly in my journal. It was so cold that first night and the building so quiet without the electric whir of appliances that I imagined a family of bears just out-side as I heard the trash bins moving. Did I just invite my friends to have a Jurassic Park experience? The idea stuck a little too strongly when I fell asleep, for I dreamed I was a character in the original *Jurassic Park* movie, Dr. Ian Malcolm, who is played by the hilarious Jeff Goldblum. I was so stressed that I couldn't help but think I had inadvertently created the same conditions for our participants to do the opposite of thriving, which was chaos, and at this point I became a chaotician like Dr. Malcolm.

The next morning, I got up to go for a run in the cold. I ran just beyond one of the campgrounds, where some of the staff lived, and stopped to talk to two young men and a young woman who happened to be outside their little cabin. They told me that they had been evacuated before, so it was not a big deal, and they were just waiting for the call. I may have been staring at their hot coffee a little too intently as they spoke, because they invited me to sit at their little outdoor table and have some out of a tin cup they quickly rinsed within the house. We sat and talked for an hour about their dreams. These young people had come to Yosemite for this experience. They were not paid a lot. They came here to have the experi-ence I was trying to cultivate: to encounter awe and wonder daily and be part of something much bigger than themselves. It was inspiring to hear their stories. I thanked them for the coffee and ran back to my room.

What if this was the event we were supposed to have? What if the weather and hardship were creating the conditions needed for us to put a stake in the ground to have the most memorable meeting for an academic gathering possible? We hadn't planned for power during the day any-ways, because when the sun rose, we were going to send the participants out into the park. After all, it was going to be over 60 degrees during the day. This was exactly why we came to Yosemite: to disconnect from the day-to-day realities we all faced; to have no cell-phone coverage, no Wi-Fi, and no emails while forest bathing in one of the most beauti-ful places on the planet; and having only the most necessary conversa-tions about how to create conditions for students and scholars of color to thrive. Of course, *heat* would have been nice, but the conditions were present for us to do our work in the best way possible. The power outage had only amplified these conditions.

It was clear to me in this moment that this gathering would work. As Priya Parker writes in the *Art of Gathering*, the most important thing is "committing to a bold, sharp purpose."[10] Creating conditions for schol-ars of color to thrive was our purpose. It was derived from a clear *what is*:

the dismal numbers of scholars of color in the academy and the limited gains in the last two decades to diversify faculty and teaching. Our *what if* was "Can we do this work in collaboration, across a network, across our institutions, and in a way that inspires people to see this work as their own, to break open their technical fixes and come up with novel, adaptive changes?" A bigger *what if* was "If we gave these leaders the time and space to think together through this, as opposed to facilitating every moment to give them *wows*, would they come up with new solutions?" To do so, we had to wow them with our convening.

No matter how much planning one does, for those of us who work in the spiritual space between planes, who connect to the above and beyond, sometimes the Spirit and spirits are already present, waiting to be seen. With all the lights that typically distract us out, people were present in ways they usually weren't—not just in academic settings but in their lives. They were present to themselves. One of the scholars of color said they were forced to sleep when the sun set because there was no power to keep their electronics running, and it was too cold to do anything but get under the blankets. They had the best sleep they'd in a long time. Others did exactly as we hoped: they went outside and stared at the sky. It may not have led to the revolution in higher education we all desired, but our leaders, partners, and friends saw the stars and were reminded that there is beauty, knowledge, and inspiration beyond their control or design. We hoped that they saw the love and attention we'd put into providing them the best experience possible so that they, in turn, could do the same for students and scholars of color.

As leaders design and build more equitable institutions and society, the temptation is to find the stars, hoping that those who shine brightest will bring about the change for the collective good. This way of thinking gives a false sense of control over how to be more equitable and of who brings about change. If, instead, we slowed down and looked for inspiration, we would see that we can bear witness to the constellation of knowledge, power, and wisdom that exists in our communities. Our work to bring about a more just and equitable society is not about extracting a star out of the sky to claim it as our own. By valuing the whole constellation, we can begin to reimagine what is good. Excellence is no longer defined by single leaders but by the health and thriving of the whole. When we look up at the stars, as we did in Yosemite, we see the beauty of constellations. The challenge for us now is to find the constellations in our institutions, in our communities, and in our streets.

Reflections

Where would you go to see stars? What constellations exist in your life that the world cannot see? What distractions do you have to turn off or leave behind to see the beauty available to you?

Mind-Set Shift: Building Constellations, Building Communities

I had no idea when I was younger that I would work at the intersection of higher education and the church. Academics and preachers, higher education professionals and faith leaders, all share an incredible talent for wanting to be stars. Rightly so, as these are leader-rich fields. It takes a lot of courage to teach and preach. Parker Palmer said it best in *Courage to Teach*: "Good teaching cannot be reduced to technique; good teaching comes from the identity and integrity of the teacher."[11] Great teachers know who they are and teach from the heart, but they don't just come from anywhere. They are leaders who are as much formed by their study and honing of their craft as they are by the experience they gain through living their vocation in community.

Today, the right conditions are necessary for great teachers to appear. COVID-19 exposed this truth a little too plainly, as many of my friends across sectors, who are incredible leaders, were not able to keep their work. The warrior myth that my colleague Matthew Wesley Williams challenges in *Another Way* would have us believe that these leaders should have been better at pivoting, adapting, and finding ways to survive.[12] A sort of leadership Darwinism would suggest that those who survive are those best fit to survive, the brightest stars, but Williams points out this idea is a myth for a reason. For those leaders, pastors, presidents, deans, first responders, teachers, and members of the helping professions who saw their fundamental ways of survival disrupted, the ground has shifted—as Walter Fluker has put it.[13] As people of faith, we have countless examples of how this myth can go terribly wrong. From Abraham to Jacob and from Moses to David, God's anointed men all prove the limitations of the singular leader model. Time and again, they lose faith or, worse, commit harmful acts against the people they were supposed to lead. To say that a single leader has the answer to the world's complex problems is where leadership often fails, where stars often burn out.

Leadership development is leveraged as training up protégés: a younger mentee under the care of an elder who seeks to choose and train their replacement.[14] We often think of a singular leader and how to develop their leadership skills so that way they are able to lead with integrity. The leadership pipeline reflects the institutions and spaces from where great leaders come. Think of the ways business schools tout which world leaders and executives graduate from their programs. We have celebrated and lauded systems that are hierarchical. I see too many well-meaning pastors, leaders, and educators point to singular leaders who were the fathers and patriarchs of institutions, historical moments, and, at times, the first movers of history. I think of my own tradition and the number of times I watch Moses lifted as a leader. He is mentioned by name more than any other figure in the Bible, but a deep analysis of Moses as a leader reveals that he is not just flawed; he is a reluctant and terrible leader much of the time. The writers of the text were aware of this, even if the movie versions of his life were not. Dr. Wil Gafney reminds us that "the biblical text does not refer to Moses as a prophet until Deuteronomy 34:10, where he is identified as the preeminent and prototypical prophet, one who has unparalleled intimate access to YHWH—face-to-face, literally mouth-to-mouth, and as a wonder worker."[15]

Moses did not want to lead. In fact, he made five excuses not to follow God's call. See Exodus 3 and 4 for a list of complaints that for the rest of us would cause us to lose us our jobs. Can you imagine your future or current supervisor or leader (let alone God) telling you exactly what to do, and you saying, "Who am I to do that?" Moses asks God for directions on what to say when it's time to bring the people of Israel out of Egypt. He complains that people will not believe him when he speaks. He says he is not a good speaker and needs an aid to do his primary purpose, which is to relay what God says to him. Finally, in Exodus 4:13, he says, "Send someone else." I cannot stand it when I hear pastors and scholars interpret all of this as "God calls even the most reluctant." Moses was a privileged whiner who sat at Pharaoh's court. His story was more akin to God's talking to a student at Harvard Business School with a guaranteed job upon graduation than to a prophet being called out of the wilderness. At one point, God rebukes Moses for smashing a rock to get water—as opposed to speaking to it as commanded. See Numbers 20:1–13 for one of the "Scratch your head" moments that has challenged rabbis, scholars, and teachers for thousands of years. There is plenty to read into the passage itself. Part of me interprets the passage as God losing patience with Moses for not being able to follow a simple direction—the kind of losing-patience moment that we all have at work or home when we tell someone exactly what we want to happen, but for whatever reason they do something else. It's the same frustration I feel when I see someone load the dishwasher the wrong way.

I often work with brilliant, burning stars who shed light so life may spring forth. They are like Moses. They have a few unique skills and the right access to the resources to execute their work, but they sometimes lose sight of the fact or are simply not aware that they are just "small" stars, embedded in one galaxy among many galaxies in an ever-expanding universe. Now, I write this not to remind Moses that he is a small star among an ever-expanding universe; it is to hold Moses, or at least our reading of Moses, accountable. It is a simple reminder that others went before us, that we are the expression of many generations' love before we even draw breath. Before Moses could even hear or see God "face-to-face," his sister, Miriam, saved him. Miriam also healed the people and counseled Moses. She, too, was a prophet. As Marian Wright Edelman, founder of the Children's Defense Fund and civil rights leader, says, we "are never alone."[16]

Reflections

Who in your life loved you before you could even discern or know your purpose? Who are the "warrior kings" whose ego drives their leadership? Who counsels you in your own leadership? What community formed you?

Finding Mastery in Community

Finding the balance between being a leader and being part of a community requires "mastery" and the intentional pursuit of one's purpose. Sarah Lewis writes in *The Rise: Creativity, the Gift of Failure, and the Search for Mastery*, "Mastery is not merely a commitment to a goal, but to a curved line, constant pursuit."[17] This sense of mastery comes as much out of failure as it does out of the pursuit of practice, not of perfection. Her opening example is the art of archery. She studied archers who pursued their craft for hours. That does not mean they were shooting arrows for hours. She watched them practice their breathing, exercise, and perform visualization and meditation practices to focus their minds. She says that in our culture and society today, there is "little that is vocational about American culture anymore, so it is rare to see what doggedness looks like with this level of exactitude, what it takes to align your body for three hours to accurately account for the wind speeds and hit a target—to pursue excellence in obscurity."[18] She remarks that these archers spend entire days together, helping one another through practice. Tacit in her argument is that pursuit of a craft only happens in community.

While her work is focused on the individual pursuit of excellence, people who have found their vocations often hang around, attract, and gather others who have done likewise. She saw how archers came together for an entire day, practicing together, breathing together, sharing meals and laughter together. Similarly at the turn of the twentieth century, writers from all walks of life found their homes together in Paris. This sense of vocational community is why university departments produce excellent scholarship and research and why countless studios and street artists cluster around the world's most renowned museums. The concentration of people pursuing their work in close proximity, collaborating on projects, will ultimately hone one's craft to change the world.[19] It is why musicians and artists know everyone in their domain; they know the techniques, nuance, and history behind their work.

The purpose gap creates the imaginary space between what people master and what they do not. If my mind is not left to wander as it should over that cup of coffee, on a long walk in the park, or under the night sky, allowing me to think more expansively about my purpose, then the purpose gap widens. If I do not have the time to find my co-conspirators, co-inspirers, who can help me on my path, then the purpose gap widens. More importantly, if we, collectively, have not created the conditions for others to pursue their purpose and find opportunity, then we, collectively, cannot achieve our communal, world-changing goals.

My three-year-old daughter tells me every day she wants to be an astronaut. And she absolutely can be an astronaut. She is smart, intuitive, and fearless. However, not everyone is provided the resources available to become an astronaut, training that requires mastery. NASA's website states that to be an astronaut a person must

- Be a U.S. citizen.
- Possess a master's degree from an accredited institution in a STEM field, including engineering, biological science, physical science, computer science, or mathematics.
- Have at least two years of related professional experience obtained after degree completion or at least 1,000 hours pilot-in-command time on jet aircraft.
- Be able to pass the NASA long-duration-flight astronaut physical.

The master's degree requirement can also be met by the following:

- Two years (36 semester hours or 54 quarter hours) of work toward a doctoral program in a related science, technology, engineering, or math field.
- A completed Doctor of Medicine or Doctor of Osteopathic Medicine degree.
- Completion (or current enrollment that will result in completion) of a nationally recognized test-pilot school program.[20]

Easy, right? Around 75 percent of master's degrees earned in the United States are earned by men, and Latinas represent a slight fraction of master's degree earners in STEM disciplines.[21] While there has been Latina representation among astronauts, such as Arnaldo Tamayo Méndez of Cuba, who was also the first Black Latino to fly in space, and Ellen Ochoa,[22] the first Latina astronaut and first Latina director of NASA's Johnson Space Center, it does not change the fact that my daughter, Carmelita, would have to break barriers just to qualify. There were 18,300 applicants with similar dreams in 2016. The odds are not in favor for my daughter to be among the stars. To create a community of geniuses, scholars, artists, educators, doctors, and so on, from all walks of life to achieve their purpose, we must first create the conditions for more children to have access to high-quality STEM education, conditions where these children who love to stargaze can come together to play and dream of flying among the stars. If they can love and support one another through the journey and if we as a public invest in seemingly impossible things—like spaceflight—more than just my daughter will be in the application pool.

NASA's now-famous "West Computing" team created the conditions for Black women to pursue excellence in mathematics. Dorothy Vaughn, Mary Jackson, Katherine Johnson, and Christine Darden are now forever immortalized in the film *Hidden Figures* as those who pursued excellence at NASA, despite being in the segregated South.[23] What they were able to do could only exist in community. They gathered and helped one another to pursue their careers. Aguilera–Black Bear and John Tippeconnic write in *Voices of Resistance and Renewal: Indigenous Leadership in Education*, "Community-based leadership is fundamental to achieving self-determination in education."[24] If we want our children to achieve their purpose, we must create the conditions for all children to thrive. We must give them the tools to actualize their purpose and surround them with people who want to help them achieve. At every internal barrier—when they struggle with a math test or with a physical exam—we will be there to provide support and guidance. We have the power to encourage children to pursue their purpose and give them the resources to do it. And we collectively need to change conditions for those who are marginalized and left out—whose purposes have barricades like hunger, abuse, and suffering, who experience homelessness, or who need a family to love them—for those who "never had a shot." We need to ensure that every child has what they need to shoot for the stars and be part of the ever-growing constellation of stars.

The "how-to-become the best version of yourself" self-help, leadership, and vocational development literature focuses on one's individual growth and self-worth. The gap in the literature is the power of creating conditions for people—plural—to thrive, to move from "stars" to "constellations." I beg you, dear reader, to help me and others create conditions for all people to thrive. I encourage you to shift your focus from developing or seeking out individual stars and trying to ensure that our children are exceptional, to building and celebrating constellations of stars and creating the space capable of hosting them.

The work is not hard. Like being in Yosemite, we need to learn to slow down and value the beauty that is already present. We do not need to control it or extract it but simply be inspired by it. For those from marginalized communities, the work is about honoring the lives of everyone who makes up the community. For those from the dominant culture, it is about looking at those places and communities that have been cast aside and violated and valuing the experience, knowledge, and wisdom that exist in that space. Even excellence, such as mastery, is communal work. We must practice together. To create conditions for future generations to thrive, we must practice a new way of seeing the world.

Reflections

What did you want to be when you grew up? Did you achieve that goal? What stars did you look up to? What do you want to be right now? What stars do you want to be among? Who else do you need to include in your dream? Who do you need to bring along to help them achieve their purpose? What is your community's purpose? What do you need to do to build constellations and set aside aspirations to be a star?

Chapter 6

The Power of Networks

In the early 2000s I was working in construction in Delano, California. We were building a medical center, doing the metal framing, exterior lath, and hanging Sheetrock. As I sat eating my lunch with my friend Andy, one of the bravest and most broken men I have ever known, an elder who lived down the street from where we were building came and sat down next to us. "You know. This is where it all started," he said as he reached for a cigarette from Andy. Confused, we both laughed and kept eating. "You don't believe me. But I saw César right there. I saw Dolores right over there. This is before you were even born, *mijo*. You don't even know what we did for you." In 1965, Delano was the epicenter for networked resistance. The Agricultural Workers Organizing Committee, led by Larry Itliong and Filipino farmworkers, joined forces with the National Farmworkers Association to take on the grape growers. The strike lasted five years but effected change from public policy to the collective bargaining of ten thousand farm workers. It was the foundation of the United Farm Workers Labor Union. This strike did not just include the farmworkers. It was a collective, networked strategy for change. It included churches and faith leaders, business leaders and everyday consumers, politicians and their constituents. It required all sectors and communities, each trying to achieve freedom for those who put the food on our tables.

Dolores Huerta traveled the country to ensure that major markets did not carry the grapes. Everyday consumers refused to purchase them. It included a pilgrimage from Delano to Sacramento. Eight thousand people walked across the Tower Bridge in Sacramento that year, and people still honor that march by crossing the bridge on its anniversary. In 1968,

101

Chávez went on a hunger strike, famously breaking his fast with communion with friends and fellow workers surrounding him. In the pictures, you can see Larry Itliong standing directly behind him. Sitting next to him was then-presidential-hopeful Robert Kennedy, who was assassinated later that year. Kennedy fell into the arms of Juan Romero, a seventeen-year-old kitchen helper, who placed a rosary in Kennedy's hand as Kennedy drew his final breaths. Many in the movement, including Dolores Huerta, were present that day. From politics to the church to the fields to the schools, the network held together until they won five years after they began the strike. Every institution and every person that was part of the network made it possible for that little bit of freedom for the farmworkers, creating the conditions for someone like myself to sit in that same space and build a health care center that would serve our community.

Building on chapter 5's claim that constellations are more powerful than individual stars, this chapter explores how these networks of connectivity can be built, sustained, and leveraged for the flourishing of all people.

Networks are different from communities or institutions. A community is a set of people bound together by geography, commitment, or interest. Peter Block in his beloved text *Community* argues that a community is something we build collectively.[1] Networks are individuals and communities stitched together by a set of relations, both formal and informal. Sometimes networks are embedded within communities, and sometimes they connect several communities.

To illustrate the difference between networks and communities, I think about eating. Every year, my family gets together to make tamales. We make hundreds in the low years, but we made thousands when my grandma was alive. The community—the Reyes, Andrada, and Contreras families—would come to help make the masa, spread it on the corn husks, add our fillings, fold or roll (depending on your perspective), cook, and package in plastic bags to freeze to be given away or sold. Many in our community, including neighbors and friends, came to participate, pick up, and, yes, eat the tamales. Between Thanksgiving and Christmas, this network of relations would generate buzz about my Grandma Carmen's tamales, and we communed with people who would otherwise be strangers. The network extended to those supporters who attended the family's annual New Year's Eve party, the Contreras Family Reunion Scholarship Fund, where the family's network raised money to support scholarships for students going to community college in Bakersfield—stars not being extracted from our community but staying home and changing it!

Networks are intentionally designed connections that serve a purpose or a larger goal that benefits all members. Like a web, the spider connects various holds, weaving together what might be a very weak connection into a strong, adaptable structure capable of sustaining the spider's life. The strength of the web is its multiple anchors and intricate weaving pattern. Sometimes, when I walk with my kids, we stop to look at each web to see the patterns of each unique design. I try to teach my children to pay attention to these webs. If you return to them day after day, they change. The conditions in the environment necessitate that the spider must add holds, change the shape, or create repairs to the web. Sometimes it will seem as if a whole family of spiders is on the web, and at other times it will be empty. And most importantly, no spider web is permanent, just as no network is permanent.

The strength of a network is not in how well it holds one shape, a permanent structure like our cathedrals or monuments. The strength of the spider web is in its flexibility and adaptability to change—its ability to lose a hold in the wind and still maintain its usefulness. Its strength is in its ability to hold well beyond its weight and distribute that weight across the entire system so that no one part is overly taxed. No part is stronger or more important than any other. The web finds its strength in the system of interconnection and in the elasticity and strength of the structure, without a single point being more necessary than the other. Similarly, the distributive power of networks allows for shared strength and shared challenges. In hierarchical structures, it is clear who makes decisions and where power lies. Drawing on our previous discussion, this is how the Powers work. Institutions, for example, may have networks within them, but they are not networks in and of themselves. Closing the purpose gap is not accomplished by a single decision maker; it requires strong networks that can leverage individual and collective power and create alternative structures for the next generation to thrive.

Networks allow for knowledge and wisdom holders to connect with one another to offer community support, peer review, and coaching and to share ideas. With networks, information is shared, critiqued, adapted, and pressure tested in a variety of settings beyond the one in which an idea was formed. The diversity of insights that are offered through networks, the shared information, the ability to check biases and see new insights and questions, all create opportunities for knowledge networks to broaden society's collective knowledge and wisdom. Networks are necessary to handle complex challenges, especially the social challenges of today.

In his definition of *complexity*, Scott Page writes, "Systems that produce complexity consist of *diverse* rule-following entities whose behaviors are *interdependent*. Those entities interact over a *contact structure* or *network*."[2] Notice that Page does not use the term *community*. The words *complex* and *network* stand out. Complexity can be found in all sorts of problems today. Closing the purpose gap is a complex issue, involving multiple interacting sectors and conditions like education, health care, private industry, or forces like the economy or regional conditions like climate and topography. In solving problems like income inequality, housing insecurity, the education gap, or the purpose gap, a broad set of conditions affects both the problem and the myriad of potential solutions. What Page is saying is that complex systems have complex solutions, where no single, one-size-fits-all solution or perspective will solve the problem. What is needed, in his assessment, are diverse teams working toward many solutions, operating each from their own perspective and toward an end. He calls this suite of solutions the diversity bonus: that is, diverse teams outperform homogenous teams every time. Diversity goes beyond race, gender, and creed to include diversity of life experience, cognitive difference, and training. The diversity bonus arises when networks pool their solutions to achieve a shared purpose.

What holds these teams and their solutions together are networks, not singular communities or individuals, but networks of either or both. For example, K–12 educational institutions attempt to create conditions for children and youth to matriculate through their respective grade levels at equitable rates. Local governments create infrastructure, raise funds through taxes, and set policies to guide efforts to support the next generation of students. NGOs and local community groups address housing and food insecurity, so children have their basic needs met. They are addressing the purpose gap for children, but they operate independently in a network often defined by local geography. For Page, the diversity bonus comes from the combined efforts of all these players.

Good networks clarify mission and purpose and streamline resources to effective ends. Bad networks are those that think a single piece solves the whole or those that serve only an individual's needs. I learned this lesson in graduate school. As someone who cut my teeth on organizing in the Salinas Valley, I came to Boston to make a difference. For my field placement, I was able to work with one of the most inspirational humans I have ever met, Br. Anthony Zuba. In my second year in graduate school, Br. Anthony was kind enough to include me as his co-presenter for a course Marshall Ganz was teaching at the Harvard

Kennedy School. The class was filled with future MBAs committed to social change and the greater good. Ganz brought in several Boston area organizers to offer presentations about the power of networks. There was more financial capital and influence in the room than I had ever had access to in my entire life. The content of organizing for power, both individual and collective, I knew in my bones. The questions seemed basic, but the network to which I was appealing was remarkably different from my own. Back home we fought for our lives and organized to collectively bargain for better wages and safer working conditions, whereas I was now in a room full of people who could pick up the phone and make the policy changes they wanted to see. These were people who, frankly, did not have a need or desire to protest. By calling influencers, power brokers, and decision makers, they could enact the change I hoped to make through organizing. In short, they represented those who lived on the other side of the purpose gap, who grew up with access to resources. They benefited from the system as it was, and they had the power to change it if they wanted to.

I had been trained in and practiced several organizing methodologies, and my strength was in the relationships with my neighbors, friends, family, and community. These relationships helped us survive. Since that day, when I had my first glimpse at institutional power, Ganz's teaching and writing have been instrumental in how I think about networks. Although I felt out of place in his class, his work is a reminder that networks, specifically my local networks, were one part of the larger system. By expanding our local networks, we could better effect change. He writes,

> The leaders' *social networks* can similarly feed the team's strategic capacity. Strong ties to people whose lives one affects and whose regard one wishes to earn can be powerfully motivating. And the more diverse the relevant social networks with which members of the leadership team interact, the broader range of useful information and feedback to which the team has access. This too increases the team's salient knowledge and enhances its approach to problem solving.[3]

Ganz is suggesting networks can build our strategic capacity but only through the diversity of people and experiences we have participating in the network.

Networks provide the mechanism through which we can collectively close the purpose gap. Like the spider, we need to build and orchestrate our own web of connections. Next we will look at the key principles involved in doing that work.

Reflections

What networks have been influential in your life? What networks can you activate in times of need? In times of joy? In your social networks, list ten people who will pick up the phone when you call. As you look at this list, ask yourself if this group of people is already connected beyond you. Draw the connections with lines to visualize the network.

Principles of Network Building

There are key principles and activities associated with networks. Understanding these principles will enhance our ability to solve our problem: closing the purpose gap. Network principles include:

- Defining a clear purpose
- Identifying leaders
- Sustaining the network by sustaining people
- Leveraging the network for collective liberation and freedom

Defining the Purpose

Unlike communities, in which we may simply exist, a clear purpose is critical for a network to achieve its aim. It is important for defining the benefits for leaders who participate in actualizing the network's purpose. Networks are often designed and reliant on the context of the times. One straightforward case study is television networks, which serve a single purpose: to broadcast programming. While many television networks create their own programming, their central business model relies on the distribution of content. These networks became powerful because if you wanted to get your television program into the world, especially through the 1980s, they were the power brokers. They had forged a set of relations that inhibited and created an almost impenetrable barrier for newcomers. As more and more networks moved from broadcasting to cable services, new players entered who could offer content that was deliverable across wired networks.

With the invention of the Internet (itself a network), the idea that content had to go through the studios and their decision makers was disrupted.

New services like YouTube allowed users to upload their content to the Internet and share it without having to greenlight their project through one of the large networks. This, along with technological innovations like smartphones, caused a revolution in content creation, giving rise to the many options of streaming services we have today. These new networks, closed and bound by a subscription, broadcast and distribute content across its services. We are all participating in a broader and more diverse set of players who are content creators, but the television networks remain the power brokers.

Examine closely any one of the networks or streaming services, and you will see that the power for who decides what content is distributed is still in the hands of a few corporations. The original "Big Three" included the American Broadcasting Company (ABC), National Broadcasting Company (NBC), and Columbia Broadcasting System (CBS). They were powerful networks that had more influence over the thoughts and minds of people than most of us care to acknowledge. What does it matter that we have replaced these four with HULU (owned by Disney), Disney+, Netflix, and Amazon Prime Video? Going back to purpose, these networks are not here to simply "stream content." Their purpose is to capture your attention over and against their competition through the distribution of content. The content is second to the control of the distribution. Amazon is one of the strongest players in this sector because it understands that the power of its network is not just the distribution of content. They have an interconnected system, with personal assistants, reading devices, delivery services, grocery, and personal amenities; anything that requires human focus can be answered and resolved by the Amazon network. As a parent, I know from experience that Disney does the same with children. You cannot have a theme park without the movies and shows, which you cannot have without toys, memorabilia, and clothing, which you cannot have without having a set of stores and experiences that bring those things to life. The purpose of this closed network of experience is to create magical memories for a family. No one part of Disney's system delivers on that purpose; it takes the whole network.

Churches and faith communities have understood the network strategy for some time. Denominational structures today have been able to scale and expand their influence globally because of their networks. From progressive to conservative, from evangelical congregational to conferences and complex legal structures like the Presbyterian Church (U.S.A.), these networks of individuals and communities have led to the global expansion of Christianity. However, unlike the moral indifference of television and entertainment networks, do these Christian networks bring "good news"? Did they close the purpose gap for those they evangelized? If you are talking about California missions, then the answer is no, for the network of missions brought annihilation to the Indigenous peoples of California and the Southwest, my people. The church in many ways has been the chaplain to empire—in some cases literally. It has led to a global expansion of Christianity, but at great cost to those on the wrong end of the gap.

Networks that can hold together both Indigenous ways of knowing and the church's teaching are few and far between. We need to acknowledge that the church is and has been a totalizing force. Antonio Gramsci, the Italian philosopher who wrote many of his theories in prison, claimed that clergy were one of the "intellectual classes." Clergy, in his mind, created and maintained a hegemonic culture. Catholic clergy, directed by Rome, leveraged their power to create sameness. The purpose of the church was to "assimilate or destroy" that which was not like the Roman Catholic Church.[4] We need to acknowledge pastoral power, as Michael Foucault named it, as the power that clergy and the church hold over individuals.[5] It is the same power exhibited by the single-star model from the previous chapter. And, as Walter Mignolo points out, it is through the relationship of the church and "the Powers," to borrow Wink's phrase, that domination and oppression are designed and maintained in the global South.[6] These networks of institutions and their leaders have not been leveraged for the common good, especially not for the Indigenous peoples of any continent. However, is there a way that they could be leveraged for good? Is there a way to build faith networks that close the purpose gap? The means are already there, untapped.

At the Forum for Theological Exploration (FTE), where I currently work, we have an institutional doctoral network comprising around ten institutions. The network's purpose is to "create conditions for students and scholars of color to thrive." Are the vocations of the institutions and their leaders always aligned with this goal? Further, is this their only work or the only network they should rely on for the many complex problems at their institutions? Certainly not. A person or institution ought to rely on multiple networks. But when these institutions and their leaders think about diversity, equity, inclusion, and access for students and scholars of color, they have a network they can activate to address their concerns for the good of their scholars and students.

For those who need to start a network or build the web of relations, naming the purpose and constantly reframing the purpose of the larger network is critical in addressing the many complex problems associated with the purpose gap. That work needs to rely on the community of leaders and needs to be constantly reflected upon by the network itself. As you will notice below, the "who" of the network is what gives it power.

Identifying Leaders

Leaders are those who inspire change—not just those who have followers. A social media influencer is not what we mean when we say leader. Leaders are, in short, storytellers. As Marshall Ganz reminds us, "The motivation, knowledge, and learning practices of a leadership team grow in part out of the combined identities of its individual members. By identity, I mean the way each person has learned to reflect on the past, attend to the present, and anticipate the future—his or her 'story.'"[7] Leaders are able to tell their own story and the story of their communities. They are important to networks because they can mobilize, motivate, and move the community to action. If one of the young adults I work with faces challenges or barriers, I can rely on members of our network to call and check in on them, to do the human and soul care that we all need at the many thresholds of our experience. I can rely on other members of our network to address the issue through leveraging their power and positions to make concrete changes to a young person's life. These leaders may not know the young adult or be in community with them, but the power of the network and its stated purpose allow the leader to act toward justice, healing, mercy, and love.

It is not just any leaders, though, that you want in your network. Good leaders are those who learn. As Stephen Preskill and Stephen D. Brookfield write, those leaders "who learn know how beneficial and broadening learning is for everyone; they work to create mechanisms, structures, strategies, and opportunities to support individual and communal learning. . . . Learning isn't only a means to some end; sometimes it is an important end in itself."[8] Leaders are those who think generatively about their experience. Great leaders are those tireless learners, never satisfied with a limited set of experiences and knowledge. They pursue new angles, perspectives, viewpoints, and wisdom with excessive curiosity. Great leaders have eyes open to the world in a way that is "premised on the idea that every voice is precious and that every person has knowledge to impart that can benefit the entire group."[9] This openness is critical to understanding that networks, unlike communities, are dynamic structures. Depending on their needs, networks may not be active all the time. Great leaders know when members need to be active and when they need to be called upon.

My wife would tell you that there is no network more beautiful or holy than a symphony. Their leader—the conductor—calls upon instruments in their turn and guides the ebb and flow of sound. The members—professional musicians each one—know their roles and perform them expertly. Many have careers as soloists when they are not playing with the symphony. Still more earn an extra living as teachers, passing on their craft to young musicians. Not every piece will require an oboe, and not every work performed will require a piano, but a strong symphony has these players ready to call upon. Networks function in a comparable manner, with leaders knowing what instrument is most useful for their chosen goal and which member to call to the stage to perform.

The best leaders are committed to the next generation. Many of our leaders today create, design, and imagine with themselves in mind. They are great at producing solutions to create conditions for themselves. But the leaders I like working with most are consistently asking, "What if?" for the generations that have yet to be born. In my experience, these are the types of leaders who are also busy. The work of the Children's Defense Fund and Freedom Schools has for decades been committed to creating conditions for the next generation to thrive. Marian Wright Edelman is a leader we should all aspire to be and the type of leader to identify in our local networks. She has placed children at the forefront of her work for more than half a century now. Her purpose, to create conditions where children can thrive, can be seen not just in the institutional work but in her daily life: "I write letters to young people with some life lessons they can take or leave and to my beloved grandchildren with my hopes and wishes for them and for all grandchildren to come and their children and grandchildren."[10] As theological educator Reginald Blount says of work with young people,

> Teaching to transform is about helping young people claim their voice and vocation, their identities for followers of Jesus, and their purpose as members of God's people who are called to join in God's mission to the world. It is about providing an environment for young people to discover they have a place and a role to play in God's unfolding drama. It involves leading young people to discover they are participants in God's story, a story worth dying for and living for.[11]

This emphasis on children's children is a rare quality in a leader. Many leaders today say they are committed to change, but often their vision is short-sighted and self-serving. They are thinking about the liberation of themselves or peers. Leaders of this sort think and say things like "this generation" is the "chosen," or "greatest."[12] They could not be more wrong. Great leaders, those who move a network toward its stated purpose, are leaders whose impacts exist outside of time. They can see backward and forward, as if looking through a window. They draw on the learnings of the past and pull themselves forward to an unrealized future. Leaders of this quality can see the potential for a better future and create the space for future generations to achieve it.

How do we know who these leaders are? In my line of work, egoless leadership is important. Returning to the last chapter, leaders of this sort know that they are not single stars but instead both part of and looking for constellations. When I extend an invitation to individuals to help build a network, they always say that they are not doing this work alone. They are the type of people who will provide you with the same attention and depth of thought on a walk in the woods as they would in a presentation behind the lectern. They would rather take the time to walk with a close friend than accept an award or speak to crowds. Great leaders are those who know the names of the neighbors, friends, and even those they do not like to be around and remember the names of all their family members. Leaders for networks are those who would shut down a strategy session to check in with your soul, to remind you of your purpose.

Perhaps you seek to become a great leader of networks. If so, remember, good leaders recognize that the power of the network is in the people who sustain the network. They are the ones who will close the purpose gap. Identify leaders of this sort, and the network can move mountains.

Sustaining a Network Means Sustaining People

Once you have identified leaders, one of the hardest parts of the network is sustaining it. Here, clarity of purpose and knowing who the network is for are critical. The network's purpose needs to be constantly framed and reframed in light of the changing context. For example, a network may have an explicit purpose to support first-generation college students. A network existing prior to 1944, when the G.I. Bill was introduced, would have focused on white men who might have otherwise gone into trade work. The supports for first-generation students of this time look quite different in today's world, not just because of the changes to the content of higher education or changes in technology but because higher education is more accessible to a larger diversity of people than before World War II. Many students today from minoritized communities remain first-generation college students. This reframing is important because communities in these two contrasting times in history require different kinds of support.

Sustaining the network requires a constant reframing of the network's core purpose and a reinterpretation of the network's mission. As conditions change, so will the tactics used by the network to carry out its strategy. *Strategy* is the road map to long-term plans and priorities that serve the purpose or mission. *Tactics* are short-term, concrete, actionable steps or initiatives that express the execution of the strategy. Knowing the difference is important. How is the network going to achieve its purpose across its disparate parts? How are those parts going to employ localized tactics that serve that strategy?

Take literacy, for example. If you build a network of people with the purpose of closing the education gap for children by starting at early childhood education, you identify leaders from across the community: grandparents, parents, caregivers, preschool teachers and directors, librarians (local libraries do excellent programming for this age group), children's bookstore owners, parks and recs department representatives, public pools, early intervention specialists, movement class instructors, pastors, philanthropists, and so on. The strategy might be to improve early childhood education so that every child in the community goes to kindergarten loving books, identifying sight words and letters, and being able to grip a writing utensil and print their name. Tactics might include a book campaign to put books in children's homes organized by librarians and bookstore owners, or a library read-a-thon, like my town's A Thousand Books before Kindergarten campaign. To identify sight words and letters, grandparents and preschool teachers may adopt similar flashcards for everyday objects, or public pools might offer children classes that begin with noticing signs around the pool. The point is that the network is aware of the larger strategy to close the literacy gap of children prior to kindergarten and that leaders employ tactics to help close that literacy gap by taking up the piece of strategy that makes sense given their own mission and resources. A network like this will always be needed if children are present. It is only when networks become too attached to their tactics or, worse, confuse their tactics with their strategy or purpose that they become too inelastic or ineffective to survive.

We have seen the networks that created social change in modernity struggle to transform themselves for today's global reality. In the United States, the 1950s saw the boom of mainline Protestant churches, including the predecessor denominations of today's United Methodist Church

(U.S.A.), Christian Church (Disciples of Christ), Presbyterian Church (U.S.A.), Episcopal Church, Evangelical Lutheran Church in America (ELCA), American Baptist Churches (U.S.A.), and the United Church of Christ. Networks such as the National Council of Churches and National Conference of Catholic Bishops (NCCB), both major players in the twentieth century regarding social issues, have all but lost their cultural relevance among the rank and file. Previously, we explored how the National Council of Churches was fundamental in the foundation of Freedom Schools. Reflecting on the National Council of Churches and the ambitions of the Methodist Episcopal Church's building offices in 1922 across from the Capitol, Robert P. Jones comments that "over the last half century, the United Methodist Church and even the National Council of Churches have been culturally disarmed. . . . built as monuments to Protestant power, they ultimately become memorials to a White Christian America that never realized its aspirations."[13] The goal of these networks, to solidify the leaders or congregations across the country to be accessible and leveraged for social change, was ambitious. However, they have lost their power with the decline of the mainline church and, in the case of the NCCB, with the changing demographics of U.S. Catholicism toward a Latinx majority for those under the age of 30. We are the church, not its diversity, as Carmen Nanko-Fernandez would say.[14] But it is more than just a demographic shift. For those progressive or social-justice-oriented faith leaders, it is more than just a political shift. Networks focused on power and influence, as opposed to people, do not survive. Power, while important, is nothing without the people.

Networks were the catalysts for social change in modernity. From the Student Nonviolent Coordinating Committee as the backbone of the Freedom Rides and Freedom Summer of the 1960s, to the United Farmworkers Union (and related unions), these networks provided the people and power necessary to produce social change. Sustaining a network requires paying attention to each of these dimensions. Without paying attention to both people and power as important aspects in framing the network's purpose, networks begin to move toward irrelevance or, worse, obsolescence.

People need to be sustained. Networks are sustained in the relationships between people. If people are not cared for, are burned out, or do not have clarity of purpose or the basic resources to survive, the network will not be sustainable. Throughout the life of the network, people must check in with one another and share resources. Too often in my work, partners treat networks as if they are a *marketplace* for the exchange of power, resources, and capital. I have worked with partners who are upset that the network did not "turn out" people for them or turn its attention to their needs. In every instance, it is a lack of relationship between that person and the rest of the network. They do not know what is going on with partners' personal lives, let alone their institutional leadership. They only seek to achieve their own ends. To close the purpose gap, networks need to care for people. People are always the priority. To go back to our conversation on design, the network must be designed by, for, and with the people most directly impacted by the network's purpose.

This is not to dismiss power. Networks must participate in a power analysis as part of its purpose. It must include looking at the pieces within the network, such as which leaders hold power in certain sectors, communities, or the network itself. How do they leverage that power? Is it for the common good, or is it leveraged for only parts of the network? Power analysis must also be conducted about the systems or ecologies the network is hoping to influence, including how strong and elastic the network is in responding to threats and its ability to be activated in its network. If a network is central to closing the purpose gap, then a purposeful network must be aware of the various systems and ecologies that are providing meaning and purpose. This includes faith communities, but also homes, community centers, occupations, and professional development organizations.

Cyndi Suarez writes in *The Power Manual: How to Master Complex Power Dynamics*, "Power is, first of all, relational."[15] Suarez reminds us that power is not about implementing a new structure or about trying to be the boss or leader of the system, the single decision maker. Power is about people moving toward freedom and liberation. It points back to people. Suarez offers a helpful reminder that it is in the interaction that power is expressed. It is why her work focuses on concrete practices that help networks, institutions, and individual leaders understand power more clearly.

Leveraging a Network

Our shared purpose is to close the purpose gap. If we are a network of purpose seekers interested in finding our own God-given purpose, then we will only participate in networks to advance our own aims. However, if we build a network committed to the next generation and do the hard work necessary to sustain the network and its people, then it becomes a powerful tool for collective action toward helping close the purpose gap for all its members.

Networks can leverage what Chris Rabb calls invisible capital—the power of our social networks to be leveraged for the common good. Rabb outlines the distinct types of invisible capital:

> Cultural capital sums up the experience afforded by access to the people you need to know . . . social capital can best be understood as the set of networks each of us have. Networks are formal or informal groups of people who share one or more affiliations, whether scholastic, religious, vocational, ethnic, geographic, athletic, and so on.[16]

As Rabb reminds us, it is not *what* you know but *whom* you know. Together, our networks are far more powerful and represent a larger amount of capital, especially for those without inherited wealth. His argument is that "invisible capital is the toolkit of our skills, knowledge, language, networks, and experiences, along with the set of assets we were born with: our race and gender, our family's wealth and status, the type of community in which we were raised, and the education we had as children."[17] Networks as one component of this invisible capital are the keys for creating conditions for people to find purpose. They create the ability for one to establish connections beyond one's neighborhood, family, or workplace. They can consist of knowledge and social networks that expand our vision of how to work together for the future our children need.[18] The most important thing is that these networks serve a purpose and that purpose serves future generations.

In my work, when we gather or host networks, we always establish agreements and covenants. While they are often agreed upon during the gathering or proposed ahead of the gathering, here are some common features:

1. Show up authentically, bring your whole-self and attention to the present.
2. Take time to discern and ask for what you need.
3. The collective wisdom is greater than any individual's insight.

For networks to be leveraged for the common good, leaders need to be authentic in who they are and how they show up. They need to be fully present to the task at hand. Members of the network need to be able to ask for what they need, but as leaders, we do not spend enough time discerning and asking for our needs. We are conditioned to assume or name what others need. Networks that consistently take the time to listen and discern what its members need and provide space for them to ask are better positioned to address the needs of its members. One of my mentors, friends, and leader of leaders, Rev. Dr. Janet Wolf, the director of the Alex Haley Farm and of nonviolent organizing for the Children's Defense Fund, consistently opens her facilitation with naming ourselves and our needs or a gratitude we may have. She says there is "power in naming ourselves into being." Whether she is facilitating on death row or having a meal with friends, she offers this invitation. It is a radical act of freedom, to name ourselves. Finally, when networks harness the full power of their network of individuals, our conceptions about what is possible expand. There are no longer limitations to resources or access to people. We only see possibility.

Reflections

What networks create conditions for future generations to thrive? What networks do you belong to or need to create to find freedom? Who is in your network currently that calls you to life? Who in your network do you need to check in with?

Chapter 7

The Hardest Place to Take
the Work Is Home

In the late 2000s, I found myself sleeping on the floor of my teenage brother's bedroom next to our family dog. I had spent over a year in graduate school, proud to be the first to go to graduate school, prouder still that the community had celebrated this "first." What the community did not know is that I had told friends at school that I was not coming back. I started working quality assurance at the packing plant where my father ran the information systems and technology, and I had resigned myself to a life that simply did not live up to its potential purpose. I had been kicked out of a class in graduate school for not being "serious enough," saddled myself with more educational debt than I could reasonably imagine ever paying off, and had nothing material to show for it. I did not have a job in my field. I did not even have a car to get me to my current job. My friends had either moved up and out of my hometown, or if they had stayed, they had found a rhythm of family life and stability in their community. I tried to talk about all the things that were critical to my formation in graduate school—the ambitious ideas, the books I read and was still reading. I tried to get people to care about the momentous change I could see for the world and tried to talk to my own family about my sense of call, purpose, and faith. Honestly, most of them just wanted me to be happy with my job in the packing sheds, get my own car, and move out. I was a depressed mess. I did not have a clue about how to articulate or actualize my purpose at home, and honestly, I did not know if I even wanted to.

Nowadays, when I go back to California, I usually make it to where I grew up in Salinas. There is something satisfying about that return after living life away from the physical space that forms you. I drive around seeing my friends, most of whom are still around, eating food, going to cookouts, hanging out at the parks, and laughing about when we were just kids. In some ways, the feelings, the emotions, the connections, and the friendships are frozen in time. I find myself cruising around town seeing those places that spur memories—good and bad. The good includes the streets where we drove low and slow and the school where teachers and classmates alike taught me to live into this Brown body, in its full complexity. There is no replacing the rows of lettuce or strawberry fields that roll across the landscape. The rodeo grounds, Little League fields, public pool, and parks where I would ride my bicycle all populate my nostalgic imagination. We all have those places where our firsts were—first time driving a car or riding a bike, first date and breakup, and first graduation. We have all done this drive before, the trip down memory lane. These are the spaces that populate our "whens." We and our community *remember when*. They remember all our triumphs and all our failures. They remember when we thought we had nothing but dreams and ideas about the future. When we had nothing but fears and joys of the present. The people who populate our memories still hold us accountable for the people we are becoming.

Then, without fail, there comes a smell, a sound, a catch of phrase, or the arrival of someone you had not expected to see or, worse, feared. Sometimes I am more intentional in creating these moments of nostalgia to remind myself of where I am from. I often return to the playground where I was around unwarranted violence against Brown bodies. Or once, while speaking to a friend on the phone while aimlessly driving through my hometown, I realized that by the end of my call I was sitting in front of the house where my childhood was stolen from me. Why?

When I return, I am home yet feel the pain of my displacement at the same time. I am committed to the land and the people, but that is a vow I took, a vocation I embody. It is not as if the land wakes up and says to all of us who were birthed, sustained, and buried in its soil, "I love you." The land returns to us something much more profound. It longs for us to reconnect to it, to settle, to express love and gratitude for hosting us. Instead we extract nutrients, wealth, and life from it. We extract without letting it rest—as the Bible commands—or even as the land demands. It is as if we no longer know how to care for our home. As the world has become more connected, we have become more disconnected from the soil that sustains our breathing. What a painful way to live. With each passing day, my heart yearns to be connected again.

Drawing on the work that focuses on building community, such as that of Peter Block,[1] Marshall Ganz,[2] and Rev. Dr. Martin Luther King Jr.,[3] we will explore what every leader knows: taking these theories, theologies, and practices home is some of the hardest work we will do. This chapter forecasts the turn toward the inward work that leaders must do to create the space and capacity not only for their own thriving but also to lead communities to create conditions for people to thrive.

Defining Home

We cannot escape those places that formed us. The stories were so profound in creating us. They are the narratives that continue to play, over and over and over. Our memories are lined with the textures and smells of these spaces. I caught a glimpse of how this happens during the COVID-19 outbreak. My daughter, Carmelita, who was only three, would go on afternoon "wonder walks" with me. We would walk around the block, stopping every few steps to pay full attention to what our senses were telling us. We would slow down enough to smell every flower on an hour-long walk, picking our favorite smells. We returned to these same flowers day after day. We would stop to watch the red-tailed hawk that lived near our building fight with what seemed like every other bird on the block. Taking slow, methodical steps, we felt the concrete or grass under our feet. As we listened to the birds, as we watched the squirrels skirmish and run up and down trees, I sometimes thought to myself that we were not just going to get through this pandemic; we were also creating joyful, wonder-filled memories.

We stopped one day in front of two trees. One was a large white-oak tree that reached fifty feet or so into the sky. The roots spread out in the soil, a mix of red Georgia clay, rocks, and sand from the neighboring street. We looked all the way up at this tree that was leaning slightly, and I walked up to put my hand on its bark and asked Carmelita to help me "hear its heartbeat." She placed her small hand on the tree. She looked up the tree, pointed at the stumps, and said, "This tree hurts." As I looked up into the tree's canopy, I noticed it had been split open at some point, pruned in unhealthy ways, with stumps that resembled the battle scars I had only previously seen on the bodies of young people who survived domestic abuse and gang violence. She closed her eyes. "It hurts, Pa." Her expression of pain for the earth was deeply moving. As I sat and stared at the tree, her three-year-old attention span took her to the next tree.

The second tree was a magnolia with big, broad leaves. It stood merely twenty feet or so, but it cast a net of branches of equal length. With only four or five feet between the bottom of the branches and the ground, the magnolia was growing in better soil than the oak. The texture and color of the soil reminded me of a well-tamped espresso shot. We went inside the tree and looked up through its branches. The afternoon sunlight filtered through the leaves, providing a little bit of warmth. The wind that afternoon did not breach the branches. As we stood and looked up, we again listened to the heart of the tree. Carmelita simply smiled. No words. Carmelita is an extremely active child. She loves the outdoors. She loves to yell, grab, throw, jump, climb, and always be moving. Here we were in the middle of a pandemic, underneath this magnolia tree, with her gazing up through its branches, listening to the heart of nature, and again I returned to the thought that she is making incredible memories.

Anticipating that her attention was ten minutes past its limit, I asked Carmelita to continue the walk with me. With her hand on the trunk, she said, "No, Pa. I stay here. I feel safe." It stunned me. I'd been interpreting my daughter's experience of the pandemic through my own traumatic childhood, thinking that she was in a magical daydream creating the wonder- and awe-filled memories she deserved. I asked her why she felt safe. With a smile, she looked at me and said, "No one get us." In a time of social distancing, when she was separated from her friends, it was clear that Carmelita had caught the emotional contagion we were experiencing together. The impact of walking on the other side of the street when we saw another person, wearing masks, and not seeing our friends face-to-face had taken its toll. She needed more than anything to feel safe. This moment in the tree created the security she needed. It was reminiscent of the Brazilian educator, Paolo Freire, who wrote about his time in both solitude and communion under the shade of a mango tree. He writes, "I find refuge under its shade when I am there alone, secluded from the world and others, asking myself a question, or talking to myself."[4] Carmelita wanted to belong to the space we were inhabiting. She wanted to feel safe and secure. She wanted a home in nature.

Jennifer Ayres writes in *Inhabitance: Ecological Religious Education* about how humans have come to inhabit God's world—how we have come to live with and could live better with God's creation. Just as we were distant from one another during the pandemic (and may still be at the time of this publication), we are alienated from the very environment to which we belong:

> When human beings do not understand themselves to be members of a community or members of an ecosystem, they fail to recognize the webs of connection that bind human and nonhuman life

together. They mistakenly begin to believe that their happiness, success, and even ecological impart are determined by the individual choices and actions. They no longer understand themselves as members of a community, with all the pleasures and obligations that attend to that membership. And so, these problems of alienation, loneliness, unchecked industrialization, and environmental degradation are fundamentally theological and ecological problems.[5]

Ayres's work reminds us that humans long for home, a place to belong together. She writes that "human beings at least partly derive their work and identity from their mythic origins in the very soil beneath their feet. By being born of the topsoil, they thus belong to it, just as they belong to their families, their communities, and the social groupings that shape them into who they are."[6] Ayres reminds us that the way to combat the loneliness and go deeper in our relationship to our collective home is to learn inhabitance, a responsible way of being part of our global household.

In many ways, Ayres's idea of home is reminiscent of Wendell Berry's fictional town of Port William or Gabriel García Márquez's Macondo in *One Hundred Years of Solitude*. Each place holds more than just the setting for these two authors. The settings become part of the lifeblood of the community. Port William serves as the backdrop for an entire range of books, my favorite being *Jayber Crow*.[7] Jayber begins his life as a ministerial student who becomes disillusioned with ministry and settles for being the town's barber. Jayber wrestles with his sense of place in Port William. Berry crafts the angst that so many of us feel when we are trying to decide if we should stay or go. Perhaps more well known, Márquez's *One Hundred Years of Solitude* tells the story of seven generations of the Buendía family. Macondo is the fictional town founded by the patriarch of that family. As the world changes around Macondo, each generation seems to be haunted by the spirits of the past and struggles to make sense of their place in the world and their community, living and experiencing the world through the lens of their homeland.

As we read Berry and Márquez together, we gain a deeper appreciation for the challenge of space, of finding one's purpose at home. Berry asks, How do we find beauty in daily living? How do we find ourselves among our neighbors, who have learned a certain respectability politics? How do we settle into our role within that community and be affirmed in our call? In Márquez's writing, we gain a deep appreciation for the struggle over multiple generations to break free from the traumas that haunt our homes. As the world turns, Márquez reminds us in Macondo that local communities fluctuate from feeling those changes to losing their relevance and purpose if the community does not change with the world. Wrestling with these questions of home and space are critical for us as we discern our purpose. It is not merely just selecting a piece of land to live on, a colonial mind-set. The tragic flaw of Macondo was that the family constructed a narrative that the town was an island. This could not be further from the truth. It was no more a literal island, as it was just next to a river, than it was a figurative one, as every generation was drawn to the wider world. The family needed to find a new purpose. The purpose of previous generations could not be the purpose of this generation. The gap caused by generational trauma is explored throughout Márquez's work. We need to find new ways of being in the world, new ways of living with this world that are responsive to the changing conditions. We need to account for our sense of epistemological and existential displacement and dispossession while at the same time claiming responsibility for a local place and people.

Reflections

How do you define home? Is it a place? Is it a community? What are the elements of home that have carried on from generation to generation? What features of home are life giving? Which are threatening? What kind of home are you creating now?

Displacement and Dispossession

One of the hardest aspects of taking the work home is that, due to the legacies of colonization, slavery, and forced mass migration, many of us are displaced and dispossessed of our homes. If the land beneath your feet was stolen from you or you were taken away from your origins, where do you actualize your purpose? It is different from the nomadic culture of U.S. young adults today, who are choosing a neighborhood, city, or school to live, work, and play in, though that is a disruption as well. If the choice has been taken from you, how can your purpose be realized at home if you do not have an experience of home?

The poet and author Édouard Glissant explores the theme of what is lost because of the transatlantic slave route. In *Poetics of Relation*, he writes about the impact of slavery and the plantation system on the imagination of future generations. From the United States, through the Caribbean Islands, the coasts of Latin America, and portions of Brazil, the deposit of enslaved bodies in the Americas occurred simultaneously with the erasure of the Indigenous peoples of the land. He writes about the impact of this violence on the soul and on the understanding of the self. The chaos these systems of domination created do not benefit the marginalized:

> Those who dominate benefit from the chaos; those who are oppressed are exasperated by it. This speeding up of relationships has repercussions on how the full sense of identity is understood. The latter is no longer linked, except in an occasionally anachronistic or more often lethal manner, to the sacred mystery of the root.[8]

He goes on to say,

> Identity as a system of relation, as an aptitude for "giving on-and-with" [*donner-avec*], is, in contrast, a form of violence that challenges the generalizing universal and necessitates even more stringent demands for specificity. But it is hard to keep in balance. Why is there this paradox in Relation? Why the necessity to approach the specificities of communities as closely as possible? To cut down on the danger of being bogged down, diluted, or "arrested" in undifferentiated conglomerations.[9]

Artists and writers have long understood the power of space, and how context comes to define so much of who we are and were. Tommy Orange's *There There* explores the way all displaced people have diverse levels of relation to their roots. As his twelve main characters journey to and through Oakland, with the Coliseum as the final destination for the climactic gathering, the role of space and place—and the trauma of being displaced for Indigenous peoples—is one of the central motifs throughout the book.[10] For Orange, there is this deep wrestling with the internal violence and struggle caused by the displacement of bodies from the land. The internal violence and the external expressions of that violence have triggered a conversation about where and how we belong to a space and to a people.

This pain of disconnection is why my favorite poet and author, Jimmy Santiago Baca, writes so powerfully in *Immigrants in Our Own Land*, his first book of poetry published in 1979. It is an expression of the deep pain of one whose history, land, and people have been stolen from us.[11] Baca tells his full story of survival in *A Place to Stand*.[12] Drawing on his experience of childhood trauma and the trauma of incarceration, Baca reminds us that to belong is not the same as to thrive. When the land has been stolen from under your feet, when your home is not a home, how do you take the work home? Baca hints at an answer. He offers a new way to define both home and belonging. Rather than long for what was, his poetry and writing are present to what is. In his poem "Who Understands Me but Me?" he pays attention to the place of incarceration. After describing the horrors of being incarcerated, of being raised in a desert without resources, he redefines it as beautiful. The deathly hallows that provide the imagery for his poem are not objectively beautiful, but the poetic process of seeing his "what is" in current reality, and finding the beauty in it, is what is beautiful. It is a powerful expression that gives testament to his later life. Rather than return home to try and create a life exclusively on the outside, Baca returned to the same prison after just a month of freedom, the same place he was held like a caged animal, to teach poetry, his language of freedom. Belonging and home were redefined not by the place but by his sense of purpose. Baca inspires because his purpose arises out of his greatest trauma, out of the state's attempt to steal his humanity. Finding purpose within his own story and gifts, he is teaching how to do this with others. He is working for the souls of our brothers and sisters locked in cages.

Baca provides the closest interpretation of one of the most troubling Scriptures for me growing up. In Luke-Acts, Jesus goes to the house of a prominent Pharisee where a man is suffering. The Pharisee is set on catching Jesus violating the law because Jesus would have to heal the man on the Sabbath. Jesus does not hesitate; he heals the man and sends him on his way. Jesus then teaches those who are present to focus on flipping our scripts about who is important, who is worthy of our love. Jesus reminds us to start with the poor. Then comes the deepest challenge. After this healing miracle, he turns to the cost of discipleship. From Luke 14:26–27: "'Whoever comes to me and does not hate father and mother, wife and children, brothers and sisters, yes, and even life itself, cannot be my disciple. Whoever does not carry the cross and follow me cannot be my disciple.'"

I didn't understand this Scripture until I experienced Baca's poetry. When I struggled to survive the violence of my neighborhood and my home, I did not want to think of those who were supposed to love me as being bad people. Through my young and jaded theological understanding, I thought that I was responsible for the safety and healing of my family. My shoulders held a heavy burden. If I believed in a God that wanted me to love my father and mother as commanded, that wanted me to forgive, and worse, if I believed that sin necessitated forgiveness, then I wanted to take on the sins of my family. I would lie awake at night, bruises on my body, saying, "God, please do not punish my mother's boyfriend; it is my fault." I had taken on the trauma of my block: "God, please forgive my friends for beating me up; they were just doing what they were told to do." The cost of discipleship, at least at home, was my suffering. The theology I learned in Sunday school appeared in the nightly prayers I recited over and over again. Baca reminded me that it was bad theology. One of the great philosophers and theologians, Enrique Dussel, writes that the oppressed are like Job in that Job's friends, Bildad and Zophar (the powerful), try and convince Job of his sins, "exonerating the real oppressors."[13]

Much later in my seminary education, I read Dietrich Bonhoeffer, who writes, "When the Bible speaks of following Jesus, it is proclaiming a discipleship which will liberate mankind from all man-made dogmas, from every burden and oppression, from every anxiety and torture which afflicts the conscience."[14] What I had been taught was what Bonhoeffer refers to as "cheap grace." I wanted cheap grace for those around me and for myself. I wanted a quick way out of my everyday experience. The cost of discipleship, however, requires costly grace, not the grace of my suffering. I have said it before, and I will say it again, there is no redemption in suffering.[15] The cost of discipleship is to follow God's call to heal. My call, my purpose, was to understand that I was not alone in this isolation. The purpose of following Jesus is to find liberation for myself and others who suffer, on the Sabbath or any other day. Bonhoeffer, like Baca, helped remind me that the burden I was experiencing while reading Scripture was superficial. To follow Jesus, however, I would need to find ways to be liberated from the shackles of abuse—physical and psychological—in order to heal myself and others. I would have to redefine to whom I belonged. I found inspiration in Baca's poetry because he learned to write with only a dictionary and paper while locked up in solitary for refusing to work in the fields. He overcame the widest of purpose gaps.

With a theology that does not prescribe my suffering, returning home feels completely different. Jesus returns home to Nazareth in Luke 4:16–21. He has already resisted the devil in the desert. He famously goes to synagogue, as is custom, and reads from Isaiah:

"The Spirit of the Lord is upon me,
    because he has anointed me
        to bring good news to the poor.
He has sent me to proclaim release to the captives
    and recovery of sight to the blind,
        to let the oppressed go free,
to proclaim the year of the Lord's favor."
                        (Luke 4:18–19)

Jesus is reading Isaiah 61, and the response from the audience was not clear until Jesus adds, "'Today this scripture has been fulfilled in your hearing'" (v. 21). Imagine that! Imagine yourself as a listener, someone who has watched Jesus grow up and who knows exactly where he has come from, because you came from there, too. My favorite passage comes from one of those who were present: "'Is not this Joseph's son?'" (v. 22). Leaders are called to "bring good news to the poor," to offer a preferential option for the poor, to honor God by becoming a healer of the world, but sometimes when we go home, our communities just do not understand. They are more likely to wonder, "What makes you think you are so special?"

I am less concerned with what Jesus feels in this moment or with poor readings of this text than I am with that question, "'Is not this Joseph's son?'" It is the same question that people of color know too well and one I've heard asked to me directly. When they hear that a Chicano from an education desert is overseeing grant making and leadership regarding meaning and purpose, I have been asked directly, "How did you get that job?" "What makes you qualified to do that work?" "I didn't realize just anyone could do that!" "But your family doesn't do this. What makes you think you can do it?" Or my favorite, which was asked to me in an invited lecture on meaning and purpose: "Do you have imposter syndrome? Are you a sellout?" They were questions about my person, not about my work or purpose. The questions are not about meaning and purpose but about not understanding their own brokenness. Imagine that question in its fullest: *Isn't that Joseph's son? The carpenter? The one who went to the same religious training as my child? The one who went away for a little bit? Our neighbor's kid? The one who grew up on this block? The one who threw a temper tantrum wanting to study Torah? He is claiming to be able to heal our wounds. What does he know? He left. We have been here.*

The internalized oppression of our communities can hold back those members who have found their purpose. Our community narrative is that *no one from here* is supposed to make it. We are, in Frantz Fanon's words, the *damné*, the damned.[16] When we return, our stories are inspiring, but our continued presence can be unsettling. Our teaching and pedagogy need to make a difference in the daily lived experiences of the people we grew up with. Taking the work home can be the hardest work because, as Jesus says in Luke 4:24, "'No prophet is accepted in the prophet's hometown.'" The hard truths of the world and the need for healing are felt deepest right at home. Soul healers are often not welcome at home because of the unaddressed trauma of shared experience. I know the pain of my own abuse—of being thrown out of my own home, or what I thought was my home. I know the pain of unjust systems designed to segregate and marginalize my community. I have sat with relatives and fought about the humanity of those locked up, talking abstractly about mass incarceration. What goes unaddressed is the police being called to patrol our communities because of systemic racism or our family members who go unvisited behind bars. I have had too many arguments with family and other community members about the pains of the last couple of years and the unbearable heartbreak of children being locked in cages, children whom I view as family. However, home symbolizes the complicated relationship between having immigrated to this country and having achieved success. Taking the work home can mean challenging traditions and practices that are not liberating or life-giving for the most marginalized members of our community. For healers, taking our purpose home can mean excavating the pains that lead to unchecked and unexamined bias in ourselves and our community. This work is hardest at home because we know what the stories are, we know the people, and we know where the bodies are buried.

For those involved in change work, whether on the local or national level, the question of belonging is always present: What is my role in the movement? As people of faith and the Book, we want to know how our commitments to *la causa* or our faith translate to the folks we live and work with most directly. But vocation is not simply about finding a place or a people to serve. When you have committed your life to end the suffering of others and the planet, it is overwhelming how big the community you serve becomes. When I first started organizing, I realized how intimately connected communities are. Organizers, by our very nature and work, are embedded in lives throughout the community. Justice work, also known as ministry, often takes place where communities feel deep pains or are suffering. Those pains can be spiritual in nature, economic, or due to the great society ills of racism, xenophobia, classicism, materialism, homophobia, transphobia, patriarchy, and the many other undergirding prejudices we hold about others. This pain can be all consuming. Often, organizing campaigns are situated around a single issue like education, workers' rights, or civil rights. In all these cases, the challenge is to see how these issues overlap and interlock.

How do young people find their place in the movement? How do they find themselves in a community of call? Every year in my work with hundreds of leaders, I ask questions about call, or how they see their own vocations. These leaders represent youth-development networks, college campus ministries, educators in higher education, pastors, nonprofit leaders, doctoral students of color, and the young people we all serve. Data from applications, reports, and evaluations where we have asked them to define and locate their vocation or call show that they always receive this call in their home or community. This fact is fundamental to how we must change our view of education. The purpose of education is not to gather and regurgitate facts and white history. Education's purpose is to heal and find freedom. We must not only prepare students to return home; we must also value the education they first received at home.

Education Everywhere

As a trained and experienced educator, I cannot get away from how important reframing education is to acknowledge our stories and lives. Teachers are everywhere, and most children's education happens outside of the classroom. If we all began to see ourselves as teachers, as those who want to see people realize their purpose, then we could transform the world. As Parker Palmer writes, "Teachers possess the power to create conditions that help students learn a great deal—or keep them from learning much at all. Teaching is the intentional act of creating those conditions, and good teaching requires that we understand the inner sources of both the intent and the act."[17] Allowing young people the chance to realize their purpose is about creating the conditions for both the inner and outer act of freedom.

One of the foundational actions people can take to close the purpose gap is to recognize and honor the education, knowledge, and wisdom that pass from one generation to the next, including that which takes place beyond formal and explicit instruction. We often limit the strategies we use to close the many gaps in our society by taking inventory of the explicit conditions we control, the stuff at the tip of the iceberg. We zero in on things like how the gap came to be. For example, in *The Color of Law: A Forgotten History of How Our Government Segregated America,* Richard Rothstein lays out the case for how legislation and judicial cases have led to a segregated America.[18] Our neighborhoods are not just segregated by accident. They are the conscious choice of lawmakers and the courts. Earlier, we explored that idea when we talked about the design of our commutes. Michelle Alexander's masterful work *The New Jim Crow: Mass Incarceration in the Age of Colorblindness* held up a mirror to America to show that our history from slavery to our present practices of mass incarceration has always been about the domination of Black bodies.[19] Bryan Stevenson in *Just Mercy: A Story of Justice and Redemption* chronicles his work as a lawyer and founder of the Equal Justice Initiative, working for justice for those facing death behind bars.[20] Stevenson has long fought for the rights of the poor, people of color, and the wrongfully accused in this country. His work has made explicit what so many people of color on this side of the purpose gap know in our bones: the system was set up to mark us guilty before we were even born—in Ibram Kendi's words, "stamped from the beginning."[21] Like Moses or Jesus, we carry a mark on our heads for death. In the face of this mark for death, our very breathing is sometimes purpose enough. Our lives are the refusal to give into the Powers that seek to destroy us.

The work of these authors is explicit. Their writing makes visible that which otherwise is invisible to many. For those seeking to cross an insurmountable purpose gap, these truths are not secrets; they have always been explicit. Our task is to acknowledge the power and legitimacy of both the implicit and tacit education that happens in our communities, spend time learning the wisdom and knowledge that exists in our homes, and share it as knowledge equal to that which the majority culture values as knowledge. We must learn to value our traditions and unlearn our miseducation. We must *generate* new knowledges.

Acknowledge
One of the biggest contributors to the purpose gap is access and equity in education. As Beverly Daniel Tatum writes in *Why Are All the Black Kids Sitting Together in the Cafeteria: And Other Conversations about Race,*

> Unless we engage in these and other conscious acts of reflection and reeducation, we easily repeat the process with our children. We teach what we were taught. The unexamined prejudices of the parents are passed on to the children. It is not our fault, but it is our responsibility to interrupt this cycle.[22]

One of the greatest educational challenges in progressive circles is to teach about equity and diversity. The tools available in the classroom and at home vary. In so many of the lessons about diversity I witness from my children's schools—diverse and progressive schools in which I have been an active member of leadership—equity work includes a celebration of difference. For example, students are asked, "What makes you unique?" Even in these progressive spaces, the response to the purpose gap is that every child is unique and special, but it teaches children a lie. It creates cognitive dissonance between the experience they have at home and what they are getting in school. What does it matter if everyone is special and unique when children know as early as preschool that the different experiences they have at home are not the same as feel-good adages? Though they are told they are special and unique, they still worry about having enough food or surviving the terror of their home or neighborhood. Some children are bussed into schools where the only healthy meal they get that day will be the one that the school provides.

It is a shame to tell these children that they are all unique in the same space. Society is designed to marginalize. Education needs to heal and be accessible. Rather than lying to future generations, we need to teach about unjust systems and create collaborative environments for change that begin with the most marginalized. The everyone-is-unique mantra becomes a cultural performance or exposure for white children. They want to know about our communities, but do not want to face the horrors they have caused. It is an extractive education system.

My son, who has Indigenous blood flowing through his veins and yet is geographically removed from his Indigenous family, was asked along with the rest of his classmates to play the "Indian" for Thanksgiving. The teacher was well-meaning, repeating the traditional Thanksgiving play that her predecessors had put on for generations. However, rather than teach the violence experienced by his ancestors and family at the hands of white people, my son's Indigenous family was dismissed, consigned to paper-feather headdresses and brown pillowcases worn by a sea of white children welcoming their new pilgrim friends with baskets of squash and corn. As you can imagine, my wife and I did not allow him to participate. My wife's mother, who is Apache, gave us some helpful advice, and my wife went in and read a children's book and talked to his kindergarten class about our family members whose traditions are very much alive today. That was the last year the traditional Thanksgiving play was put on at his school. This small change, however, is not enough to bridge the gap for Indigenous children, or for any other children of color who continue to experience the aftereffects of the cruelty that ripped their ancestors from their land and took the land from their ancestors. The current education system is not set up for our collective freedom.

Teaching about white privilege assumes that if the white community becomes more *aware* of their part in the purpose gap, they will make changes. However, privilege is the wrong framework for thinking about the passive and implicit education that comes with race and culture. One thing my children must learn is that the weapons of white supremacy are available to white people all the time. The potential destructive power of these tools, even if you never use them, is what causes fear for the rest of the world. It is a nuclear stockpile that some white people refuse to use, but they continue to benefit from the fear caused by its very existence. The term for this sort of power is not *privilege*, it is *deterrence*, a strategy used by the U.S. military and militaries around the world. Deterrence theory says that another party will not use force for fear of being destroyed as a result. If people willingly allow racist policies like housing discrimination through redlining and refusing to grant home loans to Black and Latinx people, then it has a direct impact on school funding because property taxes go to the schools, furthering the wealth and opportunity gap. The wealth white families have accumulated has provided them unique advantages in a society founded on unjust systems. As Thomas Shapiro writes in *Toxic Inequality*, it is not enough to teach that everyone is equal, because we are not. He writes,

> Looking at a representative sample of Americans in 2013, the median net wealth of white families was $142,000, compared to $11,000 for African American families and $13,700 for Hispanic families. This racial wealth gap means that even black families with incomes comparable to those of white families have much less wealth to use to cushion unemployment or a personal crisis, to apply as a down payment on a home, to secure a place for their families in a strong, resource-rich neighborhood, to send their children to private schools, to start a business, or to plan for retirement.[23]

There is a quantifiable difference between the wealth of white families and Black and Brown families. Our students and children know this. Shapiro notes that there is evidence that this inequality compounds "stress-inducing events, including community violence, accidents, life-threatening illnesses, loss of economic status, and incidences of racism. We also know that financial resources shield family from economic and social trauma, lessen the impact of some trauma, and enable more rapid recovery, and reduce the risk of subsequent adverse events."[24] These are material differences our children feel in their bones. Celebrating difference in a one-dimensional way teaches our children to ignore material differences. What we should be doing is teaching our children and future generations to interrogate the differences and to challenge them.

Even this diversity- and equity-focused education system deters from addressing underlying issues within our society. It keeps systems in check and in place. Said differently, it keeps Black and Brown children in their social place. When white people have amassed the wealth, capital, and power to design systems that advantage their children, they may not be openly racist, but they still benefit from racist structures. Shapiro's research is clear that "parental wealth while children are growing up foreshadows how well they will do in their adult lives. The parents' well-being and the child's future opportunities are contingent on wealth accumulated during the child-rearing years."[25] Children on the other side of the purpose gap are taught and know these material differences in their skin. Formal education has tried to diffuse the difference or teach it away, preferring to perpetuate lies that everyone can be whatever they want to be. The current system benefits white students in the same way that American citizens benefit from a nuclear arsenal. As an American citizen, I benefit from the fear and deterrence our nuclear stockpile creates in the same way that white people benefit from a history of white supremacy. These weapons of wealth, capital, and past violence provide white children with material advantages in the world. White parents can personally be antiracist or live an antiracist life, but the racist system that is in place provides a sort of cover, a deterrence from destabilizing the systems that benefit their children. It is the same fear that causes people of color to rethink jogging, to notice people watching them in stores and in public, and to see the way their kids are policed and kicked out of class as early as preschool. The fear that white supremacy causes has shifted education in my own home, for I have to teach my children a completely different history curriculum and have conversations about the news where their bodies are implicated. Until the systems created and sustained by the deterrence provided by white supremacy are destroyed, we cannot be free. This is part of the acknowledgment.

To talk about race and difference in militaristic terms seems like a far stretch from the literature I read on the subject matter, which is mostly focused on how to talk across difference. These resources, while incredibly helpful, do not help parents have the talk with their children about the weaponization of white supremacy.[26] It was weaponized explicitly when that fifth-grade teacher spat in my face and said he could "handle" my Brown dad. It is also implicitly weaponized when I sit in school board meetings and hear parents leveraging "differentiation" to separate their children into peer learning groups based on racial and socioeconomic class or when we look at school-district maps and see the impacts of redlining, gentrification, and white flight. Another example of explicit weaponization is when parents tell their children they are not allowed to play with their school friends who live on the wrong side of town, as was said about me growing up. The purpose gap exists when a white family moves in and the property values go up, but when a Latinx or Black family moves in, the property values go down. It affects the purpose gap because it is educating a future generation not to think through the economic, political, and social impact of displacing, distancing, or replacing people of color from the education pipeline.

Unlearn

The stories we tell matter. Where we tell them, how we tell them, and why we tell them matters. My favorite educator, theologian, psychoanalyst, and writer is the late Rubem Alves. The Presbyterian Church of Brazil gave Alves's name, along with five others, as dissenters to the Brazilian government to avoid further implication by the U.S.-backed military coup. He fled to the United States with the help of the Presbyterian Church (U.S.A.) and completed his PhD at Princeton Theological Seminary. With this backdrop, Alves eventually left the theological academy to work toward the education of children more broadly. His writing spans disciplines and genres, and it weaves poetry and imagination together to help readers "unlearn" violent ways of knowing. Alves wanted to return to the sacred encounter of everyday life.[27] Specifically, he writes about children's imagination, using stories and metaphors that they can understand. From cooking and spinning webs to imagining the actual resurrection of the dead, Alves can help us unlearn so we might pursue our curiosity and creativity.[28] He claims that for children, curiosity is their purpose: to stay curious about the world, to be fully immersed in the stories of their culture and traditions, to be curious about the natural world, and to listen to their own internal voices. Children have no problem imagining friends and talking or singing to themselves. They have no inhibitions about asking the most basic of questions and not being satisfied with a generic or unsatisfactory answer. They can stay focused on a parade of ants, following the path that exists between the ants' home and their destination. Children's curiosity and thirst to learn are the very unlearning Alves gestures us toward. It is the inner learning to which Fred Rogers and *Sesame Street* were so attuned.

The inner life of the child is where meaning and purpose are constantly being worked out. It is where they navigate their place in the world, in their community, in the home, in the family, and in themselves. When a child's mind sees the astronaut on TV, it does not shy away from saying, "I want to do that." To unlearn to the point where all things are possible, even resurrection in Alves's case, is to be returned to the mind and curiosity of the child. This curiosity is what will close the purpose gap.

Our purpose must be to unlearn our own miseducation, as Carter G. Woodson writes,[29] or undo the extraction and dehumanization of education typified in the removal of Indigenous children and placing them in U.S. boarding schools.[30] Roxanne Dunbar-Ortiz reframes how we must unlearn our own storytelling:

> Anishinaabe (Ojibwe) historian Jean O'Brien names this practice of writing Indians out of existence "firsting and lasting." All over the continent, local histories, monuments, and signage narrate the story of first settlement: the founder(s), the first school, the first dwelling, first everything, as if there had never been occupants who thrived in those places before Euro-Americans. On the other hand, the national narrative tells of "last" Indians or last tribes, such as "the last of the Mohicans," "Ishi, the last Indian," and *End of the Trail*, as a famous sculpture by James Earle Fraser is titled.[31]

To dive deep into the grief of our miseducation of extraction and colonization is to begin the healing process of education. Leanne Betasamosake Simpson reminds us that the starting place of education for Indigenous people, specifically from her place as a decolonial scholar, a Michi Saagiig Nishnaabeg writer, and activist, is to recognize that there needs to be healing from this generational trauma.[32] It is violence that continues to strip not just the land from the people, but the culture as well. She writes,

> Our most sacred places have been made into provincial parks for tourists, where concrete buildings cover our teaching rocks. Our burial grounds have cottages built on top of them. The rivers have lift locks blocking them. The shores of every one of our lakes and rivers have cottages or homes on them, making it impossible for

us to launch a canoe. Our rice beds have been nearly destroyed by raised water levels from the Trent-Severn Waterway, boat traffic, and sewage from cottages. We live with the ongoing trauma of the Indian Act, residential schools, day schools, sanatoriums, child welfare, and now an education system that refuses to acknowledge our culture, our knowledge, our histories, and our experience.[33]

We need to unlearn the myths that our education system teaches us and recognize that their silence on our truths is a form of erasure. From my own context, the historical myths are best exemplified in colonization and conquistadors. We are all taught the same story: Hernán Cortés conquers the Aztecs because the local people thought he was a god. How naïve! My ancestors were so stupid, right? Camilla Townsend reframes the story as a

> tale of military rather than spiritual loss on the part of the Indians. The Mexica did not believe the god Quetzalcoatl walked among them, nor were they impressed by a vision of Mary or one of the saints. Moctezuma, the king, simply found himself in possession of less military power than the newcomers, and he recognized this. Part of the story lay in the hands of the people whom the Mexica had rendered enemies ... the war against the Spaniards was a horrific period in which all kinds of people—Malinche (translator for the Spaniards), for instance, as well as Moctezuma's captive daughter ... simply did their best to stay alive. Aside from the destruction of the war, the death toll from the smallpox brought by the Spaniards led some native people to believe that they would all die.[34]

Our ancestors were not naïve. The opposite is true! We are the descendants of survivors. Undoing this miseducation is essential in closing the purpose gap. I have a proud history to tell. I am not the descendant of people who found spiritual enlightenment through the sight of these pale conquistadors. I am descended from the survivors of attempted genocide through warfare, where guns, germs, and steel forced new tactics of survival.[35] It is a powerful reframing of our story and lineage, one that is long documented and recovered by Chicana and Latina feminist scholars.[36] To unlearn these myths that were lifted up as historical truths allows me to reclaim a story and purpose.[37] My ancestors from this soil did what they had to do, in the face of certain death, to ensure that future generations may survive and maybe, one day, thrive.

We must acknowledge that a set of conditions has defined our explicit and implicit education. We must reframe our histories in order to change the rules of the imagination. Acclaimed educator bell hooks has been bridging this educational divide for decades, trying to alert the wider audience to this weaponization of race against people of color.[38] Her own vocation was tethered up in the act of writing and education: "Teaching was about service, going back to one's community. For black folks teaching—educating—was fundamentally political because it was rooted in antiracist struggle. Indeed, my all-black grade schools became the location where I experienced learning as a revolution."[39] She adds that the teachers in her life modeled for her the vocation, the purpose of education. She writes that her teachers "knew our parents, our economic status, where we worshipped, what our homes were like, and how we were treated in the family . . . my effort and ability to learn was always contextualized within the framework of generational family experience."[40] We have to unlearn the idea that education only happens in our institutions, the same institutions that preserve and protect power for the few. Education happens in our communities. This education was evocative for hooks and reinforced her sense of purpose. Hooks's moving from the home to primarily white institutions reminded her that there was also a "shift from beloved" to "interlopers, as not really belonging." It taught her the difference between "education as the practice of freedom and education that merely strives to reinforce domination."[41] In my California schooling, from kindergarten through my college classes, I had only three Latine/o/a teachers. Even my ethnic studies class in college was taught by a white man. I learned about bell hooks from a white man. This lack of nonwhite teachers is one of the deepest plagues of the purpose gap along racial and ethnic lines. Salinas Union High School District serves just under 15,000 students, 13,000 being Hispanic or Latinos/as, comprising 87 percent of those fully enrolled. Only 35 percent of those Latino/a students meet University of California or California State University admissions standards. Latinx faculty are only 30 percent of the faculty, whereas 62 percent are white. Fifty percent of white students are college ready as of 2019. There is a correlation between who tells or teaches the stories and what counts as knowledge. Education is the pathway to freedom, a pathway to closing the purpose gap, but if our public institutions, while improving, are not creating the conditions for students to realize their purpose, then we might have to redefine what we mean by education, or, more specifically, redefine where education takes place.

Brazilian educator Paulo Freire's foundational work *Pedagogy of the Oppressed* is one of the most cited works in education. For Freire, meaning and purpose are about "humanization," one that is always bending toward freedom.[42] Freire focuses his work on education at home. He sees that oppression has limited the ability of children to dream. For Freire, teaching students how to read and write gives them access to the political process, to the ability to participate in civic life and change their conditions.[43] He claims that starting with the critical reflective practices of the fundamentals of our lives, like cooking, eating, and sleeping, changes the very nature of the conversation about education and its purpose. Education is everywhere. Further, "to teach is not to *transfer knowledge* but to create the possibilities for the production or construction of knowledge."[44] If the collective redefines knowledge as those things that are indispensable to our very survival, then the greatest teachers are those with whom we spend the most time. It is not enough for me to learn my grandma's recipes from a card. The instructions are merely the transfer of knowledge. But if we count all those hours I sat with her in the kitchen, listening to her tell stories of our family and ancestry, then what she has empowered me to do is more than just to cook a recipe. She has taught me how to love myself, our history, and our traditions. Kneading tortilla dough is an act of love. And given the change in the world since she has gone to the above and beyond, these stories get nuanced and reframed with every generation. I have found my own ways of creating knowledge. I take the stories she told me and nuance them for today. I take the literal story of my sitting with my grandmother in the kitchen while she made tortillas, place it in this book, and generate new knowledge that centers around my grandma's tiled floor kitchen, the gas burners, and a comal always ready for a good flip. I found freedom in her kitchen. If we can reframe education as the reclaiming of lives, histories, and traditions and work for justice and not a diffusion of difference, then our entire society will benefit.

Share

Education everywhere requires us to pay closer attention to who and what we value. Day-care workers, after-school caretakers, teachers, parents who stay at home, and parents who work outside the home—they are all teachers. The history-and-culture curriculum at my son's school does not even come close to the family and cultural storytelling we do over the dinner table or the prayers and songs we sing at night. It does not compare to the ways we unpack current events and reflect on what has happened each week during Shabbat. Like a modern midrash, my spouse and our community are creating the texts that interpret our traditions and stories for today's world.

If education is the practice of freedom, then we must begin to take a better inventory and value the education we receive outside of formal education structures. I am not suggesting that we abandon formalized education. Following Freire, knowledge generation is the purpose of the scholar. Scholars read and research *everything* in their field. They write novel work, and then other scholars expand that work. The attention to craft is how scholars achieve knowledge and separate a casual opinion about a topic from one that is vetted by sources many of us are not even aware exist. In this age of anti-truth, social media, and shorter and shorter attention spans, that work is even more critical.

What I am arguing for is that education be understood more broadly, especially for those who are staring at an insurmountable purpose gap. To close the purpose gap, education needs to be accounted for and valued. When I lived with my grandparents, my grandpa and I would sit on his front porch most nights while he smoked his Pall Mall cigarettes. Some nights we sat in complete silence; other times he would share stories about the family. Our front porch served as a small confessional. One evening, Grandpa Julio told me about his time in the military when he was both a bugle boy and a driver for an officer. The person he drove was a white officer, "a mean *pendejo*," he called him. He said he learned quickly that he would never be the person someone else drove around, that he must do his best to hide his accent, and that he always had to look ready to work. "That's what they want. They want you to be ready to do whatever they say, because if you don't . . . well, you know." These lines educated and formed me. Was this the reality I was going to live into? Keep my head down, and do exactly as I am ordered? That was the way to success, he would tell me. Such conversations educate and form. But they were far from when he and I would talk about Emiliano Zapata, the Mexican Revolutionary, who said it is better to die on your feet than live on your knees, and "*la tierra es de quien la trabaja con sus manos*," the land belongs to those who work it with their hands. The education of our daily lives and the teachings from our elders inform our approaches to life. They can help close the purpose gap or widen it. Taking inventory and being more intentional about what we are teaching means that we are taking responsibility for the next generation and their education.

Critical pedagogues have known about this for some time. The educator Lev Vygotsky created the idea of the zone of proximal development, or the social context where learning takes place. Key to his idea is that students have artifacts, resources, and tools all around them, but these tools and resources are highly contextual.[45] The idea of the "organic intellectual" is foundational to critical pedagogies' concern with education everywhere. The organic intellectual stemmed from Italian theorist Antonio Gramsci, whose works were mostly written while he was imprisoned over ten years. Gramsci writes about how intellectuals are the creators of culture and longs for an intellectual class to emerge from the ground up, from our communities on the other side of the purpose gap. He writes, "It must be recognized that no occupation is ever totally devoid of some kind of intellectual activity, and, finally, that apart from his own occupation, every individual carries on some intellectual activity: he is a philosopher, he shares a conception of the world and therefore contributes to sustain it or to modify it, that is, to create new conceptions."[46] The idea that every task requires some intellectual activity, that everything teaches, is mirrored in the works of writers like Michael Apple,[47] Henry Giroux,[48] bell hooks,[49] Joe Kincheloe,[45] Ira Shor,[50] John Smyth,[51] and Peter McLaren.[52]

If education happens everywhere, what can we do to close the purpose gap everywhere? Marketers have already figured this out. In a study to look at whether or not television could teach preschoolers, Mary Morrisett, one of the founders of *Sesame Street*, who saw "education as a sacred duty," set out to answer that question.[53] The answer was far more intuitive and could be boiled down to a few lines: "'Can television teach?' Cooney said. 'Well, we knew the answer. I knew the answer right away. Every child in America was singing beer commercials. Now, where had they learned beer commercials?'"[54] Like my sitting on the porch with my grandpa or helping in my grandma's kitchen, everything teaches. There is no escaping it. And what we teach influences how we see our potential and purpose. The stories and narratives that we tell ourselves and our children are the primary forms of education: no education could matter more.

To close the purpose gap, the hardest place to take the work may be home, but that is precisely where the gap closes. It closes in the imagination of the child or the adult when a loved one believes in you and believes you were destined to follow your many purposes. That need to be affirmed in one's purpose does not end in childhood but continues to form us throughout our lives. If we can acknowledge that education happens everywhere, work to unlearn the lies that serve our domination, and share our salient knowledge with future generations, then we can create the conditions for freedom and liberation.[55]

Reflections

Who were your greatest teachers beyond the classroom? What do you have to unlearn from your education? What knowledge do you have to acknowledge and value? What wisdom do you have to share with the world? If education is the practice of freedom, then how are you contributing to the liberation of future generations?

Part 3

What Is My Purpose?

I am no longer in a cage
Freedom
Somewhere between a history stolen
And a story to be told
I am finding my voice
Colonized, certainly
Resisting erasure, actively.
I can feel it.
They want me to conform, assimilate.
Just say "thank you." You made it.

PURPOSE

We are not free until we are all free.
Your children are my children.
The cycle will be broken.
Never again. ¡Basta!
We are not the same.
We will be free.
Thriving is liberation.

Chapter 8

Carry Your Corner

Chapter 8 is the last of the "how" chapters and serves as a transition to the "What does thriving look like?" section of the book. This chapter bridges the literature between the power of conditions and the power of the human spirit to work toward thriving. In Rev. Dr. Otis Moss III's analysis of Jesus' healing of the paralytic man (Luke 5:17–26), the four men carrying the mat on which he lay needed to carry their own corners to get the paralytic man to Jesus. People, likewise, need to be able to "carry their corners" to heal and lead others. Chapter 8 explores the importance of all the gifts of the community coming together to move individuals and the community toward healing, justice, and accomplishing the impossible. It draws on the narratives of groups and organizations that are creating the conditions to solve impossible tasks. Drawing inspiration from the work of Frank Rogers[1] and Augusto Boal,[2] I argue that by setting big goals, attempting to tackle seemingly unanswerable questions, practicing and training to accomplish unimaginable feats, and working toward a common purpose, we can create the ideal conditions for people to thrive.

How did Jesus get his disciples, and why is it important? The Gospel of John claims that John and Andrew, followed by Peter, Philip, and Nathanael, were Jesus' first disciples. The call was achieved through word of mouth, and it all occurs in the first chapter. Strangely, gathering his disciples is one of the first things that Jesus does in the book of John. Writing later than the other Gospel writers, the author(s) of John assume that we can skip over the part where Jesus built up enough notoriety to gain followers. In the Synoptics, Jesus must work to get his followers. In Matthew's Gospel, Jesus does not call disciples until the fourth chapter, after he has been tested in the wilderness by the devil and begins to preach. This call narrative is a little more dramatic with Jesus calling Simon (Peter) and Andrew, who are fishing. The famous line he says to these two fishermen is "'I will make you fish for people.'" (Matt. 4:19). Luke offers something incredible, though. In the previous chapter, we looked at how hard it was to take the work home. In Luke, Jesus resists the temptation in the desert, but then he goes back to Nazareth, his hometown. He proclaims the Scripture has been fulfilled, and his neighbors, many of whom he grew up with (social mobility then was not what it is today) run him right out of town.

In Luke, he does not call disciples as his first acts, as in John, nor does he go and preach and call folks at the water, like in Matthew. Right after the desert, he returns home and is rejected. In Luke 4:33–35, he drives out an impure spirit, just as he was run out of his hometown. Before Jesus casts him out, the demon recognizes Jesus, saying, "'Have you come to destroy us? I know who you are.'" The text says that afterward he went to the home of Simon where he healed Simon's mother-in-law, and the people cheered him. Jesus then returns to solitude, to discern his purpose, reemerging to say that he needs to preach in other towns. Jesus does all this work without disciples; no one is following him yet.

It is not until Luke 5 that Simon, James, and John follow him. When the chapter opens, they are fishing and not catching anything. Jesus goes out on the boat with Simon. The text says they go out after Simon has a long night of working and not catching anything. Jesus tells Simon to put his nets down deep. Sure enough, Simon catches a lot of fish; he now has his livelihood. If Simon had left to follow Jesus when he was not catching anything, that would have been cheap grace. But here, in the middle of abundance, Simon, along with his crew, give up their livelihood to follow Jesus. Now that Jesus has a crew, Luke 5 concludes with the healing of the paralyzed man (Luke vv. 17–26) mentioned previously. The text is clear that multiple people brought the man in and lowered him. Jesus is no longer rolling solo. And there is a reason for it.

Now that Jesus has disciples, his message and his works have a broader impact. More importantly, each of these disciples would learn to carry the burden of taking care of the community. Rev. Dr. Otis Moss III, at the Alex Haley Farm in Clinton, Tennessee, spoke about this text in 2019. He reminded us that each of the four disciples who brought the man in on the mat had to carry his own corner. If any of them dropped his corner, the man would not make it to Jesus. Rev. Dr. Moss claims that this is what discipleship is: we alone are not the movement, and we alone cannot heal the world. We need to be good disciples who carry our corners. It's not a novel idea, but to focus on this one piece of Scripture, to zero in on how Jesus' first healing act with his disciples is an act that requires the community, is profoundly telling about how people of faith might live out the call to its fullest. We are not meant to carry the burden of the world, just our corner.

If you capture nothing else from this book, I hope that you take away this one idea: to overcome the purpose gap, we must do this work together. We must ask better questions about the narratives and stories we tell ourselves about how to close the gap, about the conditions in which we find ourselves, and about our various purposes and vocations. Do not believe the self-help literature that finding your purpose is the key to happiness. This work is not a solo act. Even Jesus could not perform his purpose alone. Asking questions in community can be a far more powerful life source than finding the work or life purpose that drives you alone.

In our work supporting young adults and doctoral students of color in finding and realizing their purpose, one thing is clear: the process of discernment is far more important than the outcome itself. Even for those who know what they want to do in life, the imagination expands once it's exposed to new practices and people who are both discerning and living into their calls. By not setting their intention on a fixed outcome and allowing themselves to be open to the multitude of possibilities of God's call, people successfully discern their next most-faithful step in community. When young people seek better questions with their peers, they receive qualitatively and quantifiably better answers, but they are not just any questions. They are the big "why" questions. They ask impossible questions, challenging the foundation of our knowledge. They push the boundaries to answer new questions. Through the practice of asking better and bigger questions in community, we are better equipped not just in finding our purpose but living into it. It is inspiring to see someone who has asked the right question and pursued it to its natural end.

One of my favorite examples is the distance runner Eliud Kipchoge, who became the greatest runner of all time and the only human to run a marathon in less than two hours. He was able to achieve his purpose not only through practice but also with the help of a community to support that purpose. In 2003, Kipchoge won his first world championship title in the 5,000-meter race. He won Olympic bronze for Kenya in 2005, bronze at the World Indoor Championships in 2006, and a silver in the 2007 World Championships, 2008 Summer Olympics, and 2010 Commonwealth Games. Following the 2010 Commonwealth Games, he was racing in Belgrade and lost his shoe! Even with one shoe, he took second place in that run. A few more seconds and thirds on the world stage, and then tragically, he came in seventh place in the 5,000-meter Olympic trial race for Kenya, missing joining his country's 2012 Olympic team.

Kipchoge persevered. Like most of us, he decided that in the face of this defeat he would just run farther, opting for the half-marathon and full-marathon events. For perspective, most runners (and humans) do not opt for a longer distance when they no longer can compete at short distances. For those who are not quick with the math, 5,000 meters is the 3-mile (5K) race that many of us run around Thanksgiving each year. The half marathon is 13.1 miles, or just over 21,000 meters. A full marathon is 26.2 miles, or just over 42,000 meters. At these longer distances, Kipchoge began to thrive. In 2013, he won the Barcelona half marathon and the Hamburg marathon with a 2:05:30 time. By 2016, he cut this down to 2:03:05 in the marathon, the second-fastest official time for the marathon on record. In 2016, he took gold in the marathon at the Summer Olympics.

I first learned about Kipchoge in 2017. Nike and National Geographic teamed up to host the Breaking2 project, featuring Kipchoge, Zersenay Tadese, who was the world record holder in the half marathon, and Lelisa Desisa, whom I had witnessed win the Boston marathon in 2015.[3] These three athletes, some of the fastest long-distance runners in the world, set out to break the two-hour barrier in the marathon, a feat that people had said was humanly impossible. The marathon comes from the Greek legend of Philippides, the messenger who ran from the city of Marathon to Athens to say that the Persians had been defeated. The legend is that he ran the entire distance, announced his message, then died of exhaustion. The Breaking2 project featured scientists, engineers, a team of pacers who were the best runners in the world in their own rights, coaches, and, of course, Nike, to prepare the athletes for a closed course and ideal conditions to beat the two-hour mark. For those who are wondering how fast you would have to run to break the two-hour barrier, it's faster than a 4-minute-34-second average pace per mile. I don't know about you, but I certainly cannot run even one mile at this pace, let alone twenty-six.

As I watched the race come to an end on the documentary, waiting to see if they were able to break the two-hour barrier, I noticed one of the pacers looked familiar. The documentary shows this athlete coaching the final runners about how they are going to get Kipchoge to the finish line to break the two-hour barrier. That runner was Lopez (Lopepe).[4] I had finished reading his memoir a few months prior. Lopez was one of the lost boys of Sudan. As a boy, rebels invaded his church, stole him from his home, and placed him in a camp where he had to learn to sift the sand out of the porridge that the rebels fed the children. He ran for his life escaping the camp where he was held during the Sudanese Civil War. Once he made it to a refugee camp, he was eventually adopted in the United States, where he ran track in high school. When you read Lopez's book, you realize what a gift of a human he is, that the purpose gap is beyond wide for some children in this world. He carried the U.S. flag in the 2008 Olympics and has won several races to date. Lopez is someone whose purpose, to run, meant far more than just going out for a jog; for him, the purpose gap was a matter of life and death.

Lopez was the runner bringing Kipchoge home to the finish line. Not only was he one of the fastest milers and 5K runners in the world, but he is one of the most inspirational humans on the planet. Kipchoge, National Geographic, and Nike were showing the world that when you set out to do the impossible, you need to surround yourself with those who carry their own corner and believe in the impossible with you. Like the four men carrying those corners of the mat to Jesus, they did not have to do the impossible themselves, but they believed it could be done. They brought the man home.

Kipchoge did not break the two-hour mark that day. He finished 25 seconds over. His quotes at the end of the documentary reveal a man who believes, "No human is limited." He tells the interviewer that it was hard for him to take the several minutes off to get closer to the two-hour mark, but perhaps in the future it will not be so hard for another person to shave off just 25 seconds. Desisa, Tadese, and Kipchoge all went on to run faster personal times after training for breaking the two-hour marathon. Desisa won the 2018 New York City marathon with a time of 2:05:59, and he won the World Athletics Championship in 2019. Tadese ran a personal-best marathon in Berlin in 2018 with a time of 2:08:46. Kipchoge set a new world record for a marathon event in 2018 in Berlin with a 2:01:39, breaking the previous world record by 1 minute and 18 seconds and finishing almost five minutes faster than the next runner. In 2019, he won the London marathon, setting the second-fastest time ever at 2:02:37, beating the London marathon record by 28 seconds, a record he had set in 2016 just prior to attempting to break the two-hour marathon. And in May 2019, true to his word that "no human is limited," he finished what he started with Nike and National Geographic in 2017. Just after his London win, he started the "INEOS 1:59 Challenge." He broke the two-hour marathon with a finishing time of 1:59:40. It is recognized by the Guinness World Records as the fastest marathon ever.

Carrying your corner is more than just doing your part. It is seeing the gap between where you are and where you want to be and also seeing others who are trying to get over their own gaps and helping them out. It is not about a single act of extraordinary healing or a one-time win. Kipchoge could not just walk out his front door and run a sub-two-hour marathon. He needed teammates. Inspiring teammates. Jesus also needed teammates; he could not do his ministry alone. Likewise, we all need people to help refine our work and get us to our starting line and over the finish.

When you ask of yourself the impossible and take the time to practice and drive toward your goal, surrounded by people who inspire you, the impossible gradually becomes within reach.

Reflections

What are your big "why" questions? What is a question that seems so big that it will take years to achieve? Is it something that has never been done in your family? In your community? Are you following in the footsteps of one of your mentors or role models? What pushes the bounds of human existence for you? For some, it is getting out of bed, just breathing. What are your big goals? What would push the bounds of your human limitations?

Practice

If you set out to do the impossible, you need a daily practice. We talked about Kipchoge; now let us look at the opposite end of the running spectrum: my daily runs. I am no professional, but about ten years ago, I took up distance running—not to improve my fitness but to suck up to the in-laws. My partner, who was at the time my fiancé, did not run, but her father, brother, and sister did. The trouble was, I knew how to run, but not like a runner. We all learn to stand, walk, and run, but few of us are taught to do it with efficiency and grace. I was celebrated for standing, walking, and running pigeon-footed, heel-striking, and being slow. When I was just learning to run, no one fixed my gait or improved my form. I remember my dad yelling, "Unhook the trailer!" There was nothing to unhook. I was just slow.

After a lifetime of running the wrong way, it's no wonder that I would step outside, and for the first five minutes of every run everything would hurt. Pounding the pavement felt more like the pavement pounding me.

I eventually started watching coaching videos on the Internet and created a running log that included my diet and fluids, and, more importantly, how I felt. At the top of every entry was a question: "What is the purpose of this run?" The opening reflections started with numbers—speeds and distances. These goals were all set without any sort of recognition of the rest of my life. For example, one speed run had this entry: "5K speed run PR—17 min." That was the goal. I did not hit that goal. The recorded time was 25 min. My goal did not match my reality. I was waking up at 4 a.m., writing my dissertation, working a full-time job, and finally getting to my run around 4:30 p.m. My best time was not going to happen, but it did not mean that my best run could not happen. I had the run's purpose wrong. I had not explored "why" I was running and, sadly, why I was always running alone. The numbers were a distraction and answers to the wrong questions. The purpose of the run could have been to gain speed, or the ability to cope with a sedentary lifestyle, or even to impress my future in-laws. I knew I needed to do something, because it seemed like I was never hitting my goals and was never having any fun. I read that reframing my purpose for runs would change my experience of running. What if I was not running for a time or distance but for something bigger?

My entries went from "To focus on training for more than two hours," "To recover from a long training session," or, simply, "To run," to more inspiring entries, including "To be a Reyes that runs" (Reyeses are known for baseball, not for distance running). Others read, "To take care of myself so I live long enough to see future generations"; "To care for my mental health"; "To work through my relationship with my brother"; "To write another chapter of my dissertation"; or my favorite: "To take myself out of the house for a long time so my partner can have a break." That last one is still the purpose of many of my runs. This practice of setting a purpose and writing down my reflections on that practice transformed how I viewed the sport. Notice that each goal always included dialogue with my community. Even the one about writing; my best writing happens after a run because, while I run, I have conversations with the authors I have read and people I have spoken to, and I formulate ideas during that conversation. I was no longer running for myself (or to kiss up to my in-laws); the purposes began to be much bigger than the act of running. Running itself was not my purpose, nor was it the purpose of any individual training session. The practice of running was a vehicle that would help achieve greater fitness, but I could accomplish my long-term goals with any number of practices. The choice was now mine about how I wanted to do that work.

With a new appreciation for running, I started to imagine how it could provide other things, like a sense of community, beauty, or wonder (they do not call it a runner's high for nothing). From participating in the "Pete the Cat" annual 5K to half marathons and full marathons, I have seen the power of daily practice and the way that it transforms not just myself but the community around me. Take the first marathon I ever ran, the San Luis Obispo marathon. My wife and I arrived the night before. Nervous, I barely slept. I had trained for months prior. I put in three 22-mile-plus training runs back home, but 26.2 miles was a new distance for me. After I woke up, I put on my running gear, ate a small bowl of oatmeal, and headed to the starting line. The course was beautiful: a series of rolling hills through wine country in the central coast of California, ending in the small college town. I ran the last five miles with a group of people who were all challenging and encouraging one another to finish. There was my friend "Sprints," who starting at mile 22 or so would run as hard as he could for 100 yards and then walk. There was "Old Reliable," a man in his late fifties who had run more than twenty marathons. He had been in this area of pain before though seemed not to exhibit any of it. He told us running stories all the way until the finish line. There was "Ms. Motivator," who seemed to be a one-person motivational poster, yelling to herself and everyone around us, "We can do this!" And there was me, "The Monk," who, with religious discipline and complete silence found only in the most remote religious communities, focused on putting one foot in front of the other, saying little prayers under my breath that we all finished. The beautiful thing about the running community is that everyone wants to see everyone else finish their best race. We know we all have been practicing this art form for months, and the encouragement and advice are always given out of love. We want to see people through to the end. Remember what I said about Reyeses not being runners? At the finish line, my dad was standing there with his camera ready, taking pictures. I have never been prouder to call myself a runner and a Reyes as I was in that moment.

There are a few key components to practicing well. The community of support includes the following categories:

- Specialists
- People who provide wisdom and salient knowledge, and who teach intuition
- Spirit workers

Exploring each category will help us understand the importance of a well-rounded community in achieving our purpose.

Specialists

Specialists are those with expertise in your area of practice. I was recently moved while watching a commercial for the online learning platform MasterClass, where astrophysicist and author Neil DeGrasse Tyson suggests that because of the wealth of information available to people today, we all have the ability to know when we are right but not enough to know when we are wrong. In other words, in today's world, because of the explosion of information and platforms to share information, such as social media, we have drastically transformed the way we think and learn. Those who used to be known as "armchair experts" are being treated as actual experts. They read headlines or brief articles intended to capture a moment of a person's attention and feel informed enough about the topic to form an opinion of equal value or merit to experts in the field.

I am constantly bombarded with opinions levied as if they are fact. The problem is especially pernicious in the church and religious leadership, where pastors and educated lay leaders feel empowered to speak authoritatively on matters far beyond their domain of expertise. Specialists, on the other hand, are clear about what they practice and what they do not. If you were to go to a cardiologist to fix a pain in your right rear molar, the doctor would kindly redirect you to a dentist. The work of a great specialist is to question and explore all the solutions related to their area of expertise, not to formulate a single solution to all problems.

For questions of purpose, it seems that we have moved away from the specialists in this area, who ask and pursue answers to our biggest questions. The current crisis in the humanities is a clear example of this turning away from those experts who are asking the "why" questions. As colleges, universities, and seminaries drop humanities courses and focus more on lucrative disciplines like business, psychology, and STEM disciplines, or take on more generic "leadership education," they do so at the peril of those poets, historians, novelists, linguists, and philosophers who spent a lifetime in the discipline of "why." Specializing in the humanities, while indeed a risky career choice to pursue, could not be more important than in this moment. The purpose gap is expanding between the haves and have-nots because of the lack of attention to questions of morality, ethics, common good, and purpose. More importantly, we have moved away from studying the works of those who have modeled this pursuit of purpose. The best example is the lack of deep study of work by Rev. Dr. Martin Luther King Jr., Nelson Mandela, Gandhi, César Chávez, Toni Morrison, Paulo Freire, Ella Baker, and other philosophers and historians from marginalized communities. Scholars who research, study, and read everything related to the works of the great teachers also formulate new works that synthesize information and wisdom from that rich background. Scholars not only work to understand their purpose in their own context, but they help provide people with answers within that context. Armchair experts reduce these great teachers to notable quotables, or memes, usually taken out of context.

It is also important for leaders in technology or business to write about meaning and purpose from their lived experiences. I have received a lot of value from leaders Cal Newport,[5] Clayton Christensen,[6] Bob Iger,[7] Howard Shultz,[8] Daniel Pink,[9] and Jake Knapp and John Zeratsky.[10] All of these white men write about things that can add value to our lives. However, none of them acknowledge the lives of women, racial and ethnic minorities, the incarcerated, the dispossessed, and the oppressed. In fact, their insights assume a level of privilege to make decisions about the lives of others. None of them go as deeply into the human spirit and our purpose for being as the writings of James Baldwin. His experience as an intellectual trying to make sense of our racist society as a Black man and attempting to discern his role in that racist society is far closer to our struggles than any of the authors listed.[11] When I read Baldwin, the sights and sounds of his writing are familiar. These white leaders never even reference Black and Brown women, and none of them reference the impact of having a nonconforming body.

As a Chicano, when I read authors and poets like Rudolfo Anaya,[12] Jimmy Santiago Baca,[13] Gabriel Garcia Marquez,[14] Esmeralda Santiago,[15] Julia Alvarez,[16] Rolando Hinojosa,[17] Erika Sanchez,[18] Elizabeth Acevedo,[19] Octavio Paz,[20] Matt De La Peña,[21] Carolina Hinojosa-Cisneros,[22] Gloria Anzaldúa,[23] Ana Castillo,[24] Cherrie Moraga,[25] Richard Rodriguez,[26] and Luis Rodriguez,[27] meaning and purpose leap from their pages. This concoction of Chicano/a, Mexican, Puerto Rican, Chilean, Colombian, biracial, and Brown authors of novels and children's books, poets, and essayists have more to say about my day-to-day reality than any of those business leaders promising to improve my life with easy-to-follow steps. These experts in the humanities, in the human condition, have helped me cultivate a sense of purpose in ways that are authentic to my life. They present a rawness of the material world entangled with wonder and awe. Our schools have shown a clear preference for the linear analysis that the business community provides on purpose: a prosperity gospel in sheep's clothing. *If you do this, your life will be blessed.*

Philosophers, theologians, ethicists, historians, linguists, writers, poets, and scholars more broadly are concerned with knowing and reading from across our various communities, getting to know the authors' theories and theologies, exploring their methodologies, assessing their value and import, and adding new, original, or adapted ways of thinking about similar questions. Laura E. Pérez explains the need to pay attention to this wisdom literature:

> We live on the crumbling faith act, the historically specific aftereffect of colonization of the Americas and the rationalization of racialized, gendered, and sexed hierarchical orders in the post-Enlightenment thought—that we are unrelated, gulfs apart from nature, from other people, even from parts of our own selves, as if our interdependence on all these levels were fantasy, delusion, superstition, or the demonic. And so, swept away are the ancient cross-cultural imperatives to know ourselves, to be true to ourselves, and to care for others as our own selves. Discovering ourselves, nonjudgmentally, is dismissed as useless navel gazing rather than the indispensable road to respective coexistence with others.[28]

She goes on to say,

> Perhaps, therefore, the crooked lines of our living are a spirit writing, traces that life forces some of us call spirit(s) and/or Spirit(s) leave, testifying to that which is disincarnate in us, not quite killed yet not fully born in us, yet the marrow of our being. Traced in us and by us in a different alphabet, markings between and beyond the social context of dominant, dominating orders: a spirit writing. Winding, returning, spiraling and seemingly dead-ended jagged paths characterize the pilgrimage toward understanding that the (re)harmonization of the mind-body-spirit and the synchronizing of humanity to the rest of the natural world is sane, healthy, necessary, a craft work that is not solely personal, but perhaps the most pressing ideological and political work, the heart of the "decolonial."[29]

When answers are needed, experts not only tell you their opinion; they can tell you where their opinion fits into the larger system of opinions.

More importantly, experts, whether credentialed or not, have spent years studying and are life-long learners of their craft or domain. There are poets, historians, writers, dreamers, humanitarians, and theologians, in Pérez's words, spirit writers among us. They walk our streets. Prophets who remind us of how the neighborhood came to be. They capture the sentiments above, spirit writers and healers. These stories need to be heard and valued. They are the specialists our soul needs for its healing. Listen to the questions and how they ask them. They offer wisdom from the spirit of the underground rivers that flow beneath our communities. They are the well-springs of our lives. We go searching for the artificial dams, draining our streams, instead of listening to the wisdom rustling over the rocks, carrying purpose and meaning downstream from generation to generation.

Wisdom, Salient Knowledge, and Intuition

We can spend years studying the experts, but there is also wisdom to be learned from experience and intuition. Before you begin to think that experts and our own intuition are antithetical, we know from research that those who learn and unlearn their biases to understand how their intuition works can make better judgments in the long run. Malcolm Gladwell in *Blink*[30] and *Talking to Strangers*[31] names in both works the strengths and limitations of our intuition. What I love about Gladwell's writing is the everyday impact of relying on bad intuition. In *Blink*, he shows how orchestras that changed to blind auditions made more equitable and diverse choices for musicians, pointing to the racial bias the same selection process had when selections were made by watching the musician audition. In *Talking to Strangers*, he tells several stories about how bad humans are at interpreting the truth from friends and strangers alike! In both cases, he suggests that we can become more aware of our limitations and practice to overcome those differences. What you will find below is a brief exhortation about cultivating intuition and how to practice it alongside the rest of the tool kit to gain deeper understanding.

Trust your intuition, unless your intuition sucks. This was some of the best advice I ever received from one of my first bosses in my professional life. A white Libertarian in his early seventies, he offered the advice as I picked him up from the train station in Norwich, England. He told me that we could figure out how to get back to the office. Here we were, two Americans in a quaint town in England, where no road is straight, trusting our intuition. I had been in the country for only two months, but I was fairly used to driving on the other side of the road. Having the very intimidating president and founder of our company next to me, however, seemed to throw me off completely. Not only did I end up going down the wrong side of the road, but I drove us into a parking garage convinced that it was the driveway to our office, which was on a private road out in the country in a converted barn. The parking garage was clearly a mistake, but it was a fun jaunt around town and also a great lesson about how men can live into the stereotype of refusing to ask for directions or look at a map, and how many of us have terrible intuition.

In truth, our idea of intuition was off. The intuitive thing to do would have been to rely on the collective intelligence of local people. *Intuition* comes from the Latin root word meaning "to consider." It provides a helpful starting place for how to understand its power. Often when people think of intuition, they think of someone who just "seems to know the answers" or "who produces the answer all on their own." This could not be further from the truth. Western thinkers have long depicted intuition as appealing to the irrational, meta- or subconscious, and inner voices. Carl Jung referred to intuitive types as those who could perceive or predict future possibilities before others could. This inner gift seemed to be limited to a few people, who then took on an almost clairvoyant status in popular culture. We all have a certain level of intuition, however.

I remember reading Octavia Butler's *Parable Trilogy* for the first time. In the first of the three books, two core concepts were developed that have later been amplified by theologians and artists alike: *empathic leadership* and the idea that "God is change." The main character, Lauren, claims that she is an empath. She can feel the pain of those around her, which allows her to make decisions based on how she anticipates her actions will affect other people and her own body. As an empath, she can guide her newly formed community. She can consider the feelings of community members, both physical and emotional, and make decisions based on these feelings. She is attentive to the world around her in a way that allows her not only to stay alive but to perceive potential threats and opportunities.

This intuition leads Lauren to found Earthseed, a new community that would provide love and safety for all who joined. The name comes from the idea that "God is change," in that seeds can be planted in new places and sprout new life. Inspired by Butler, adrienne maree brown wrote *Emergent Strategy*. Emergence, for Brown, is recognizing that everything participates in an iterative process, providing more and more data that can inform and shape how we interact with the world. Emergent strategy is thus being an active, generative participant in world building.[32] In a similar way to Sasha Costanza-Chock's notion of design justice being a communal endeavor,[33] emergence is the collaborative process that is informed by the people who are closest to the experience, taking into the account notions of power, equity, and liberation. Emergence is the considering of data that is often left out or dismissed. Inspired by Butler, brown develops the idea of emergence as a deep listening and attention to our worlds. She arrives at this concept from her own intuition, her own attentiveness to the world.

Think of intuition as the expression of guides and spirits. In many ways, the wisdom and spirit of my ancestors live in my very bones. The sum of my experiences, to borrow from brown, makes up my intuition. For those who cultivate their intuition, who pay attention to the wisdom that lives in their bones, and who leverage it for communal change, one of the most helpful strategies is to mystify—as opposed to demystify—one's intuition. We are not algorithms. When we slow down and pay attention to the gut, which by the way has a lot to do with our responses to the world, we can be more in tune to what that collection of experiences is telling us.[34] When we name what is emerging, we are able to better distill the thoughts that are necessary for our own thriving. To cultivate one's intuition requires deep reflection and practice. Learning to hone our intuition can help close the purpose gap and build new worlds.

To cultivate your intuition, *slow down*. It is often said that the world is speeding up. Scientists can tell us how fast the rotation of the earth is relative to a spot on the equator. They can also tell us how long it takes for us to orbit the sun. As you read this sentence, we are each moving just under 70,000 mph through the solar system. Scientists can tell us how fast the sun is moving toward the star Lamba Herculis: just over 43,000 mph. They can also tell us that our solar system is orbiting the center of the galaxy at 446,400 mph.[35]

We are speeding up, and we are moving extremely fast, but our perception is limited to the here and now. Human beings, without math and instruments to observe the speed of the universe, cannot perceive this speed in our bodies. When writers and thinkers say that the world is speeding up, a reference to the rapid pace of industrialization and technological innovation, it is a helpful reminder that speed means truly little on a universal scale. We are inherently very slow beings. We are already perceiving life slower than it is. If we slow down to appreciate that slowness, then we can better attune ourselves to the rhythms of our lives. We are but ants sitting on the passenger seat of the world's fastest jet. To say that we are moving fast as we crawl around on the seat is to miss the beauty of being carried at an extraordinary speed. And to say that we are faster than our fellow ants, to race them across that seat, is comical when you think about the difference between the speed of the ant and the jet.

Second, *pay attention to the ground beneath*. Name your current reality. We discussed in previous chapters the need to start from "what is." We need to learn to sit with ourselves for a moment, to be present to ourselves, and to offer our own souls the gift of love. It pains me to see some of the most caring and loving people demonstrate great mitzvoth to the world but still be unable to extend the same love and grace to themselves. We treat our technology better than we treat ourselves or our loved ones. When a battery is low, we go and let it recharge. We do not disturb it. We do not unplug it early but wait for a full recharge. If we are not near a charger, we give it space to preserve what is left in the battery. When our devices are fully charged, we give them our full attention. We do not let others distract us, no matter how pressing the issue is. We take our technology with us, check in on it every now and then, sometimes not even having a reason to do so. When it runs out of memory, we clear some room or delete unused information and social connection apps that drain the battery quickly. If we treated ourselves and our loved ones like we do our technology, we would all be well rested, recharged, seen, and loved, with space in our heads and our hearts to receive others. Paying attention to the ground underneath our feet is a way to create new earth seeds, to plant ourselves exactly where we are and foster our own growth.

This planting does not mean a singular version of one's self either. As the world shifts and changes, so do we. Slowing down to pay attention means we must also pay attention to "who is" slowing down exactly. To whom am I being present? What parts of me are expressed at different times? The way I function in church is different from how I speak when I am sitting in a board meeting. It's not that I'm a different person or disingenuous, but various parts of me are called on at different moments. If we are going to live our many lives, we must pay attention to the many selves that make up our person. We must take inventory and love every one of them. It means naming our many selves and expressing grati-tude for and being curious about the many selves that live within us. We know these parts by name and by experience and must have compassion for them and treat them like a friend.[36] Richard Schwartz and Martha Sweezy have offered invaluable advice to name these parts in their work *Internal Family Systems Therapy*.[37] They claim that "Internal Family Sys-tems (IFS) therapy is a synthesis of two paradigms: the plural mind, or the idea that we all contain many different parts, and systems thinking. . . . IFS invites therapists to relate to every level of the human system—the intrapsychic, familial, communal, cultural, and social—with ecologically sensitive concepts and methods that focus on understanding and respecting the network of relationships among members."[38] Their practice, first introduced to me by my teacher and mentor Frank Rogers,[39] helps clients separate out the voices, people, and experiences of themselves from the idea of a singular, blended self. It helps provide distance from the idea that we have only one expression of ourselves.

In many ways, Schwartz and Sweezy's approach is not unlike an Internet challenge where users of multiple social networks would post their profile picture for the separate platforms. The joke was that for a social network like Facebook, which is mostly social, pictures were fun and filled with friends whereas with LinkedIn, a service for potential employment, the picture was often a formal headshot. That does not mean the person was different, but it shows that we have different expressions of ourselves in different situations. Schwartz and Sweezy call these "parts" only because that is the language clients used. They might say something like, "A part of me wanted to scream," or, "This part of me was angry, but another part wanted to forgive." We all do this. We recognize that we often do not react or respond to situations with our full selves but sometimes with only a part. We find ourselves saying these things all the time: *A part of me wants to go to work and be incredible at my job, but another part of me wants to stay home and be the best parent on the planet. Part of me wants to cook a great meal to enjoy with my beloved, and another part just wants to throw something in the microwave and binge-watch my favorite show.*

When we give ourselves space to see into our many parts, we can express far more compassion and love for ourselves. We learn that all our parts are doing their absolute best to keep us safe and secure. Naming the community that lives within can provide power in our everyday lives. Our parts are an acknowledgment that we are not the singular identity placed on us by society, or worse, by our own internalized oppression. Name your parts. What parts keep you alive? What parts help you navigate conflict? What parts want to enjoy life? What parts burn the midnight oil to push that project to the next level? For example, I have come to know the defensive part of me as the older brother. Whenever I perceive a threat to myself or those whom I love, I get defensive, ready to fight. The older brother first emerged in my life when I was looking out for my siblings in those moments when an abusive man who lived with my mom would hurt us. The older brother in me wants to protect those I love as well as those with less power than me. When my defenses are up, it is my body caring for our survival. It comes out of that same space of love. I am grateful for that piece of me. It kept me and my siblings alive when we were growing up, and it keeps me alive today. By acknowledging its presence, especially when it emerges in situations like parenting, staff meetings, or community gatherings, I can thank it for trying to take care of us. I can also acknowledge the older brother's presence and tell him he is not necessary at every moment. This practice provides grace to myself when I find I am just reacting to a situation. That reaction comes from a healthy, loving, and caring space.

Another part of me is the scholar. When the rest of the world said I was not good enough for school, when my fifth-grade teacher spit in my face, when a college professor told me, "ESL students don't belong in my class," and when my grad professor kicked me out of their class because I was "a distraction to the more serious students," she was there to assure me of my worth. She reminds me that I am more knowledgeable in multiple histories, traditions, and canons than those who challenge me, and she is the perfect mix of the hopes of my people and the work ethic they taught me. The downside of the scholar, the one that needs to be called back sometimes, is the smart-ass that is a little too quick to correct others. Does she really need to look up the origins of a word to settle an argument at the dinner table? I can acknowledge her presence because she is doing her best to survive in a white knowledge world, where her people are constantly dismissed. I can thank her for always being ready to learn and also acknowledge that correcting my partner at the dinner table is not helpful in the long run (and because, at the end of the day, my wife, Carrie, is always right). For those confused by the pronoun, the scholar in me is indeed a woman, because my grandma is my greatest teacher, and she continues to guide my inner workings.

When we slow down to recognize the many parts within us, we can better acknowledge the benevolent self. We are good people. Cultivating intuition is just putting those parts to work in the right direction. When we can step back and acknowledge our inner gifts, we are better positioned to work toward the future we want. As Freire reminds us,

> While I am physically alone proves that I understand the essentiality of to be *with* . . . by isolating myself I get to know myself better while I recognize my limits, and the needs that involve me in a permanent search that would not be viable through isolation. I need the world as the world needs me. Isolation can only make sense when, instead of rejecting communion, it confirms it as a moment of its existence.[40]

Before we turn away from intuition, and if naming your internal parts has not scared you off, we must make a turn toward the spiritual. For those who are committed to an intuition that is born from the lifeblood of our people, there needs to be a recognition of the spirits and Spirit among us. Just as we took a step back to name our various parts, we need to step back and name those spirits and the Spirit among us.

Spirit Work

We must not be afraid of the spirits among us, those who guide and watch over us. We must have respect and proper fear of the supernatural, just as the disciples did in the upper room, or Thomas in front of the risen Jesus who was still marked with his wounds. We must be able to journey to the underside of our imagination and contemplate the lessons in the space where life should not rightly exist. I am talking about the lessons of Flannery O'Connor and the heartbreak of a young boy mourning his mother in "The Lame Shall Enter First." The harrowing last words of a young person trying to reunite with a loved one reduce me to tears every time I read this story.[41] O'Connor never turns away from the suffering of young children. Their spirits inform her work, as they do mine. As poet Octavio Paz says, "In the hubbub of a fiesta night our voices explode into brilliant lights, and life and death mingle together."[42] We need to be able to examine the pain and trauma of this world. We must write in order to never forget.

The late Rudolfo Anaya reminds us not to look away from the supernatural, from Ultima's power, the power of the natural world.[43] We must become possessed by the mythic ancestor and the Cross in the way of Chaim Potok.[44] In *My Name Is Asher Lev*, Potok shows us that it is only through confronting the suffering of our inner life, meeting our ancestors, and journeying beyond the aesthetic that we come to know our own gifts, our own purpose in life. We must learn to live with the spirits of our people as have authors like Isabel Allende and other magical realists.[45]

I once caught a vision of an ancestor in a dream in which I was sitting at a table watching her work. The smells were potent, a mixture of cooking on open flame and a misty wet morning in the high desert. The room was dark but lit by candles. The clay tiles, a faded orangeish red, created a clear path from me to my ancestor. The tiles were spaced like stepping stones, and I walked toward her with intention. Above where she was working were two figures: an empty crucifix, dripping blood, and just below it, a small statue of the Mother Guadalupe—Brown skinned, holding a bowl like the one that hangs just inside the doors of the church that you dip your fingers into and make the sign of the cross. The bowl was catching the drops of blood and was adorned with graffiti that I couldn't read in the dream.

A coyote sat next to my ancestor, facing me, not moving, just watching me as I started to move toward her. As I got closer, the coyote stood up. My ancestor grabbed the bowl, offering it to me. I drank from it. It was no longer blood, just water. I looked up to her face but could not see it. I offered the bowl back. She refused and pointed to the door. The coyote started walking to the now clearly defined doorway. I followed the coyote through the door, and with every step my feet felt like they were made of stone. I struggled to get through the door. I did not know if I could carry my own weight. The coyote looked back. My ancestor's arm was on my shoulder. I stopped walking. My body then became weightless, and the door, the threshold, no longer existed. We were just in the desert. My ancestor. The coyote. And me. She smiled. And I woke up.

When I awoke, it was clear that I had walked with my grandma's grandma. I have not heard many stories about her, nor do I know her. Carmelita Araújo was her name. I know next to nothing about her, but she appeared clearly in this dream. To be perfectly clear, I only know her face from the ancestry work a family member did prior to a family reunion. The first time she visited me in the dream, I was on the third day of mourning after the passing of her granddaughter, my grandmother, Carmen Reyes. My grandma passed away on orientation day of my doctoral program, and afterward I considered quitting graduate work. I was prepared to say it was not worth it. After all, the main reason I chose my program was that it was the closest geographically to my grandma and would allow me to study her wisdom. Given my commitments to the liberation and freedom of my people, I was suddenly doubtful that theology was the best way to do this work. Carmelita came to me during this discernment. It is not inconsequential that a mentor of mine, Elizabeth Conde-Frazier, visited the campus the next day, reminding me that we do this work on behalf of our people.[46] Guiding spirits exist in our dreams and are embodied in our daily lives, too.

Educator Laura Rendón advocates for a socially engaged spirituality where individual and communal needs are met.[47] She invokes images of personal dreams and Mayan poetry that fuel her vision of a spirituality that engages the entire community in the spiritual practices that have sustained generations past. She delineates between knowledge and wisdom. Knowledge is what we can find in our formal education systems whereas wisdom is what we can glean from our communities and our spirits. Rendón believes that recovering Aztec and Mayan spiritual practices educates more than just the mind; it reconnects one to stolen histories, philosophies, and epistemologies: ways of knowing one's communities and oneself. She calls upon educators to become "spiritual warriors" who are on a journey to find freedom. Spiritual warriors are those of us who have connected with the infinite wisdom of past generations, current realities, and future possibilities. They are remarkably different from the previously mentioned warriors of the human spirit to which Margaret Wheatley refers.[48] Wheatley's warriors are those who know how to fight for the human spirit and all life in times of great crisis. Spiritual warriors, in contrast, are not bound by the material conditions of today. The earliest Christian disciples were spiritual warriors. Though they witnessed the torture and death of their friend and teacher, they also witnessed and testified to the resurrection and ascension. They were not bound by the material world in their belief.

These are not inconsequential differences. Spiritual warriors are those who can exist between planes and discern their next steps based on information not limited to human and material observation. Spiritual warriors draw on the wisdom of the ancestors, like the Medium of Endor. In 1 Samuel 28, the medium at Endor, referred to in pop culture and many interpretations as the Witch of Endor, is called upon by Saul to summon the spirit of Samuel. Now, we must keep in mind that Saul had already driven out all of those with similar gifts, so he must look for her in secret. In verse 9, she rightly responds, "'Surely you know what Saul has done, how he has cut off the mediums and the wizards from the land. Why then are you laying a snare for my life to bring about my death?'" She does not know it is Saul in front of her. She then calls Samuel for Saul, who tells Saul that he would experience a great defeat and be wounded. All these things come true. Rather than punish the medium of Endor as being outside of our tradition or try to reinterpret her power, we should reclaim her. We offer grace to Jacob, Moses, David, and Peter for far more horrendous things than being able to talk to the spirit of a prophet. The medium at Endor is a spiritual warrior that can provide a connection to the above and beyond. What if our leaders were less fearful than Saul to go in private to seek the wisdom and council of spiritual warriors? Rendón calls on these spiritual guides to "breathe through the cracks of our open hearts. And may our collective breath be the vision of a transformative dream of education that speaks the language of heart and mind and the truth of wholeness, harmony, social justice, and liberation."[49] By engaging what Rendón calls "dreamfields," where a diversity of spiritual practices come together to fuel a pedagogical vision of social justice and global community that is multilingual and compassionate, leaders and educators can begin to see beyond our current ways of knowing. A spirituality that engages this sort of wholeness and Rendón's "dreaming" invokes all our senses, allowing us to listen and investigate ancestral wisdom traditions and thus reach beyond the confines of academic language and places of traditional leadership.

Sometimes the spirit is a wandering companion or is expressed in animal form, such as a goose or dove. The creation of new traditions to symbolize the spirits can also guide us, as is the case with the *alebrijes* now famously depicted in Disney's *Coco*. This tradition began around ninety years ago when Mexican artist Pedro Linares saw them in a dream. Diego Rivera[50] and Frida Kahlo[51] immortalized these dream creatures in their paintings, spawning new visions about drawing on the wisdom of the many guides between this world and the above and beyond. Imagining that we are accompanied by spirits that walk between worlds allows us to see fully the material world. They provide guidance and wisdom in ways that our Western rationale and theological modes of thinking cannot.

As children, we know the power to imagine. We can fly and have conversations with friends near and far. We imagine the inanimate fully animating our lives to express some of our deepest fears and greatest joys. A stick has endless uses—a magical staff, a building, a unicorn horn, a snake to jump over, or home for small bugs. I long for the days when I had the creativity I see in my daughter's imaginary parties. Stuffed animals sit all around her, and they are fully alive, each bringing its own personality, thoughts, and gifts to the communal table. By being present with each of these "lovies," my daughter is learning to be more present to herself. As adults, we must reclaim this deeper way of knowing the spirits that walk among us, where we can acknowledge and have conversations with the different parts of ourselves and seek wisdom from those parts in ways that we have learned to ignore or write off as childish.

The last step in cultivating intuition is surrounding yourself with intuitive people and spiritual warriors. If you want to be more intuitive, learn the practices of those who have achieved mastery. Sit with masters of spirit work. Communities of healers and intuitive beings are out there. It is not a matter of just finding your tribe,[52] but a matter of practicing with others to perfect and hone your own craft. Malcolm Gladwell quantified mastery in his book *Outliers: The Story of Success*, suggesting that there is a 10,000-hour rule: If you spend 10,000 hours at any particular thing, you can achieve mastery.[53] The rule is slightly misleading in that mastery is crafted, shaped, and honed through practice with other masters. The good news is there are spiritual teachers everywhere. Sarah Lewis writes that mastery can only come through recognized challenges, where we push beyond where our guides can necessarily take us. More importantly, we need a community of teachers who can recognize when we have pushed beyond our limits, tell us what to do when we have, and help us recover well.[54]

For example, I have studied with some of the greatest teachers on the planet. In my formal education, I signed up for classes and sat with Dr. Frank Rogers, Dr. Sheryl Kujawa-Holbrook, and Dr. Martha Bárcenas-Mooradian. From these teachers, I learned the art of compassion for self and others. They taught me that education is about freedom and liberation and that it was up to the educator to help facilitate the transformation of individuals and communities. I learned that it is through languages of the heart, through the connection to people through communication, that we can learn the stories of a people. People today have less care for mastery. With so much information available, the deep study of tradition, art, and culture seems to be lost. Our patience to sit and practice over sustained periods has diminished. We want easy fixes, and we use technologies to ease every aspect of our life. In the process, we have destroyed our connection to the spirits and the spirit realm. We suffer from this loss.

With these formal teachers I invested in the time to study over coffee, runs, and walks between classroom buildings. I sat with them to learn their practices and adapted them into my own forms. However, these teachers were not the only experts in my life. Long before I entered the formal education system, my greatest teacher was my grandma. She had to listen to her intuition. Her 10,000 hours came out of necessity. My grandma's love came from her ability to listen to the above and beyond and to hear the wisdom of her ancestors informing the rhythm of her hands. It was not just from listening to us talk about our problems or claiming our needs for food and shelter. Anyone can offer that basic level of hospitality. It was in her ability to slow us down and draw on the deep ancestral wisdom she carried in her very body. Intuition is not another form of problem solving. It draws on the love that threads its way through generations. I remember a time when I was in college. I came to her house after a breakup. Heartbroken, not knowing my own value or self-worth. It was one of those breakups where my heart felt completely shattered. A part of me was lost, and I felt empty. My grandma did not respond with even a single word. She just gave me a hug, fed me, and invited me to her garden in the backyard. She handed me a small plastic rosary to take with me. The hug helped, the food fixed the pain in my stomach, but her presence with me in the garden taught me the power of distance and perspective. She sat me down on one of her white plastic chairs while she tended to her roses.

If you have experienced heartbreak, you know that at the time it feels as though your purpose, your vocation—defined by loving this other person—has been taken from you. A part of you no longer has a purpose. Helpless and hopeless, we sit in the pain of wondering if we are worthy of being loved. My grandma could sense this feeling in me. "*Mijo*, look at this!" I got up and walked toward her. A monarch butterfly had just flown over the cinderblock fence and landed on one of her flowers. As we sat and watched the monarch with its beautiful orange, yellow, and black coloring flap slowly as it rested, she began telling me a story about one of her earliest memories of seeing monarch butterflies. She remembered the slow flapping of their wings and recalled one time when she was young that a butterfly landed on her. As she told the story, the butterfly took off and landed on my shoulder. "You are blessed, *Mijo*." I smiled.

I stayed motionless, doing my best not to disturb this butterfly, to be present to this moment. As I did that, a hummingbird joined us in the garden. It was a Costas hummingbird, showing off its green back and purple chin. We both sat and watched as it danced all over her garden, zipping from left to right. I tried to stay motionless to keep my little monarch friend on my shoulder. The bird zipped between the statues of Guadalupe and Francis, between Tonantzín and the Huitzilopochtli, not knowing exactly where it belonged. I sat motionless, just watching the tiny dancer. "How beautiful!" my grandma offered. I remember smiling, again. "Can you see the wings flapping? Can you feel how fast?" she asked. I stared intently, doing my best to count the beats of the hummingbird's wings. It all appeared as a blur. I kept still, watching the small spirit dart from flower to flower. It was close enough that I could hear the buzz of the wings. While I could not count the flapping, I could sense the wings' movements. Then, in perfect harmony, the butterfly and the hummingbird took off over the wall. My grandma went back to tending her roses, and I was overcome with calm, peace, and serenity. I must have sat in that chair for another hour, occasionally helping my grandma but mostly just sitting still, waiting to catch a glimpse of another monarch or hummingbird in the backyard.

Within Chicano, Mexican, and Mexican American culture, both the butterfly and hummingbird are sacred and holy creatures. One incredible thing about both animals is their migration patterns extend from the United States down into Mexico. Some species of hummingbird stay all season, but most of these magical creatures have been traveling across my family's own migratory patterns for as long as we have been on these lands. It is not lost on me that the butterflies leave many of the spaces in the United States and arrive around Día de los Muertos in Mexico, where many believe they are the spirits of our ancestors. It is not lost on me that one of these spiritual beings came to rest on my shoulder on its journey to see my primos/as in another part of the world. One billion butterflies, each the descendants of the previous generation, coming and going. Not to stop and view this beauty, to recognize that the divine exists within the slow flap of their wings, to understand that the small insect carries with it the wisdom of generations, would be to miss the spirits of this moment.

While I might never be able to count the flaps of a hummingbird's wings, I learn through new senses the power of the tiniest of birds. I learn to see through my other senses. I can *hear* the buzz of its flight, *smell* the flowers from which it feeds, and anticipate its movement. Slowing down to perceive the natural world around me was the greatest medicine my grandma could have offered. It connected me to the spirits that travel across nations without any regard for artificial borders and taught me singular ways of being present to myself and the world. The hummingbird awakens me to the spirits that cross cultural and religious boundaries, that extend to the above and beyond, that reverberate between my Catholic upbringing and my ancestral ways of knowing the divine. It leads me to a more intuitive place than when I first entered my grandma's home heartbroken. I was not just loved by my grandma. God loved me. I was loved by generations prior to her. I was more connected than disconnected. She already knew intuitively that I would and could find love again as I waited with patience and stillness for beauty to return to my life, in the way I waited for the butterfly and hummingbird. My grandma taught me to trust the seasons, because both the butterfly and hummingbird always return and bring the love of generations before them. Closing the purpose gap is not just about changing the material world. It requires us to connect with and find healing with the spirits that guide our journey.

It is not easy to write about ancestors, intuition, and a community's spiritual warriors. Despite growing up under the loving tutelage of my grandma's intuition, I received my academic training in the Western academy. Finding freedom from this way of knowing is incredibly difficult, and several strategies need to be excavated within your own context. When writing this section, I struggled with how many of my community's and my own practices, traditions, and wisdom to include in the text, knowing it will be read by outsiders. Not everything we do in our communities is to be extracted for personal use or for the public. Colonization has commodified our work and practices for centuries. Some of it needs to be preserved in underground reserves and wellsprings for traditions to survive.

There is wisdom in the Christian tradition that mirrors the above. Dietrich Bonhoeffer rightly notes,

> There is a kind of listening with half an ear that presumes already to know what the other person has to say. It is an impatient, inattentive listening, that despises the brother and is only waiting for a chance to speak and thus get rid of the other person. This is no fulfillment of our obligation, and it is certain that here too our attitude toward our brother only reflects our relationship to God. It is little wonder that we are no longer capable of the greatest service of listening that God has committed to us, that of hearing our brother's confession, if we refuse to give ear to our brother on lesser subjects. Secular education today is aware that often a person can be helped merely by having someone who will listen to him seriously, and upon this insight it has constructed its own soul therapy, which has attracted great numbers of people, including Christians. But Christians have forgotten that the ministry of listening has been committed to them by Him who is Himself the great listener and whose work they should share. We should listen with the ears of God that we may speak the Word of God.[55]

Bonhoeffer, writing from the underground seminary under Nazi-led Germany, recognizes that in this violent and chaotic world, to slow down, listen, and see our fellow humans into being is to see and hear God. This takes spirit work. Howard Thurman, similarly, reminds us that "the basis of one's inner togetherness, one's sense of inner authority, must never be at the mercy of factors in our environment, however significant they may be. Nothing from the outside can destroy a man until he opens the door and lets it in."[56] By paying attention to the wellspring of our inner parts, our guiding spirits, and our faith in God, which occurs internally and externally simultaneously, we can find freedom.

We too often want to divorce the parts of us that inform us. As a trained Christian theologian committed to unlearning and decolonizing my own practice and thinking, I constantly practice listening to the voices of my ancestors. Included in those voices are Bonhoeffer and Thurman. My grandma's grandma and her coyote, the butterfly and the hummingbird, the spiritual warriors in my life, require deep study, deep listening, and it is now left to me to write their wisdom on paper. If we do not pay attention to these spirits, practice our intuition, and listen to our elders, that wisdom will be lost, or worse, intentionally destroyed by the destructive powers that render our communities mute. To recover their voices is an act of liberation. To follow the spirits is to educate a new generation of spiritual warriors.

Reflection

What parts of you keep you safe? What stories form those parts of you that encourage you to flourish? Who are your sacred guides? What ancestors guide your path? How do you connect with them and acknowledge their presence? What do you need to cultivate your intuition?

Chapter 9

What Does Daily Thriving Look Like?

I was sitting on the shores of South Lake Tahoe. We had just completed one of our workshops for writing and publishing for scholars of color who are writing their dissertations. For a full week, the routine was the same. I would wake up around 4:30 a.m. and call my children who were on the East Coast to say good morning as they went to school. When I was on the phone with them, I would go out and look at the stars that lit up the waters below. I would eat a small breakfast, rich in protein and heavy on coffee. I wrote my daily gratitude (a practice I use to rewire my brain for happiness), which included things I am excited about, one thing to focus on, and then a schedule of the day. Once I had my day planned, I would take my computer to the deck that overlooked the water. I would listen to the water ripple and watch the morning sun rise, welcoming the new day with my plan in mind. I would then write some words for this manuscript. At about 8 a.m., I joined the other writers, ate breakfast, shared stories, and then would journey with colleagues to the mountains for a run. The Rubicon trail on the shore of South Lake Tahoe was my favorite run. I would do somewhere between five and twelve miles through the woods, along the water, over rocks, avoiding bears the whole way. I would return from the run for lunch, take a shower followed by a twenty-minute nap on my rocking chair overlooking the water. I would wake up and write for a few more hours before going to dinner with our scholars. I would return to the porch for reading until friends, colleagues, and the doctoral students we worked with would join us on the porch for conversation, laughter, and tears.

The exception to this routine was the day I had to go back down into Sacramento to pick up a few students who arrived a few days after we began. I arranged with a mentor from my undergraduate alma mater to talk to her students of color. When I closed my speech in the class, a young man in the back of the classroom was beaming from ear to ear, hand raised high. "Eh! What high school did you go to?" After class, we talked about back home. An aspiring educator, first in his family to pursue an education, he wanted to go back and teach high school. He wanted to inspire the people back home. He wanted to close the purpose gap.

It was clear from this trip that I had made it—I am on the other side of the purpose gap. While I still need guides and mentors, it is for a different reason. I no longer need access to basic resources to survive. Instead, I am responsible for ensuring that the resources in my care close the purpose gap. Resources are far more than the grants and fellowships that my organization awards, and they are more than serving on boards or working with schools regarding diversity, equity, inclusion, and access. Closing the purpose gap takes more than just reading or drafting books and articles on the idea.

To close the purpose gap is to remain close to the people and stories that are still seeking their opportunity, or "their shot," as Lin Manuel Miranda reminds us in *Hamilton*. Retreats offer a place for renewal, for life to regain a little balance and perspective, but closing the purpose gap happens in moments like talking to the young Chicano scholar from my part of town and other scholars of color who are dedicated to changing the narrative others write for us. We must change the narratives we tell ourselves or that we allow others to tell about our lives. As I mentioned earlier, Brené Brown says it best about the revolution of our soul and the process of rising strong:

> The ultimate act of integration is when the rising strong process becomes a daily practice—a way of thinking about our emotions and our stories. Rather than running from our SFDs [shitty first drafts], we dig into them knowing they can unlock the fears and doubts that get in the way of our wholeheartedness.[1]

We need to start telling the liberative stories where our communities thrive, where purpose meets opportunity.

Closing the purpose gap is about daily living. It is about developing a "good day." To have a good day does not mean experiencing no (a)d(i)versity. That is for the conversation on white supremacy and white privilege. But people who have closed the purpose gap, who understand their purpose and pursue it on behalf of their community and future generations, sleep better, have better physical health and increased cardio function, are psychologically healthier, and report higher levels of happiness, hope, and sense of achievement.[2] Scholars and researchers at the Greater Good Science Center at UC Berkeley have gathered together studies and practices to help people find and feel happiness. Interestingly, their keys to happiness and well-being do not include money, job, or occupation. Their conditions for a happy and meaningful life include promoting others' well-being even at risk to one's own; experiencing awe and wonder; bridging differences; having compassion, empathy, forgiveness, and gratitude; and being mindful and socially connected.[3] To have a good day, you don't have to be rich, powerful, or influential nor wake up and have every box checked on your bucket list. To have a momentous day, to live a life of purpose, you simply need to recognize that you already have everything you need. The tools and resources to accomplish your purpose are right in front of you. A good day is a day where we practice abundant love together. If you take nothing else away from this book, remember that to love and be loved is central to thriving and to closing the purpose gap. Austin Channing Brown writes it best. When asked where she finds hope, she answers,

> It is working in the dark, not knowing if anything I do will ever make a difference. It is speaking anyway, writing anyway, loving anyway. It is enduring disappointment and then getting back to work. It is knowing this book may be read only by my Momma and writing it anyway. It is pushing back, even though my words will never be big enough, powerful enough, weighty enough to change everything. It is knowing that God is God and I am not.[4]

Closing the purpose gap is a daily grind. It is working toward nonfixed outcomes and relying on the things we know in our bones. If we can learn to love our neighbor's children as our own and filter our decisions for how we structure and design our worlds, then we can close the purpose gap.

In *Nobody Cries When We Die*, I claimed that vocation is a call to life. In that book, I discuss domestic abuse, addiction, gang violence, witnessing trauma and death, and the importance of having elders who call us to life—people like my grandma, teachers, and my dad. In short, I have been writing about bad days, the opposite of thriving. I've been telling hard and violent stories for the better part of a decade now, and prior to that, I was living them. I recently told a colleague, "I don't want to tell another story where a child dies because it is taking its toll on my mind and soul." It was after I presented "Wanted: Dead or Alive"[5] for TheoEd talks, in which I relate being strangled within moments of my life, after which I was a miserable partner, friend, colleague, and father for a whole week as I tried to pull myself out of reliving memories of trauma and abuse. Even in my doctoral work, I focused on survival. I worked with youth and young adults affiliated with gangs and community members who worked in the fields. I explored the spiritual and religious practices of those field workers that help them survive. All my writing since has held some thrust toward survival, and it challenged me to explore thriving for my community.

The need to do more than just account for survival came in the spring of 2019. I facilitated and helped cowrite the theology for the Ending Mass Incarceration event hosted by Ebenezer Baptist Church and Rev. Dr. Raphael Warnock.[6] The Temple, a historic synagogue that was bombed in the 1950s for their activism alongside Rev. Dr. Martin Luther King Jr.'s church, Ebenezer Baptist, cohosted the event. It was led by a group of inspirational rabbis, including Peter Berg and Lydia Medwin. Organizing the entire campaign was Billy Michael Honor, one of the most inspirational pastors I know. We talked for three days about locked-up bodies in cages and the connection to slavery, Jim Crow, and contemporary, caged Black bodies. Yale professor Walter S. Gilliam, director of the Edward Zigler Center in Child Development and Social Policy and associate professor of child psychiatry and psychology at the Yale Child Study Center, opened the morning with a video of a five-year-old being handcuffed at school and then provided his research about how the cradle-to-prison pipeline can be evidenced in the expulsion rate of Black and Brown children as early as age three.[7]

We talked about the incarcerating and caging of families, including children, at the border. As a Chicano scholar, I find the interning of children, the separation of families, and the arrest and incarceration rate of those waiting deportation hearings so overwhelming and heartbreaking that sometimes I just cry. I am overwhelmed by the images, data, and narratives that come out of my own community and the violence and trauma *los inocentes* are experiencing in my lifetime, those innocent children who want nothing more than to thrive. When I visit people who are separated from their families, hear their stories, sit with them, and see their faces, which look like my own, it pulls my soul out of my body. The world now has access to these images. How did we let this happen? We have stolen the purpose of their children and their children's children. Every act of violence is an act of violence against the generations that follow, including our own. It pains me to know that my children and their children will wonder what we did in these moments. How could my generation allow this to happen? You can hear chains echoing through generations: history's death rattle.

In preparation for the event about mass incarceration, I was on a conference call at home talking about Latinx, Central American, and Mexican children being locked up at the U.S. border. At one point in the meeting, I became distraught over the group's lack of capacity to empathize with and care for the families at the border. I found myself screaming at the top of my lungs, "Those are our babies!" When the call was over, I took my headphones off and turned around to see my son, who was only six at the time, standing wide-eyed and silent, looking as if his mind could not keep up with his thoughts. Deep fear and trepidation were written all over his face. After a moment of silence, during which we exchanged looks of concern, he asked me, "Am I ever going to get put in a cage? Are you going to be taken away?"

That happened to be the day in school where he was learning about and observing Yom HaShoah, Holocaust, and Heroism Day. Can you imagine being six and a Chicano, Latino, Mescalero Apache, Jewish child (through his mom and myself), trying to make sense of this world at this moment? Imagine that you are a six-year-old wondering if you or your parents are going to get locked up—wondering, "Will I be next?" That kind of terror perpetuates the purpose gap. As a parent, I wonder, "How do we get to the point of thriving in a world that wants us dead?" Every ethnic identity my son has inherited is a marker of violence and genocide. He learns these histories. They inform his spirit. He learns by overhearing conversations or when we attend vigils and phone calls to recognize those who have been killed for who they are. Children are taking in the energy of the world. I remember experiencing that fear as young as five. As Walter Gilliam's research has shown, children of color experience this discrimination as soon as preschool in measurable ways: Expulsion rates for preschool students of color are three times the rate of that for white students. Students of color, specifically Black students, are often treated as years older than they are, and their behavior is scrutinized at a rate far higher than for white preschool children.[8] As a scholar and a leader, I want to dive deeply into the stories, pain, and memories of these moments, but, as a father, I want my son to know none of that. I want my children to experience nothing other than hope and joy.

While the liberation of bodies, hearts, and minds is core to my purpose, the role of telling stories that make people smile and laugh, that provide hope, that lift them up is equally important to the truth, the "what is" of the moment. I do not want to mask the trauma in the world, but I do want to say to this broken world, "I see your violence, and I will raise you hope and love." I want these stories to be told from the perspective of people who have been marginalized and forgotten because we are more than the abuse, violence, and oppression we suffer. We are more than the hate the world has for us.

I love the movie *Spider-Man: Into the Spider-Verse*, about Miles Morales, an Afro-Latino young person growing up in Brooklyn, who (spoiler alert) is surrounded by Spider-men and -women from different universes. I was teary-eyed through the whole movie, first, because we have a Latino superhero, Miles Morales! Morales! You know how many superheroes we have with a Latinx last name on the big screen? Not a lot. Throughout the film, Miles is overwhelmed by life and trauma, yet, in the end, he has to live into what it means to be Spider-Man, to save his community, his father, his family, and do it all in his own way. Even for this fully grown Chicano, to see an African American and Latino superhero on screen brings me to tears. It is not inconsequential that Miles is also a teenager, growing up in a time when dominant culture tends to lock up young Black and Brown bodies instead of making them heroes. To put it in perspective, young men turning eighteen in 2019 had a one in three chance of being incarcerated over their lifetime if they were Black and a one in six chance if they were Latino.[9] Black children and Latino children are far more likely to be criminals or the bad guys in popular stories than we are to be heroes. I was delighted to be able to show my son how this young, Black-Latino superhero goes from surviving to thriving in his own unique way, rocking Jordan1s. What a powerful image and story that sends to him and to our community.

When doing my research and literature review on thriving, I often found the insights to be trite and not at all helpful. And they did not reflect kindly on minoritized communities. A group of psychologists researching *thriving* wrote a literature review and came up with this succinct definition: "*Thriving* can be broadly defined as the joint experience of development and success," and in order to achieve thriving, "an individual needs to experience holistic functioning."[10]

What does that even mean in our context? What does it mean for people of color? What does it mean for communities plagued by poverty, violence, and mass incarceration or for those of us who have not had access to wealth generation? Let us try to imagine it for the students and scholars of color I support. Surely the most educated among us, who represent single digits in all our communities as graduate degree holders, are experiencing thriving?

At the Forum for Theological Exploration (FTE), we facilitate an institutional doctoral network. As mentioned previously, this network has included the presidents and deans from a group of ten institutions in theological education. We focus on what thriving looks like for scholars of color. To guide our network, we pulled the entire system together to help us define *thriving* in our work. The collective of leaders in philanthropy, presidents, deans, directors of doctoral programs, faculty of color, students of color, and partners in education equity produced the following definitions.[11]

For individual scholars of color, *thriving* means that they are

- Intellectually strong and imaginative
- Financially secure
- Community oriented
- Vocationally clear
- Holistic in their sense of self
- Prepared to be agents of change

However, how many doctoral students of color across the country can look at this list and say that they are thriving daily? When I ask this question to a group of them, not a single hand rises to offer a response. The question is met time and again with silence.

How do people experience daily thriving if it means getting in and through a PhD program in a primarily white institution? The average debt load of an FTE Fellowship applicant is more than $70,000; to be community oriented, scholars of color are forced to spend most of their time in isolation reading and writing and, in most cases, mimicking the white, colonial academy to get through their doctoral program. To be vocationally clear, they need to maintain a long view of their work. It is not just the average seven years to finish a PhD program but nearly fourteen years total from the first day of class to getting through the additional academic hazing of the tenure process. And that assumes one is fortunate enough to land a tenure-track job, when in our academic fields fewer than 50 percent are fully employed. Moreover, scholars are pursuing a vocation that is so specialized that they will have only three to five people review their dissertation and around ten faculty (plus the trustees) review their tenure file. Finally, if they are prepared to be change agents, how do they navigate the fact that the consumption of academic monographs is an extremely limited way to reach the people and communities that they want to impact?

And this is just doctoral students of color—a very privileged subset of people of color. Can you imagine how long this list would be if we challenged these assumptions for other leaders in the church and nonprofits, educators, doctors, nurses, bus drivers, lawyers, day laborers, those experiencing incarceration or homelessness, caretakers, those who work the fields, and countless other professions and vocations?

Can we, those on the other side of the purpose gap, really thrive? I was reading the definitions of *thriving* listed previously, and not one fit my own journey, and I direct the program! At FTE, an organization focused on creating conditions for the next generation to thrive, our own definitions of *thriving* with regard to ministers and doctoral students seemed to still be tethered to a litmus test of excellence defined by white and Western notions of success. To thrive, young adults pursuing ministry and doctoral students of color have a powerful sense of vocational trajectory but having the resources to actualize that vocation and call creates a new set of challenges. Fellowships and grants are not treated as awards as intended but are lifelines to pay for basics like housing and rent. The institutions our students study at, whose vocations are to generate and create knowledge, are not creating conditions for students and scholars to thrive in their whole person.

I was on a call with community college students a few years back—all Latinas, who attended community colleges in Salinas, Gilroy, Fresno, and a few other towns in the central valley of California. We were talking about access to our own stories and narratives and reflecting on families and our shared struggles. They talked about the stepping stones to higher education, and I assured them if they worked hard enough, they could go on to get PhDs. Reading their work, I had no doubts about their talents. Listening to their stories and their current work as organizers and change makers, I could see that they had the grit to make their dreams come true. I was convinced I was going to have a class of fellows in a few years that included many of these incredible women. They knew the purpose gap in their bones and had the spirit of our people coursing through their veins. The spirits and their grandmothers would guide them. They were not only going to make it, but they were going to bring our community with them.

However, I also knew that it would not be easy. They were in a community college program. Only 13.1 percent of Hispanics (the term used by the U.S. Census) receive a bachelor's degree, 4.4 percent have a master's degree, and less than 0.7 percent have a PhD, the lowest percentages of any ethnic group.[12] The first outcome listed for students in California community colleges is transferring to a four-year university. In California, the next step is either the prestigious, competitive, globally recognized, research-oriented University of California system or the regional, far more accessible California State University system. Former community college students in the California State system make up 51 percent of graduates whereas only 29 percent of graduates at University of California schools started in community colleges.[13] The majority of these students do not go on to receive a master's degree in any program, and an even smaller amount of that group go on to get a PhD. By the time students might get to the FTE Fellowship application, the group of students from community colleges has been whittled down to statistically insignificant numbers. To have a student who emerged out of the community college system from my homeland go on to get a PhD in any field is closer to zero than it is to a 1-percent chance.

These young women demonstrated every one of the categories of thriving, even being financially secure. They were not wealthy by any means, but community college provided affordable education that could advance their vocational outcomes. They were academically strong, as expressed in their writing. All of these young women were emerging faith leaders and community organizers. They had committed themselves to transforming their local communities. They said that they wanted to advance in their theological studies and that there was a part of them that viewed faith and spirituality as critical to leadership in the community. And finally, they were holistic in that while they saw education and organizing as important aspects of their lives, equally as important were caring for their families, hanging out with friends, and organizing the community. They were clear on their purpose that they were going to make a difference in the world through the church and the academy.

If this definition of thriving includes these students, why was it so unlikely that I would ever see an application from them? The more hopeful reader will say, "Surely there is an exception among them!" Looking back at Figure 1.1, we might visualize an exception among the group that could be helicoptered out of their community and flown across the purpose gap. But it does not close the purpose gap. The exception is not the rule. We want to *rewrite* the rules. Granted, it is a pipedream for me to imagine seeing an application from all of those women in a few years. If I don't shepherd this group as a mentor, would it be my fault if they never made it into our fellowship pool? As one who made it out, who crossed the bridge successfully, as seen in figure 1.2, do I not have a responsibility to shepherd any individuals I thought could make it? When I look at my applications and the list of those we award, I see that those from Ivy League and top-tier research universities make up many of our applicants and awardees. On a micro-level, even my work advancing scholars of color and helping young people find their voice and place in ministry does not change the stubborn statistics of an entire industry and field. The purpose gap is so wide that, even by our own standards of thriving, we alone cannot address the many barriers designed by a system that is attempting to re-create itself. The paradox and beauty of our work, however, is that the purpose gap only widens without leaders and institutions that are attempting to close it. Exceptions are still needed and desired. And all these women are still making change in their local communities, organizing for change and justice. They are closing the purpose gap.

Leaders must interrogate and question our purpose. We need to ask if we are indeed closing the purpose gap. Have more people found life or come fully alive because of our work? Have those who might not have thought they were called to purpose and meaning found their call and, in turn, helped others to do the same?

When we ask critical questions of the systems we inhabit, we can better understand how to create conditions for thriving. What if your own identity amplified or muted your sense of call? What if you were a person of color from a community with a lack of access to education and resources? What if during your formative years, you were in an education desert? Or a food desert? What if you were surviving abuse or systemic and pervasive violence because of your race or socioeconomic class, sexuality, or gender? What if you were still surviving? Could you thrive? For those of us with traumatic pasts, amplified by the experience of oppression and violence experienced by people of color and marginalized groups, can we heal from our many traumas—or at least get a respite long enough for us to breathe and reflect? If the news media, newsfeeds of social media, and larger structures remind us of the violence to which we are still subject, can our imaginations be freed?

It's not a matter of *wanting* to change the narrative; we must *do the work* to change the narrative. We must create new systems. There is no reason every young person, but especially those most marginalized, should not be able to achieve their many purposes in life. The question is not about the technical changes necessary to make it happen. We need an entire mind-set shift. We need a new imagination about our desired future.

Reflections

What is your definition of *thriving*? What stories redefine thriving for you and your community? What stubborn statistics and violent histories are you overcoming?

The Purpose Gap Is about Daily Life

My challenge is how to break the data and question down further, from thriving in general to smaller, more meaningful and actionable bites. People living into their purpose understand that purpose on a daily level. Author Roxane Gay writes about her body and the many pressures and struggles, both internal and external, to knowing, understanding, and loving her body. Her memoir reflects a deep truth, an insider's guide to finding purpose. She writes, "This is my truth. This is a memoir of my body because, more often than not, stories of bodies like mine are ignored or dismissed or derided. . . . This is a book about learning, however slowly, to allow myself to be seen and understood."[14] We have to learn to love ourselves in our daily realities because we are beautiful, and we must define *beauty* on our own terms.

When I was growing up, I knew a family of social-justice-oriented Catholics. They worked at a soup kitchen on Thanksgiving, gave to charity, and supported socially progressive causes. The oldest son played on all my teams with me or competed against me in various leagues. After playing together in a series of YMCA leagues as kids, we ended up at the same junior high and high school. I went out to his house one afternoon when I was sixteen, even though he had never once come to my dad's house because, I found out later, he was not allowed "on that side of town." I loved his house. He had a whole gym at his grandparents' house that was on the property down the road. There was a full basketball court in a barn that we would convert into our own batting cage if we wanted to play baseball. He also had a whole field that was just for his dirt bikes and go-carts. He had his own room, a TV, and a bunch of video game systems, and his mom used to bring us snacks all the time. Never-ending snacks and then dinner—I loved it.

I was sitting at their table for dinner one night, sweating after basketball practice. There is nothing more satisfying than a day of play and time with friends. It had been a good day, so far. Someone offered a prayer for all the hungry and needy in the world, and then we started eating. They told me to eat whatever I wanted, so I started adding to my plate. I come from a large

Latino family in which eating is a sign of being polite. To refuse a plate from Grandma Reyes was a sure sign of your relationship with the devil.

As I was politely and happily eating what was placed on my plate, I may have even been humming as I fed myself to my heart's content. As I reached for another helping, his younger sister cuts me off. She is in third or fourth grade at the time.

"Patrick, do you know what we named our pig?"

"No, what?" I said.

"We named him Patrick because he eats like you, smells like you, and he came from the pig fields like you!"

Her mom quickly told her that was not polite and said, "She just means that you eat a lot when you are here." Everyone was laughing.

I returned their laughter with silence and a blank stare. I was completely taken aback. I had known this family for a decade; I had grown up with them. I was invited over as a friend. My feelings were genuinely hurt.

The pig fields were the rodeo grounds where they showed off their pig, which was out on the north side of Salinas where my dad lived. They only knew I lived out there because when we were younger, my friend's Little League baseball team had to come all the way out to our neighborhood to compete with us. I was angry. I felt betrayed and disrespected, as though I was being treated like another Catholic charity. Their feeding me was just another social-justice project. I felt unloved by my friend and his family because, even in their private spaces, they had compared me and *mi gente* to pigs.

Two elements of this early experience translate to my work today. First, this story is a perfect reflection of the primarily white, colonial academy and church. They say they want us all to thrive. They invite us in, feed us with whatever they have in their pantry, in this case, or in other cases, with their degree offerings or ecclesial spaces. They say we are welcome but are including us out of charity. "It is the right thing to do," they might think. They are happy to have us participate in the thriving of their kids' lives if our diversity makes the school, church, organization, or community look better. They do not see or treat us as humans because to do so means having to recognize our cultures, histories, traditions, families, practices, and lives as equal to their own.

The second thing I learned is that my work is bigger than their manure or, in this case, their pig shit. In the research for my dissertation, I interviewed friends and family who worked the fields. My question was simple: "What in your religious and spiritual lives helps you survive life in the fields?" They offered many answers. One that stands out is that those same fields that little girl was trying to shame me for were named in the interviews as sacred spaces. Those spaces—the soccer fields off Constitution Park, the rodeo grounds, and parks in the north and east side—were sacred spaces for my community because that is where the question between surviving and thriving was flipped. It is where they watched their children play and celebrated them—where at least one day a week they could have fun, joy, laughter, and hope for what might be. It was shared space with neighbors and friends who shared stories, dreams, and aspirations for their children, who, for the rest of the week, were surviving just like them. On Saturdays, it is where my community came together to share meals, gossip, play, and love one another. I knew this in my bones because I had always experienced joy in these spaces. But I was still learning that my purpose could *also* be found in my community. My purpose was not in this home where I was treated like a charity project and thought of as livestock.

These "pig fields" were where we came to have a good day, to practice abundant love together. We were able to play games, dance to the music, and tell the stories of our people without trying to make it in a white world. It was thriving on our own terms and was designed around the joy and happiness of our children. It was the space where our histories and marginalized position in the larger society no longer mattered, at least for a couple of hours. What if this could be our daily reality? What if this vision could structure our very lives?

What fascinates me about this question, boiling down meaning to a day, is that what comes back is both mundane and eternal. Borrowing from Elizabeth Conde-Frazier, Orlando Espín, Carmen Nanko-Fernandez, and others, the concept of *lo cotidiano* is one that resonates with readers of theology. María Del Socorro Castañeda-Liles's *Our Lady of Everyday Life* is the most recent example of how Latinas, inspired and informed by their mothers, pass on the sacred wisdom that helps all our people survive and thrive, daily.[15] By focusing on daily living, we move away from the fuzzy, supermarket self-help literature and turn toward what Boaventura de Sousa Santos calls epistemologies of the South, which are ways of knowing that are "technically and culturally intrinsic to certain practices—the practices of resistance against oppression. They are ways of knowing, rather than knowledges. They exist embodied in social practices."[16] For me, these ways of knowing include social practices of gathering at the soccer fields to watch our *niños* and *niñas* run, play, eat, be creative, and enjoy at least one day when the threat of colonial, political, social, economic, and spiritual violence does not beat down on their backs like the sun overhead, or at least does not feel like it is. To have a good day follows Santos's thesis in that we are trying to "identify and valorize that which often does not even appear as knowledge in the light of dominant epistemologies, that which emerges instead as part of the struggles of resistance against oppression and against the knowledge that legitimates such oppression. Many such ways of knowing are not thought knowledges but rather lived knowledges."[17] To survive daily is to take the many trips to the public library as my family does for community programming and exploration of ideas and stories. It is an afternoon spent on the playground. It is time spent sitting on a rocking chair, reflecting on the work needing to be done and the work ahead. We are slowing down and going to those places in time and space where laughter, leisure, and love abound. Thriving is not an outward expression of success or reward.[18] It is our daily survival. It is knowing we are loved by our community and by the divine. Closing the purpose gap is recognizing our individual and collective power to create the conditions for the next generation to thrive.

Thriving is the feeling you have when you see the next generation running, playing, and laughing without care. It is the smile on a child's face when they eat an orange slice, leaving the peel in their mouth to do that peel smile that only children and the childlike at heart seem to do. Thriving, for those on the brink of survival, is celebrating those moments when love overcomes the threat of oppression and freedom of the mind and body take hold for even just a moment. To create conditions for people to thrive is thus to expand and multiply those times and spaces where this love can abound. And there are ways to cultivate more of these moments, regardless of socioeconomic position.

When we focus on a single day, it allows us to be more creative about our work as scholars, pastors, religious leaders, organizational leaders of nonprofits, educators, parents, friends, siblings, people of moral courage, and more importantly, humans. I often speak to the people I serve and say that their work, their vocation, their call, is always far more important and valuable than I can ever imagine, that they will contribute to the thriving of our collective lives by honoring our ancestors and neighbors. My role—both at FTE and in my chosen vocation and research—is not in service to research but to the lives of those around me.

The markers of a good day are found when we practice abundant love together. This requires daily practice. Throughout this book, you have been given a set of practices in the reflection questions that can help you become more aware of the purpose gap. However, I also hope that they help you identify points where you have unique power to effect change. In addition, I am going to leave you with three core practices that will help close the purpose gap for both you and your community. They can be adapted or changed given your context and are intimately tied to everyday life. They are like corn meal (or flour), eggs, and sugar. How you combine, use, or add to these ingredients can lead to making everything from tortillas and tamales to huevos rancheros and cakes. They are principles as much as they are practices. But if you practice them daily, I guarantee you will be closing the purpose gap not only for yourself but for us all.

Practice 1: Telling a New Story

We need bold visions for thriving. Consider Christiana Figueres, the executive secretary of the United Nations Framework Convention on Climate Change who led the efforts to curb the devastation of climate change that eventually were codified in the Paris Climate Agreement in 2016. A Costa Rican diplomat, Figueres was able to change the way the world talks about global climate change. After the 2009 United Nations Climate Change Conference in Copenhagen, when the world could not agree on the problem the world faced, let alone the solutions, she reframed the whole conversation. When the world looked and only saw limitations, a near impossible task, she saw her challenge as not one of technical expertise but of storytelling. What story was the world telling itself about the future? She reflected that Copenhagen sounded like so many conversations we have about the "system." We are great at diagnosing the problems, those things that get in the way of our thriving, but great leaders rarely emerge to offer alternative storylines, to offer a "dream," a vision of the future where we all thrive.

Just seven years after the disastrous conference in Copenhagen, Figueres was able to bring all the major players together again to commit to the Paris Climate Agreement. She said she was able to do this with "global optimism." It was not misplaced optimism but optimism in the face of the truth of daily life. In *The Future We Choose*, Figueres and Global Optimism cofounder Tom Rivett-Carnac were unrelenting in stating the facts. What the world needed was not optional if we wanted to survive, but more importantly, it could also be an opportunity to tell the story of a desirable—and hopeful—future where we all thrive:

> To have at least a 50 percent chance of success (which in itself is an unacceptably high level of risk), we must cut global emissions to half their current levels by 2030, half again by 2040, and finally to

net zero by 2050 at the very least. A chance of this magnitude would require major transformations in almost every area of life and work, from massive reforestation to new agricultural practices; from the cession of coal production by 2020 and of oil and gas extraction soon thereafter to the abandonment of fossil fuels and even the internal combustion engine.[19]

No big deal, right? To save our planet or at least have a shot at saving our planet, we just need to change the way we fundamentally live around the globe on a daily level! They continue,

> If you do not control the complex landscape of a challenge (and you rarely do), the most powerful thing you can do is change how you behave in that landscape, yourself a catalyst for overall change. All too often in the face of a task, we move quickly to "doing" without first reflecting on "being"—what we personally bring to the task, as well as what others might. And the most important thing we can bring is our state of mind.[20]

In facing the many purpose gaps in our life, we have no control over entire, complex landscapes. If I want to close the purpose gap by closing the educational outcomes of young people of color in this country, it would be far easier if I had that magical wand that gave everyone access to high-quality, equitable education that celebrates the languages, histories, traditions, and communities from which we all come. It would be far easier for my work and purpose if every time I saw a barrier or gap, I could simply remove it or close it unilaterally.

But no one has this power. We do, however, have the power to see each barrier and gap as an opportunity to determine how we are going to approach it. The purpose gap exists, but we can reframe how we address it. Building a bridge—a singular, costly, and time-consuming endeavor—is a way but not the only way to address the gap. What if we took the energy, power, and resources necessary to build the bridge and built institutions and networks that served our community instead? What if we built support systems that allowed us to venture all the way to the bottom of the gap to recover the parts of the many who attempted but could not succeed in crossing the gap? What if we filled in the gap, ensuring future generations will have access to the other side? In fact, if we do this correctly, there will not *be* another side. All will be within reach. The white destination will no longer be the goal, and the stories of Brown and Black bodies will not be extracted for white purposes. Yelling across this chasm, trying to convince those who have extracted, dominated, and colonized our communities to build bridges wide enough for our whole community, to backfill the gap, or, even more radically, to redefine our communities as places to come and learn and invest resources is futile. Our words, like the bodies of so many of our ancestors, fall to the bottom of the divide.

For people of faith, is this not what God did when God walked among us? Certainly, my approach and the approach of many of the people with whom I work is to build a bridge, a short-term solution to bring people across. But if we choose to rewrite the narrative of our daily lives to ensure future generations can thrive, we must work steadily toward a future where bridges are no longer necessary.

Global Optimism, of which Christiana Figueres is a founding partner, encourages a three-pronged approach to the global climate crisis: stubborn optimism, endless abundance, and radical regeneration. These mind-sets are reminiscent of Viktor Frankl's approach to the search for meaning in the face of imminent death in the concentration camps. The reality is that we are facing global devastation. We are creating a world incapable of sustaining life. To put it bluntly, if my daughter Carmelita is the namesake going back five generations, then we are designing a world in which her future namesake, five generations in the future, will live on a planet where survival will be incredibly difficult. Our daily decisions affect not just our children, but all the generations to follow.

How do we reframe the narrative? Our Scriptures offer guidance for how we can affirm life even against impossible goals. For example, instead of reading Lamentations as a book of complaints, read it as a book of mourning and grieving the loss of a culture, a space, and favor with God. *Ekah*, the Hebrew for Lamentations, is translated to "How?" Figueres and Rivett-Carnac do not allow us to simply stare back at the problem. They want us to look at the problem, ask a question, and collectively produce many solutions. When we reframe the "how," we can begin to see ourselves as part of a network of change makers, who collectively have the power to rewrite the global narrative.

In the simplest of forms, and despite the great challenges before us, the Global Optimism team, who call themselves "Stubborn Climate Optimists," believe that we can change and transform this world. Everything to make the change we need is right here, for nature is abundant, and everything can be regenerative, which is a step beyond sustainable. Regenerative studies show that we can create systems that operate in harmony with the natural world. These core beliefs create a different story from that of even the most ardent of climate-change activists, who know the problem but cannot envision a future where we all thrive. In *The Future We Choose* Figueres and Rivett-Carnac sketch out a vision of the world in which children inherit clean air, where individuals do not own cars but instead ride in energy-efficient vehicles that pick us up at our doorsteps and take us directly to where we want to be. It envisions not just stacks of offices where we sit and work at desks but buildings that grow agricultural products. They paint a picture of people living in balance with nature, each providing for the other.

After reading this book, I was inspired, especially by coauthor Christiana Figueres. How does this leader from the tiny country of Costa Rica manage to shift the minds of our world's leaders, helping them to reframe the narrative, in the time span of just seven years? What if we could reframe our lives in that same way? Not just in the regenerative sense, but what if we populated it with a purpose-filled universe? What would it look like? What if we put into practice all that we have learned thus far? What would the story of all members of society thriving look like?

I tell my children stories every night. We also call family members on the phone and ask them to tell stories of their childhoods. Every narrative focuses on their knowing they are loved, and each is interactive and imaginative. The people in these stories ask questions, interrupt, challenge, laugh, and celebrate.

Storytelling for thriving is easy. We just need to pay attention. Stories from the natural and supernatural world come from paying attention to the land, as authors Octavia Butler, Rudolfo Anaya, Toni Morrison, and Isabelle Allende did. It is paying attention to the world we inhabit and dreaming of new worlds. I told my children a story the other night about the sacred birds of our block. A hawk, who wished to steal from their community, kept sweeping in, trying to take the eggs and babies out of their nests. The community of sacred birds that live on our block got together and chased the hawk off. No single bird could do it alone, so they had to build a network to protect the little ones. On our walk just a few days later, the thrushes and thrashers, along with the tiny wood warblers, sounded the alarm, crying out. "Did you hear that, Pa?" my daughter asked. "They cry." And just then a red-tailed hawk came flying around the building, with blackbirds pecking and driving it off. "The babies are safe," she said.

Stories we tell our children don't just have to cast a vision for them as grown adults. The lessons and stories about our role in the natural world cast a vision for communal thriving. I am convinced my daughter will grow up to be part of the network of those who work on behalf of others. She will create the conditions for future generations to thrive. She does not want to be a hawk. And for those who ask, "What about the red-tailed hawk?" They provide a metaphor for all those who have stolen our babies, locked them in cages, and continue to oppress us. Too literal a reading of the text or hearing of the story does not give them room to breathe and take on the purpose they serve.

Practice 2: Designing for Purpose on Our Terms

We will use Liedtka and Ogilvie's four design questions, discussed in chapter 3, to redesign purpose on our terms. "What is, what if, what wows, and what sticks" will be our guiding framework for telling a new story that liberates both the oppressor and the oppressed.[21] It will not start from a place where we are all holding hands on the playground; it will begin just as this book has, in a place of deep trauma and pain. We will follow the Global Optimism team's lead and start from the stark reality of the world we are looking at, and then we will turn to reframing the story. What if Octavia Butler's Earthseed community were our reality? How do we move it from fiction (science fiction, fantasy, magical realism) to the material conditions our children inherit?

What Is?

Many of us wake up knowing hunger pains. My body knows trauma and abuse, and the pain of my suffering makes just opening my eyes a monumental and liberative act. By choosing to breathe this morning and expressing gratitude for that breath, to pray the *Modeh Ani* (Heb., "I give thanks"), we are also choosing to live in this violent and complex world.

Closing the purpose gap means closing the education, opportunity, and wealth gaps. To actualize our purpose, we also need to account for the violent histories of colonialism and slavery, and calculate a new distribution of resources. Closing the purpose gap requires truth telling, reparations, and a radical redefinition of who our purpose serves. Earthseed belongs to all of us.

What If?

What if children had access to high-quality education? What if we invested in stronger communities that were not so reliant on consumer capitalism? What if we designed our educational, financial, political, social, and religious institutions with the field worker who picks our food in mind? What if their families were the focus of our many purposes? Instead of creating exceptions, what if we treated essential workers as not only essential but as holy and sacred? What if the thriving of *their* children were placed at the center of our work? How would that change how we design our classes? City planning? Financial investments? What if instead of funding police or military to instill fear in the world and in our communities, we hired healers, mental health workers, educators, and researchers, and invested in infrastructure and local agriculture?

To close the purpose gap, we must look at the conditions affecting children and youth, specifically children of color. It means investing in the education centers that our grandmothers, *tías*, and community offer our children. It means valuing the education that happens in our homes and creating conditions for all generations, not just the wealthy, to spend time developing our future leaders. What would it mean if my grandma had a basic income that included educational supplies in her home? Paper, books, electricity, high-speed Internet, and a computer? What could she have grown in her backyard if she'd had access to more resources? That means more than just more rose bushes or statuettes guarding and protecting our past. She could have taught me how to cultivate the earth and grow the food that feeds our soul. If we incentivized this kind of work, how would that change the lives of our children?

It would mean reducing the number of children who have been exposed to or experienced violence to near zero. It is a communal effort. One in four young people have experienced or witnessed domestic violence.[22] One in three young women will be exposed to sexual violence.[23] If women and children are afraid for their lives, that fear can paralyze their imaginations about what is possible. It widens the purpose gap. No one chooses to suffer or wants to experience abuse. There is no redemption in suffering. To close the purpose gap, we need to imagine a world where the most vulnerable do not live with the fear of that violence. It would mean reducing childhood poverty. One in six children lived in poverty in the United States as of 2018.[24] If we are not working to end poverty for every child, then we do not believe in the holiness of every child. Childhood violence is highest among people of color, but is especially prevalent in Native American, Black, and Latinx children. This statistic is the result of compounding oppressions, including the lack of basic resources, the high rate of incarceration, concentrated poverty, and a lack of access to education.

What Wows?

Imagine these wows: Our children have found freedom. Our vigorous work is paying off. Our systems are more equitable. The education and opportunity gaps are closing. Our children can dream more freely. They are inspired by people who share their Brown skin and their religious and cultural practices. There are more institutions with the foundations and purposes of historically Black colleges and universities and Hispanic-serving institutions. Tribal colleges are the example of how to educate! What if those institutions became the places that marked excellence for the entire population and funded them accordingly? We can build this pluriverse, the space that can hold the histories, traditions, knowledges, and the practices from our communities that have been denied freedom and purpose. In the words of Walter Mignolo:

> Pluriversality means unlearning, so to speak, modernity, and learning to live with people one does not agree with, or may not even like. Conviviality is not holiday, but a hard and relentless effort toward cosmopolitan localism and pluriversal futures. . . . Now if the goal were to build not only a peaceful world but also a world in which everybody, because of its humanity, is equal to every other body and thus has the basic right to food, shelter, health, and education, and not to be bothered by solicitors (evangelicals, mini-credit saviors, anxious financial agents, military interventions, irresponsible corporations, promoters of socialism, etc.), the pluriversality would be the universal project to which decolonial thinking and doing aspire, and which they promote.[25]

Mignolo is calling for us to build worlds where people have their basic needs met. He is also arguing for a world free of colonization and domination, not just of human bodies but of culture as well. He is calling for a world where the gap between purpose and opportunity does not exist.

What wows is building the communities and institutions that are not reliant on the same systems that stole our histories, our people, and our children. It is not about reforming or creating more pipelines. That is not what wows. It is not about being the firsts; it is more important not to be the last. We can build the system where our people and cultures are central and not just a difficulty to leave behind. What wows is not about creating or finding exception to the rules, but rewriting the rules on our terms.

What Sticks?

What institutions and systems are we creating for future generations to thrive? If you ask, people usually know what changes they need to make on a daily level. What sticks are those things that change the daily lives of people. Every sacrifice and decision we make is done with the faith that the tiny things we do, like my dad's long commute and his working long hours at thankless jobs, make a difference in our children's lives. One of my Latina mentors, who was one of the first Latinas in both local and state politics, said to me, "I can change the conditions of our community by focusing on parks, libraries, and potholes." Parks, as I said earlier, are where our community comes together to find freedom, to find joy, and to celebrate life. Libraries are a public good where we find freedom and where our imaginations are expanded, and, in many cases, they provide public services for our children. On our daily commutes, we all know the potholes we avoid or drive over. By ensuring people have access to the public goods that liberate and create freedom and by fixing the potholes that plague our daily commutes, we are taking steps to improve our day-to-day living.

Asking, "What sticks?" addresses daily conditions, but we also need to make sure that our solutions serve a greater purpose. For example, if the solution is to invest in libraries, those working to close the purpose gap ask questions like the following: What books do you put in the building? In my home community, what are the hours? Do they have books in our many languages? Are there people who work there who can help in our languages? Are there private spaces for social workers and tutors to work with our families to ensure we have what is necessary to survive? Are there places for the young to crawl and learn to be part of the community? Do playgrounds have lights? Are they accessible? Do they have ramps for those who cannot climb? Are they in our neighborhoods? Are there sidewalks for families to walk to them? Are there tables for us to celebrate and play together? Are there open spaces where children can run and laugh freely? If the solution is to plug potholes, we must ask, Are the roads going in the right direction? Would a rail system be better in place of the road to get people to where they need to be? Do long commutes need to happen in the first place? Does the road serve to connect communities or to demarcate lines between them? Can places of work move closer to the workforce? Are people able to live close enough to work that a car may not even be necessary? Are parks, libraries, and roads closing the purpose gap and providing equity to our world, or are they perpetuating the purpose gap? What sticks is designing with our children and communities in mind.

Practice 3: Closing the Purpose Gap Is about Today

Most importantly, closing the purpose gap is not about making plans for tomorrow. It is about today. Of course, we need to tell new narratives and stories grounded in our current reality. We also need to design for the future we collectively want. But all that dreaming, storytelling, and designing does not matter if you and I do not act today. If we do not make daily progress toward loving others every day, then all our work is for naught. If we must struggle daily, as many of us do, we must also work toward healing and freedom daily.

Imagine your answers to the following series of questions: Did you get enough sleep last night? Are you able to find time for healthy food and reflection in the morning? Do you welcome the next generation with love and affection? Are you fully present to your activities during the day? Do these activities serve their purpose? Do you find time to wander and think? Are you able to find time for a healthy meal in the evening? Do you find time for reading, imagining, and daydreaming? Do you have time to laugh and play? Will you close your day with some form of ritual and practice? Can you remind yourself throughout the day that you are loved? Can you find connection with your ancestors and the divine? Can you reflect on what you are grateful for? Have you made amends with those you have wronged? Have you planned or visualized tomorrow? Does your vision serve your purpose?

These questions were first asked of me by my community, and they were asked without judgment or direction. They were questions of care. When I worked on the night shift in the packing sheds, the Latinas who worked the shift with me helped me on our lunch break to reframe questions tied to purpose. They would ask me how I was sleeping, and if I was eating right. They would tell me they worked the night shift so that they could be present with their children during the day. They always asked what I was reading, for I have carried books with me ever since I was a kid. They asked me how my family was doing and held me accountable to my family and community. When I felt wronged or I had wronged someone, they were the first to remind me that it is our community that loves us and to make it right. They always asked what I had going on the next day and were curious about how my studies were going. That paragraph of questions could have been lifted out of a meaning-and-purpose or leadership development book, but there is a difference in tone and care when they come from our community. The daily-lived realities of people who are trying to close the purpose gap—in my case, the community that literally puts the food on your table for you to survive—ask questions of what is going on in one's daily life because they know what the stakes are. It is the same conversation that my grandparents had in their house when people came to visit; they talked about things that were happening in the community or with any of its members. Conversations went from health to loved ones, all out of care for the next generation, wanting them to have it just a little bit better than they did.

Reflections

How are you going to design your day? What will wow your community? What does the world look like if you live into your purpose? How do you create conditions for future generations to thrive?

Closing Words

Closing the purpose gap is about the small steps we all take today toward our desired future. By thoughtfully answering the reflection questions and reading this book, you have created a communal road map for freedom in your context. This is life-saving work, not just for us but for generations to follow.

Together, we have named the purpose gap. We have witnessed the design of the gap and imagined otherwise. We have reflected on and shortened our cultural commute. We have named the Powers and reflected on institutional vocations. We have reflected on institutions whose purposes have been to find freedom. We have gone stargazing and reset our intentions on not just becoming a star but on building constellations. We built networks and returned home to close the purpose gap. We have turned inward and reflected on the ancestors and spirits that have kept us safe, who guide our intuition. Finally, we have designed and dreamed of a good day, a day when the purpose gap is closed for us and our community on our terms.

My dream is for us to create the conditions for future generations to thrive, to find meaning and purpose. We are spiritual warriors and teachers, and I am grateful for your life and work. This work does not happen without people coming fully alive, living fully into their purposes.

Know that we were loved by generations before we arrived on this earth, and our ancestors are still watching, loving, and supporting us. We have everything we need. To close the purpose gap, we only need to have courage to trust our intuition and build the institutions, networks, and communities that future generations will inhabit. If we can do this work well, we will give a five-generation gift, just as my daughter, Carmelita, carries her name forward from five generations past. We will be spirits among the living—guiding and loving a generation we will never know in the flesh but whose purpose will be realized because of our work today.

Notes

Introduction

1. I use the terms *Latinx*, *Chicano/a*, *Xicanx*, *people of color*, *Black*, *Indigenous*, etc. intentionally. I also do not define each term in the text, for there are cultural nuances to each term, and each is highly contested. This book does not take up the identity debate between Latinx and Latino/a, for example, nor does it try to justify the fluidity of going between identities like Latinx and Xicanx or Chicano/x. Culture is always under construction. Because *mi gente* continue to decolonize identity formation and naming our experiences, the terms used throughout the text are not definitive. Instead they are meant to be generative. Each generation has to navigate a new era of survival. The importance is not finding the right identity marker for our people for all time but building on the traditions and values that have helped our people survive.

2. Gilly Segal and Kimberly Jones, *I'm Not Dying with You Tonight* (Naperville, IL: Sourcebooks Fire, 2019); Kimberly Jones, "How Can We Win," https://www.youtube.com/watch?v=sb9_qGOa9Go&t=91s.

3. "Six Migrant Children Have Died in U.S. Custody. Here's What We Know about Them," *Los Angeles Times*, May 24, 2019, https://www.latimes.com/nation/la-na-migrant-child-border-deaths-20190524-story.html.

4. Richard A. Oppel Jr. and Derrick Bryson Taylor, "Here's What You Need to Know about Breonna Taylor's Death," *The New York Times*, July 31, 2020, sec. U.S., https://www.nytimes.com/article/breonna-taylor-police.html.

5. Richard Fausset, "What We Know about the Shooting Death of Ahmaud Arbery," *The New York Times*, June 24, 2020, sec. U.S., https://www.nytimes.com/article/ahmaud-arbery-shooting-georgia.html.

6. Evan Hill et al., "How George Floyd Was Killed in Police Custody," *The New York Times*, May 31, 2020, sec. U.S., https://www.nytimes.com/2020/05/31/us/george-floyd-investigation.html.

7. Giulia McDonnell Nieto del Rio, "Questions Surround Police Killing of Latino Man in California," *The New York Times*, June 20, 2020, sec. U.S., https://www.nytimes.com/2020/06/20/us/andres-guardado-police-shooting.html.

8. Malachy Browne, Christina Kelso, and Barbara Marcolini, "How Rayshard Brooks Was Fatally Shot by the Atlanta Police," *The New York Times*, June 14, 2020, sec. U.S., https://www.nytimes.com/2020/06/14/us/videos-rayshard-brooks-shooting -atlanta-police.html.

9. Simon Romero, Giulia McDonnell Nieto del Rio, and Nicholas Bogel-Burroughs, "Another Nightmare Video and the Police on the Defensive in Tucson," *The New York Times*, June 25, 2020, sec. U.S., https://www.nytimes.com/2020/06/25/us/carlos -ingram-lopez-death-tucson-police.html.

10. Bill Burnett and Dave Evans, *Designing Your Life: How to Build a Well-Lived, Joyful Life*, (New York: Knopf, 2016); Bill Burnett and Dave Evans, *Designing Your Work Life: How to Thrive and Change and Find Happiness at Work* (New York: Knopf, 2020).

11. Yuyi Morales, *Dreamers* (New York: Scholastic, 2020).

12. Jim Cullen, *The American Dream: A Short History of an Idea That Shaped a Nation*, 9th print edition (Oxford: Oxford University Press, 2004).

13. Robert D. Putnam, *Our Kids: The American Dream in Crisis* (New York: Simon & Schuster, 2016), 229.

14. Jonah Sachs, *Winning the Story Wars: Why Those Who Tell (and Live) the Best Stories Will Rule the Future* (Boston: Harvard Business Review Press, 2012).

15. Sachs, *Winning the Story Wars*, 59.

16. Sachs, *Winning the Story Wars*, 61.

17. Ibram X. Kendi, *Stamped from the Beginning: The Definitive History of Racist Ideas in America* (New York: Bold Type Books, 2017).

18. Ibram X. Kendi, *How to Be an Antiracist* (New York: One World, 2019), 11.

19. *Ishmael* translates to "God hears."

20. Marian Wright Edelman, *The Measure of Our Success: A Letter to My Children and Yours* (New York: Harper Perennial, 1993), 15.

Chapter 1. Conditions

1. "What We Know: Family Separation and 'Zero Tolerance' at the Border," NPR.org, https://www.npr.org/2018/06/19/621065383/what-we-know-family-separation-and-zero -tolerance-at-the-border.

2. Simon Romero, "Migrants Are Detained under a Bridge in El Paso. What Happened?" *The New York Times*, March 29, 2019, sec. U.S., https://www.nytimes.com/2019/03/29 /us/el-paso-immigration-photo.html.

3. Associated Press, "Guatemalan Boy Sought Care for Family in U.S. and Died Crossing Border Desert," *The Guardian*, July 2, 2014, sec. World News, https://www .theguardian.com/world/2014/jul/02/boy-died-border-crossing-guatemala-ramos -texas.

4. Patrick B. Reyes, *Nobody Cries When We Die: God, Community, and Surviving to Adulthood* (St. Louis: Chalice Press, 2016).

5. Mark R. Schwehn and Dorothy C. Bass, eds., *Leading Lives That Matter: What We Should Do and Who We Should Be* (Grand Rapids: Wm. B. Eerdmans Publishing Co., 2020).

6. David S. Cunningham, ed., *At This Time and in This Place: Vocation and Higher Education* (New York: Oxford University Press, 2015); David S. Cunningham, ed., *Hearing Vocation Differently: Meaning, Purpose, and Identity in the Multi-Faith Academy* (New York: Oxford University Press, 2019).

7. Kathleen A. Cahalan, *The Stories We Live: Finding God's Calling All around Us* (Grand Rapids: Wm. B. Eerdmans Publishing Co., 2017).
8. Dori Grinenko Baker and Joyce A. Mercer, *Lives to Offer: Accompanying Youth on Their Vocational Quests* (Cleveland: Pilgrim Press, 2007).
9. Diana Butler Bass, *Grounded: Finding God in the World—A Spiritual Revolution* (New York: HarperOne, 2015).
10. Parker J. Palmer, *Let Your Life Speak: Listening for the Voice of Vocation* (San Francisco: Jossey-Bass, 1999); Parker J. Palmer, *The Active Life: A Spirituality of Work, Creativity, and Caring* (San Francisco: Jossey-Bass, 1999).
11. David Brooks, *The Social Animal: The Hidden Sources of Love, Character, and Achievement* (New York: Random House Trade Paperbacks, 2012); David Brooks, *The Second Mountain: The Quest for a Moral Life* (New York: Random House, 2019).
12. William C. Placher, ed., *Callings: Twenty Centuries of Christian Wisdom on Vocation* (Grand Rapids: Wm. B. Eerdmans Publishing Co., 2005).
13. Thomas Merton, *No Man Is an Island* (San Diego: Mariner Books, 2002); Thomas Merton, *The Seven Storey Mountain* (San Diego: Mariner Books, 1999).
14. Dorothy Day, *The Long Loneliness: The Autobiography of the Legendary Catholic Social Activist* (San Francisco: HarperOne, 2009).
15. Rick Warren, *The Purpose Driven Life: What on Earth Am I Here For?* 10th Anniversary Edition (Grand Rapids: Zondervan, 2013), 22.
16. Jennifer Harvey and Tim Wise, *Raising White Kids: Bringing Up Children in a Racially Unjust America* (Nashville: Abingdon Press, 2018).
17. Brené Brown, *Rising Strong: How the Ability to Reset Transforms the Way We Live, Love, Parent, and Lead* (New York: Random House Trade Paperbacks, 2017), 113.
18. Brené Brown, *Rising Strong*, 114.
19. Robin DiAngelo and Michael Eric Dyson, *White Fragility: Why It's So Hard for White People to Talk about Racism* (Boston: Beacon Press, 2018).
20. For historians, theologians, sociologists, cultural theorists, social scientists, and any scholar in a field in the broader humanities, there is simply too much evidence of the colonization, enslavement, and attempted genocide of humans to even come close to saying, "People are doing their best." That is not to say that the work of Brown and others is not necessary for activating our purpose. For some of us, our daily bread is central to our entire being, and we live with a heightened awareness that our survival mode is by design. This knowledge necessitates a fundamentally different starting line.
21. Toni Morrison, *Beloved* (New York: Vintage, 2004).
22. Thomas Craemer, "Estimating Slavery Reparations: Present Value Comparisons of Historical Multigenerational Reparations Policies," *Social Science Quarterly* 96, no. 2 (2015): 639–55, https://doi.org/10.1111/ssqu.12151.
23. Zora Neale Hurston, *Barracoon: The Story of the Last "Black Cargo,"* ed. Deborah G. Plant, foreword by Alice Walker (New York: Amistad, 2020).
24. Angela D. Sims, *Lynched: The Power of Memory in a Culture of Terror* (Waco, TX: Baylor University Press, 2017).
25. Octavia Butler, *Kindred* (Boston: Beacon Press, 1979).
26. Elie Wiesel, *Night*, trans. Marion Wiesel (New York: Hill and Wang, 2006).
27. Viktor E. Frankl, *Man's Search for Meaning* (Boston: Beacon Press, 2006), 79.
28. David Treuer, *The Heartbeat of Wounded Knee: Native America from 1890 to the Present* (New York: Riverhead Books, 2019), 97.

29. Roberto D. Hernández, *Coloniality of the US/Mexico Border: Power, Violence, and the Decolonial Imperative* (Phoenix: University of Arizona Press, 2018); Walter D. Mignolo, *Local Histories / Global Designs: Coloniality, Subaltern Knowledges, and Border Thinking*, with a new preface by the author edition (Princeton, NJ: Princeton University Press, 2012); José David Saldívar, *Trans-Americanity: Subaltern Modernities, Global Coloniality, and the Cultures of Greater Mexico*, ed. Donald E. Pease (Durham, NC: Duke University Press, 2011).
30. Prison Policy Initiative and Wendy Sawyer, "Youth Confinement: The Whole Pie 2019," https://www.prisonpolicy.org/reports/youth2019.html.
31. "Family Separation by the Numbers," American Civil Liberties Union, https://www.aclu.org/issues/immigrants-rights/immigrants-rights-and-detention/family-separation.
32. "Six Migrant Children Have Died in U.S. Custody. Here's What We Know about Them."
33. Press, "Guatemalan Boy Sought Care for Family in US and Died Crossing Border Desert."
34. Alexandra Kelley, "Attacks on Asian Americans Skyrocket to 100 per Day during Coronavirus Pandemic," TheHill, March 31, 2020, https://thehill.com/changing-america/respect/equality/490373-attacks-on-asian-americans-at-about-100-per-day-due-to.
35. Thi Bui, *The Best We Could Do: An Illustrated Memoir* (New York: Harry N. Abrams, 2018).

Chapter 2. Retelling the Story of Purpose

1. Howard Thurman, *For the Inward Journey: The Writings of Howard Thurman* (San Diego: Harcourt Brace Jovanovich, 1984), 60–61.
2. I served for many years on the board of ARC (Arts/Religion/Culture), an organization that Joseph Campbell started whose mission is to shepherd this legacy toward new forms of storytelling. The organization still does incredible work to expand this vision. See Joseph Campbell, *Joseph Campbell's The Hero with a Thousand Faces* (Novato, CA: New World Library, 2008).
3. Paulo Coelho, *The Alchemist*, 25th ann. ed. (San Francisco: HarperOne, 2014).
4. J. D. Salinger, *The Catcher in the Rye* (Boston: Back Bay Books, 2001).
5. Herman Melville, *Moby Dick: Or, The Whale* (Open Library, independently published, 2019).
6. Charlotte Bronte, *Jane Eyre* (CreateSpace Independent Publishing Platform, 2015).
7. David Brooks, *The Second Mountain: The Quest for a Moral Life* (New York: Random House, 2019), 98.
8. To be fair, I think Tolkien was aware of this, for his stories constantly veer from the main arc to tell the backstories of individual characters, places, and histories. He was world building. The more critical point is the way we tell and interpret these stories of finding meaning.
9. Ivan Petrella, *The Future of Liberation Theology: An Argument and Manifesto* (Burlington, VT: Ashgate, 2004).
10. Jim Collins, *Good to Great: Why Some Companies Make the Leap and Others Don't* (New York: Harper Business, 2001).
11. John Rollin Ridge, *The Life and Adventures of Joaquín Murieta: The Celebrated California Bandit*, foreword by Diana Gabaldon, introduction by Hsuan L. Hsu (New York: Penguin Classics, 2018).

12. Octavia Butler, *Kindred* (Boston: Beacon Press, 1979); Octavia Butler, *Bloodchild and Other Stories* (New York: Seven Stories Press, 2005); Octavia Butler, *Dawn* (New York: Warner Aspect, 1997).

13. Rudolfo A. Anaya, *Bless Me, Ultima* (New York: Grand Central Publishing, 1999).

14. Malcolm Gladwell, *Outliers: The Story of Success*, reprint edition (New York: Back Bay Books, 2011).

15. "Transcript of Brown v. Board of Education (1954)," https://www.ourdocuments.gov /print_friendly.php?flash=false&page=transcript&doc=87&title=Transcript+of+Brown +v.+Board+of+Education+%281954%29.

16. "Westminster School Dist. of Orange County v. Mendez, 161 F.2d 774 (9th Cir. 1947)," Justia Law, https://law.justia.com/cases/federal/appellate-courts/F2/161/774 /1566460/.

17. Patrick B. Reyes, "Practical Theology as Knowledge of Origin and Migration: An Essay," in *Let Your Light Shine: Mobilizing for Justice with Children and Youth*, ed. Virginia A. Lee and Reginald Blount (Chester Heights, PA: Friendship Press, 2019), 121–34.

Chapter 3. Designing Purpose

1. Ocean Vuong, *On Earth We're Briefly Gorgeous* (New York: Penguin Press, 2019).

2. Martin Luther King Jr., Vincent Harding, and Coretta Scott King, *Where Do We Go from Here: Chaos or Community?* (Boston: Beacon Press, 2010).

3. Nelson Maldonado-Torres, *Against War: Views from the Underside of Modernity* (Durham, NC: Duke University Press, 2008).

4. Daniel J. Siegel and Tina Payne Bryson, *The Power of Showing Up: How Parental Presence Shapes Who Our Kids Become and How Their Brains Get Wired* (New York: Ballantine Books, 2020).

5. Clayton M. Christensen, *The Innovator's Dilemma: When New Technologies Cause Great Firms to Fail*, repr. ed. (Boston: Harvard Business Review Press, 2016); Clayton M. Christensen, James Allworth, and Karen Dillon, *How Will You Measure Your Life?* (New York: Harper Business, 2012).

6. Kevin M. Kruse, "How Segregation Caused Your Traffic Jam," *The New York Times*, August 14, 2019, sec. Magazine, https://www.nytimes.com/interactive/2019/08/14/maga zine/traffic-atlanta-segregation.html.

7. Sara McLafferty and Valerie Preston, "Who Has Long Commutes to Low-Wage Jobs? Gender, Race, and Access to Work in the New York Region," *Urban Geography* 40, no. 9 (October 21, 2019): 1270–90, https://doi.org/10.1080/02723638.2019.1577091.

8. Jessica Trounstine, *Segregation by Design: Local Politics and Inequality in American Cities* (New York: Cambridge University Press, 2018), 3.

9. John E. Arnold and William J. Clancey, *Creative Engineering: Promoting Innovation by Thinking Differently*, Stanford Summer Seminars, 1959, Kindle edition.

10. Jeanne Liedtka and Tim Ogilvie, *Designing for Growth: A Design Thinking Tool Kit for Managers* (New York: Columbia Business School Publishing, 2011).

11. Jeanne Liedtka, Randy Salzman, and Daisy Azer, *Design Thinking for the Greater Good: Innovation in the Social Sector* (New York: Columbia Business School Publishing, 2017).

12. "California City Fights Poverty with Guaranteed Income," *Reuters*, June 6, 2018, https://www.reuters.com/article/us-california-income-idUSKCN1J015D.

13. Jake Knapp, John Zeratsky, and Braden Kowitz, *Sprint: How to Solve Big Problems and Test New Ideas in Just Five Days* (New York: Simon & Schuster, 2016).

14. Burnett and Evans, *Designing Your Life*.
15. Burnett and Evans, *Designing Your Life*, 221.
16. Burnett and Evans, *Designing Your Work Life*.
17. Tim Brown, *Change by Design: How Design Thinking Transforms Organizations and Inspires Innovation* (New York: Harper Business, 2009).
18. Michael Wolf, *Designing the New American University* (Baltimore: Johns Hopkins University Press, 2015).
19. Kathleen Fitzpatrick, *Generous Thinking: A Radical Approach to Saving the University* (Baltimore: Johns Hopkins University Press, 2019).
20. Angela Duckworth, *Grit: The Power of Passion and Perseverance* (New York: Scribner, 2018).
21. Sasha Costanza-Chock, *Design Justice: Community-Led Practices to Build the Worlds We Need* (Cambridge, MA: MIT Press, 2020).
22. Costanza-Chock, *Design Justice*, 23.
23. Costanza-Chock, *Design Justice*, 6.
24. Arturo Escobar, *Designs for the Pluriverse: Radical Interdependence, Autonomy, and the Making of Worlds* (Durham, NC: Duke University Press, 2018).
25. Paulo Freire, *Pedagogy of the Oppressed*, trans. Myra Bergman Ramos, 30th ann. ed. (New York: Continuum, 2000).

Chapter 4. Vocation of Communities and Institutions

1. Everett Public Library, "Library Mission," https://epls.org/230/About.
2. Walter Wink, *Engaging the Powers: Discernment and Resistance in a World of Domination* (Minneapolis: Fortress Press, 1992), 9.
3. Wink, *Engaging the Powers*, 10.
4. Andy Crouch, *Playing God: Redeeming the Gift of Power* (Downers Grove, IL: IVP Books, 2013), 170.
5. Crouch, *Playing God*, 17.
6. Wink, *Engaging the Powers*, 64.
7. Wink, *Engaging the Powers*, 164.
8. Robert Chao Romero, *Brown Church: Five Centuries of Latina/o Social Justice, Theology, and Identity* (Downers Grove, IL: IVP Academic, 2020).
9. Romero, *Brown Church*, 31.
10. Romero, *Brown Church*, 65.
11. Romero, *Brown Church*, 53.
12. Bartolome de Las Casas and Anthony Pagden, *A Short Account of the Destruction of the Indies*, trans. Nigel Griffin (New York: Penguin Classics, 1999).
13. Theresa A. Yugar, *Sor Juana Inés de La Cruz: Feminist Reconstruction of Biography and Text* (Eugene, OR: Wipf and Stock, 2014), 4.
14. Luis D. Leon, *The Political Spirituality of Cesar Chavez: Crossing Religious Borders* (Oakland: University of California Press, 2014).
15. Andrés G. Guerrero, *A Chicano Theology* (Eugene, OR: Wipf and Stock, 2008).
16. Wink, *Engaging the Powers*, 182.
17. Wink, *Engaging the Powers*, 179.
18. "Divided Decade: How the Financial Crisis Changed Housing," *Marketplace* (blog), December 17, 2018, https://www.marketplace.org/2018/12/17/what-we-learned-housing/.

19. Albert Camus, *The Rebel: An Essay on Man in Revolt* (New York: Vintage, 1992).

20. James H. Cone and Cornel West, *Black Theology and Black Power*, ann. ed. (Maryknoll, NY: Orbis Books, 2019).

21. Bessel van der Kolk, *The Body Keeps the Score: Brain, Mind, and Body in the Healing of Trauma* (New York: Penguin Books, 2015).

22. César Chávez, "1984 Cesar Chavez Address to the Commonwealth Club of California" gvlibraries.org, http://www.gvlibraries.org/content/1984-cesar-chavez-address -commonwealth-club-california.

23. Stephen Lewis, Matthew Wesley Williams, and Dori Baker, *Another Way: Living and Leading Change on Purpose* (St. Louis: Chalice Press, 2020), 49.

24. "Our Mission," *Catholic Charities USA* (blog), https://www.catholiccharitiesusa.org /about-us/mission-vision/.

25. The Y, "About Us," https://www.ymca.net/about-us.

26. "Mission & Values," https://www.redcross.org/about-us/who-we-are/mission-and -values.html.

27. "Our Mission," Homeboy Industries (blog), https://homeboyindustries.org/our-story /our-mission/.

28. "Christian Leadership Incubator/Forum for Theological Exploration," https:// fteleaders.org/about.

29. "About Us," *Airbnb Newsroom* (blog), https://news.airbnb.com/about-us/.

30. "How Google Search Works / Our Mission," https://www.google.com/search/how searchworks/mission/.

31. "Disney—Leadership, History, Corporate Social Responsibility," The Walt Disney Company, https://thewaltdisneycompany.com/about/.

32. Josh, "Disney World Statistics—The Truly Fascinating Numbers behind Disney," *Magic Guides* (blog), https://magicguides.com/disney-world-statistics/.

33. David Kamp, *Sunny Days: The Children's Television Revolution That Changed America* (New York: Simon & Schuster, 2020).

34. Crouch, *Playing God*, 178.

35. "Racial/Ethnic Patterns of Child Opportunity," Diversity Data Kids, http://www .diversitydatakids.org/research-library/data-visualization/racialethnic-patterns-child -opportunity.

36. Jon Hale, *The Freedom Schools: Student Activists in the Mississippi Civil Rights Movement*, repr. ed. (New York: Columbia University Press, 2018).

37. Ben Dawson, "CDF Freedom Schools Program," Children's Defense Fund (blog), https://www.childrensdefense.org/programs/cdf-freedom-schools/.

38. "Our Mission," Homeboy Industries (blog).

39. Gregory Boyle, *Tattoos on the Heart: The Power of Boundless Compassion* (New York: Free Press, 2011), 35.

40. Gregory Boyle, *Barking to the Choir: The Power of Radical Kinship* (New York: Simon & Schuster, 2018), 167.

Chapter 5. From Stars to Constellations

1. Sheryl Sandberg, *Lean In for Graduates: With New Chapters by Experts, Including Find Your First Job, Negotiate Your Salary, and Own Who You Are* (New York: Knopf, 2014).

2. Marie Kondō and Scott Sonenshein, *Joy at Work: Organizing Your Professional Life* (New York: Little, Brown Spark, 2020).

3. Marie Kondō, *Spark Joy: An Illustrated Master Class on the Art of Organizing and Tidying Up*, Illustrated edition (Berkeley, CA: Ten Speed Press, 2016).
4. Coelho, *The Alchemist*.
5. Robert B. Reich, *The Common Good* (New York: Vintage, 2019).
6. Joseph Gordon-Levitt, *How Craving Attention Makes You Less Creative*, https://www.ted .com/talks/joseph_gordon_levitt_how_craving_attention_makes_you_less_creative.
7. "These American Cities Are Losing the Most Brainpower," *Bloomberg.Com*, November 1, 2018, https://www.bloomberg.com/news/articles/2018-11-01/california-s-non -silicon-valley-works-to-reverse-brain-drain.
8. Liedtka, Salzman, and Azer, *Design Thinking for the Greater Good*, 163.
9. Ronald Heifetz, *Leadership without Easy Answers* (Cambridge, MA: Harvard University Press, 1998).
10. Priya Parker, *The Art of Gathering: How We Meet and Why It Matters* (New York: Riverhead Books, 2018).
11. Parker J. Palmer, *The Courage to Teach: Exploring the Inner Landscape of a Teacher's Life* (New York: Jossey-Bass, 1997), 10.
12. Lewis, Williams, and Baker, *Another Way*.
13. Fluker, *The Ground Has Shifted: The Future of the Black Church in Post-Racial America* (New York: NYU Press, 2018).
14. Colin Powell, *It Worked for Me: In Life and Leadership* (New York: Harper Perennial, 2014).
15. Wilda C. Gafney, *Daughters of Miriam: Women Prophets in Ancient Israel* (Minneapolis: Fortress Press, 2008), 3.
16. Edelman, *The Measure of Our Success*, 77.
17. Sarah Lewis, *The Rise: Creativity, the Gift of Failure, and the Search for Mastery* (New York: Simon & Schuster, 2015), 8.
18. Lewis, *The Rise*, 7.
19. Adam Grant and Sheryl Sandberg, *Originals: How Non-Conformists Move the World* (New York: Penguin Books, 2016).
20. Debbie Collins, "Astronaut Requirements," NASA, http://www.nasa.gov/audience /forstudents/postsecondary/features/F_Astronaut_Requirements.html.
21. Hironao Okahana and Enyu Zhou, "Graduate Enrollment and Degrees: 2008 to 2018," (2019), 82. https://cgsnet.org/graduate-enrollment-and-degrees-2008-2018.
22. Patty Rodriguez and Ariana Stein, *The Solar System with Ellen—El Sistema Solar Con Ellen*, biling. ed. (Los Angeles: Lil' Libros, 2020).
23. Margot Lee Shetterly, *Hidden Figures: The American Dream and the Untold Story of the Black Women Mathematicians Who Helped Win the Space Race* (New York: William Morrow Paperbacks, 2016).
24. Dorothy Aguilera–Black Bear and John W. Tippeconnic III, eds., *Voices of Resistance and Renewal: Indigenous Leadership in Education* (Norman: University of Oklahoma Press, 2015), 13.

Chapter 6. The Power of Networks

1. Peter Block, *Community: The Structure of Belonging* (Oakland, CA: Berrett-Koehler Publishers, 2018).
2. Scott E. Page, *Diversity and Complexity* (Princeton, NJ: Princeton University Press, 2010), 17.

3. Marshall Ganz, *Why David Sometimes Wins: Leadership, Organization, and Strategy in the California Farm Worker Movement* (New York: Oxford University Press, 2010), 17.

4. Antonio Gramsci and Antonio Callari, *Prison Notebooks*, trans. Joseph A. Buttigieg, vol. 3 (New York: Columbia University Press, 2011), 207.

5. Michel Foucault, *Power*, ed. James D. Faubion, trans. Robert Hurley (New York: New Press, 2001).

6. Mignolo, *Local Histories / Global Designs*; Walter D. Mignolo, *The Idea of Latin America* (Oxford: Blackwell Publishing, 2005).

7. Ganz, *Why David Sometimes Wins*, 14.

8. Stephen Preskill and Stephen D. Brookfield, *Learning as a Way of Leading: Lessons from the Struggle for Social Justice* (San Francisco: Jossey-Bass, 2008), 5.

9. Preskill and Brookfield, *Learning*, 22.

10. Marian Wright Edelman, *The Sea Is So Wide and My Boat Is So Small: Charting a Course for the Next Generation* (New York: Hyperion, 2008), xix.

11. Reginald Blount, *Cultivating Teen Faith: Insights from the Confirmation Project*, ed. Richard R. Osmer and Katherine M. Douglass (Grand Rapids: Wm. B. Eerdmans Publishing Co., 2018), 118.

12. Tom Brokaw, *The Greatest Generation* (New York: Random House Trade Paperbacks, 2001).

13. Robert P. Jones, *The End of White Christian America* (New York: Simon & Schuster, 2017), 29.

14. Carmen Nanko-Fernandez, *Theologizing En Espanglish: Context, Community, and Ministry* (Maryknoll, NY: Orbis Books, 2010).

15. Cyndi Suarez, *The Power Manual: How to Master Complex Power Dynamics* (Gabriola Island, CA: New Society Publishers, 2018), 11.

16. Chris Rabb, *Invisible Capital: How Unseen Forces Shape Entrepreneurial Opportunity* (San Francisco: Berrett-Koehler Publishers, 2010), 61.

17. Rabb, *Invisible Capital*, 6.

18. Paul Hildreth, *Knowledge Networks: Innovation through Communities of Practice*, ed. Chris Kimble (Hershey, PA: IGI Global, 2003).

Chapter 7. The Hardest Place to Take the Work Is Home

1. Peter Block, *Community: The Structure of Belonging* (Oakland, CA: Berrett-Koehler Publishers, 2018).

2. Marshall Ganz, *Why David Sometimes Wins: Leadership, Organization, and Strategy in the California Farm Worker Movement* (New York: Oxford University Press, 2010).

3. Martin Luther King Jr., Vincent Harding, and Coretta Scott King, *Where Do We Go from Here: Chaos or Community?* (Boston: Beacon Press, 2010).

4. Paulo Freire, *Pedagogy of the Heart* (New York: Bloomsbury Academic, 2016), 29.

5. Jennifer R. Ayres, *Inhabitance: Ecological Religious Education* (Waco, TX: Baylor University Press, 2019), 4.

6. Ayres, *Inhabitance*, 7.

7. Wendell Berry, *Jayber Crow* (New York: Counterpoint, 2001).

8. Édouard Glissant, *Poetics of Relation*, trans. Betsy Wing (Ann Arbor: University of Michigan Press, 1997), 141.

9. Glissant, *Poetics of Relation*, 142.

10. Tommy Orange, *There There* (New York: Vintage, 2019).

11. Jimmy Santiago Baca, *Immigrants in Our Own Land & Selected Early Poems* (New York: New Directions, 1990).

12. Jimmy Santiago Baca, *A Place to Stand* (New York: Grove Press, 2002).

13. Enrique D. Dussel, *A History of the Church in Latin America: Colonialism to Liberation* (Grand Rapids: Wm. B. Eerdmans Publishing Co., 1982), 8.

14. Dietrich Bonhoeffer and Eric Metaxas, *The Cost of Discipleship* (New York: Touchstone, 1995), 37.

15. This is a central theme in my book *Nobody Cries When We Die*.

16. Frantz Fanon, Jean-Paul Sartre, and Homi K. Bhabha, *The Wretched of the Earth*, trans. Richard Philcox (New York: Grove Press, 2005).

17. Parker J. Palmer, *The Courage to Teach: Exploring the Inner Landscape of a Teacher's Life* (New York: Jossey-Bass, 1997), 6.

18. Richard Rothstein, *The Color of Law: A Forgotten History of How Our Government Segregated America* (New York: Liveright, 2018).

19. Michelle Alexander, *The New Jim Crow: Mass Incarceration in the Age of Colorblindness* (New York: New Press, 2020).

20. Bryan Stevenson, *Just Mercy: A Story of Justice and Redemption* (New York: One World, 2015).

21. Ibram X. Kendi, *Stamped from the Beginning: The Definitive History of Racist Ideas in America* (New York: Bold Type Books, 2017).

22. Beverly Daniel Tatum, *Why Are All the Black Kids Sitting Together in the Cafeteria? And Other Conversations about Race*, rev. ed. (New York: Basic Books, 2017), 87.

23. Thomas M. Shapiro, *Toxic Inequality: How America's Wealth Gap Destroys Mobility, Deepens the Racial Divide, and Threatens Our Future*, Kindle edition (New York: Basic Books, 2017), 17.

24. Shapiro, *Toxic Inequality*, 20.

25. Shapiro, *Toxic Inequality*, 35.

26. Carolyn Helsel and Y. Joy Harris-Smith, *The ABCs of Diversity: Helping Kids (and Ourselves!) Embrace Our Differences* (St. Louis: Chalice Press, 2020).

27. Rubem Alves and Jo Ind, *Poet, the Warrior, the Prophet* (London: Hymns Ancient & Modern Ltd, 2002).

28. Rubem Alves, *Tomorrow's Child: Imagination, Creativity, and the Rebirth of Culture* (Eugene, OR: Wipf & Stock Publishers, 2011).

29. Carter Godwin Woodson, *The Mis-Education of the Negro*, ed. Tony Darnell (Suwanee, GA: 12th Media Services, 2017).

30. Roxanne Dunbar-Ortiz, *An Indigenous Peoples' History of the United States* (Boston: Beacon Press, 2015).

31. Dunbar-Ortiz, *An Indigenous Peoples' History*, 9.

32. Leanne Betasamosake Simpson, *This Accident of Being Lost: Songs and Stories* (Toronto: Astoria, 2017).

33. Leanne Betasamosake Simpson, *As We Have Always Done: Indigenous Freedom through Radical Resistance* (Minneapolis: University of Minnesota Press, 2017), 5.

34. Camilla Townsend, *Fifth Sun: A New History of the Aztecs* (New York: Oxford University Press, 2019), 10.

35. Jared Diamond, *Guns, Germs, and Steel: The Fates of Human Societies* (New York: W. W. Norton, 2017).

36. Rolando Romero and Amanda Nolacea Harris, eds., *Feminism, Nation and Myth: La Malinche* (Houston: Arte Publico Press, 2005).

37. The great fiction writer Laura Esquivel reimagined this story masterfully, centering survival and love. Laura Esquivel, *Malinche*, trans. Ernesto Mestre-Reed (New York: Atria Books, 2007).

38. bell hooks, *Killing Rage* (New York: Holt Paperbacks, 1996).

39. bell hooks, *Teaching to Transgress: Education as the Practice of Freedom* (New York: Routledge, 1994), 2.

40. Hooks, *Teaching to Transgress*, 3.

41. Hooks, *Teaching to Transgress*, 3.

42. Paulo Freire, *Pedagogy of the Oppressed*, trans. Myra Bergman Ramos, 30th ann. ed. (New York: Continuum, 2000), 84.

43. Paulo Freire, Stanley Aronowitz, and Donaldo Macedo, *Pedagogy of Freedom: Ethics, Democracy, and Civic Courage*, trans. Patrick Clarke (Lanham, MD: Rowman & Littlefield Publishers, 2000).

44. Freire, Aronowitz, and Macedo, *Pedagogy of Freedom*, 30.

45. Joe L. Kincheloe, *Critical Pedagogy Primer: Second Edition* (New York: International Academic Publishers, 2008), 69.

46. Antonio Gramsci and Antonio Callari, *Prison Notebooks*, trans. Joseph A. Buttigieg, vol. 2 (New York: Columbia University Press, 2011), 215.

47. Michael Apple, ed., *Knowledge, Power, and Education* (New York: Routledge, 2014).

48. Henry A. Giroux, *Between Borders: Pedagogy and the Politics of Cultural Studies* (New York: Psychology Press, 1994); Henry A. Giroux, *On Critical Pedagogy* (New York: Continuum, 2011); Henry A. Giroux, *Fugitive Cultures: Race, Violence, and Youth* (New York: Routledge, 1996); Paulo Freire and Henry A. Giroux, *The Politics of Education: Culture, Power and Liberation*, trans. Donaldo Macedo (South Hadley, MA: Bergin & Garvey Publishers, 1985).

49. bell hooks, *Teaching Community: A Pedagogy of Hope* (New York: Routledge, 2003); bell hooks, *Teaching Critical Thinking: Practical Wisdom* (New York: Routledge, 2009).

50. Ira Shor, *Empowering Education: Critical Teaching for Social Change* (Chicago: University of Chicago Press, 1992).

51. John Smyth, *Critical Pedagogy for Social Justice* (New York: Continuum, 2011).

52. Kendi, *Stamped from the Beginning*.

53. David Kamp, *Sunny Days: The Children's Television Revolution That Changed America* (New York: Simon & Schuster, 2020), 14.

54. Kamp, *Sunny Days*, 24.

55. Enrique Dussel and Linda Martín Alcoff, *Pedagogics of Liberation: A Latin American Philosophy of Education*, trans. David I. Backer and Cecilia Diego (Santa Barbara, CA: Punctum Books, 2019).

Chapter 8. Carry Your Corner

1. Frank Rogers Jr., *Practicing Compassion* (Nashville: Fresh Air Books, 2014).

2. Augusto Boal, *Theatre of the Oppressed*, trans. Charles A. McBride (New York: Theatre Communications Group, 1993).

3. "Breaking2," https://www.nike.com/us/en_us/c/running/breaking2.

4. Lopez Lomong and Mark Tabb, *Running for My Life: One Lost Boy's Journey from the Killing Fields of Sudan to the Olympic Games* (Nashville: Thomas Nelson, 2016).

5. Cal Newport, *Deep Work: Rules for Focused Success in a Distracted World* (New York: Grand Central Publishing, 2016); Cal Newport, *Digital Minimalism: Choosing a Focused Life in a Noisy World* (New York: Portfolio/Penguin, 2019).

6. Clayton Christensen, *The Innovator's Dilemma: When New Technologies Cause Great Firms to Fail* (Boston: Harvard Business School Publishing, 2016); Clayton Christensen, James Allworth, and Karen Dillon, *How Will You Measure Your Life?* (New York: Harper Business, 2012).

7. Robert Iger, *The Ride of a Lifetime: Lessons Learned from 15 Years as CEO of the Walt Disney Company* (New York: Random House Large Print, 2019).

8. Howard Schultz and Joanne Gordon, *Onward: How Starbucks Fought for Its Life without Losing Its Soul* (New York: Rodale Books, 2012).

9. Daniel H. Pink, *Drive: The Surprising Truth about What Motivates Us* (New York: Riverhead Books, 2011).

10. Jake Knapp and John Zeratsky, *Make Time: How to Focus on What Matters Every Day* (New York: Currency, 2018); Knapp, Zeratsky, and Braden Kowitz, *Sprint: How to Solve Big Problems and Test New Ideas in Just Five Days* (New York: Simon & Schuster, 2016).

11. James Baldwin, *The Fire Next Time* (New York: Vintage, 1992).

12. Rudolfo A. Anaya, *Bless Me, Ultima* (New York: Grand Central Publishing, 1999).

13. Baca, *A Place to Stand*; Baca, *Immigrants in Our Own Land & Selected Early Poems*.

14. Gabriel Garcia Marquez, *One Hundred Years of Solitude*, trans. Gregory Rabassa (New York: Harper Perennial Modern Classics, 2006).

15. Esmeralda Santiago, *Almost a Woman* (Reading, MA: Perseus Books, 1998).

16. Julia Alvarez, *Afterlife* (Chapel Hill, NC: Algonquin Books, 2020); Julia Alvarez, *In the Time of the Butterflies* (Chapel Hill, NC: Algonquin Books, 2010); Julia Alvarez, *How the Garcia Girls Lost Their Accents* (Chapel Hill, NC: Algonquin Books, 1991).

17. Rolando Hinojosa, *The Valley / Estampas Del Valle*, biling. ed. (Houston, TX: Arte Publico, 2014); Rolando Hinojosa, *A Voice of My Own: Essays and Stories* (Houston, TX: Arte Publico, 2011).

18. Erika L. Sánchez, *I Am Not Your Perfect Mexican Daughter* (New York: Knopf Books for Young Readers, 2017).

19. Elizabeth Acevedo, *The Poet X* (New York: Quill Tree Books, 2020); Elizabeth Acevedo, *Clap When You Land* (New York: Quill Tree Books, 2020).

20. Octavio Paz, *The Labyrinth of Solitude: The Other Mexico, Return to the Labyrinth of Solitude, Mexico and the United States, the Philanthropic Ogre* (New York: Grove Press, 1994).

21. Matt de la Peña, *Mexican White Boy* (New York: Ember, 2010); Matt de la Peña, *Carmela Full of Wishes* (New York: G. P. Putnam's Sons Books for Young Readers, 2018); Matt de la Peña, *Love* (New York: G. P. Putnam's Sons Books for Young Readers, 2018).

22. Carolina Hinojosa-Cisneros, *Becoming Coztōtōtl* (McAllen, TX: Flower Song Books, 2019).

23. Gloria Anzaldúa, *Borderlands / La Frontera: The New Mestiza*, 3rd ed. (San Francisco: Aunt Lute Books, 2007); Gloria Anzaldua, *Light in the Dark / Luz En Lo Oscuro: Rewriting Identity, Spirituality, Reality*, ed. AnaLouise Keating (Durham, NC: Duke University Press, 2015).

24. Ana Castillo, *So Far from God* (New York: W. W. Norton, 2005); Ana Castillo, *Black Dove: Mamá, Mi'jo, and Me* (New York: Feminist Press at CUNY, 2016).

25. Cherríe Moraga, *Loving in the War Years: Lo Que Nunca Pasó Por Sus Labios* (Boston: South End Press, 1983); Cherríe L. Moraga, *A Xicana Codex of Changing Consciousness: Writings, 2000–2010* (Durham, NC: Duke University Press, 2011); Cherrie Moraga and Gloria Anzaldúa, eds., *This Bridge Called My Back: Writings by Radical Women of Color* (San Francisco: Third Woman Press, 2002).

26. Richard Rodriguez, *Darling: A Spiritual Autobiography* (New York: Penguin Books, 2014); Richard Rodriguez, *Brown: The Last Discovery of America* (New York: Penguin Books, 2003); Richard Rodriguez, *Hunger of Memory: The Education of Richard Rodriguez* (New York: Dial Press Trade Paperback, 2004).

27. Luis J. Rodriguez, *Always Running: La Vida Loca: Gang Days in L.A.* (New York: Atria Books, 2005); Luis J. Rodriguez, *It Calls You Back: An Odyssey through Love, Addiction, Revolutions, and Healing* (New York: Atria Books, 2012).

28. Laura E. Pérez, "Writing with Crooked Lines," in *Fleshing the Spirit: Spirituality and Activism in Chicana, Latina, and Indigenous Women's Lives*, ed. Elisa Facio and Irene Lara (Tucson: University of Arizona Press, 2014), 23.

29. Pérez, "Writing with Crooked Lines," 24.

30. Malcolm Gladwell, *Blink: The Power of Thinking without Thinking* (New York: Back Bay Books, 2007).

31. Malcolm Gladwell, *Talking to Strangers: What We Should Know about the People We Don't Know* (New York: Little, Brown, 2019).

32. adrienne maree brown, *Emergent Strategy: Shaping Change, Changing Worlds* (Chico, CA: AK Press, 2017).

33. Sasha Costanza-Chock, *Design Justice: Community-Led Practices to Build the Worlds We Need* (Cambridge, MA: MIT Press, 2020).

34. Giulia Enders, *Gut: The Inside Story of Our Body's Most Underrated Organ* (Vancouver: Greystone Books, 2018).

35. "What Is the Speed of the Solar System," Stanford SOLAR Center, http://solar-center .stanford.edu/FAQ/Qsolsysspeed.html.

36. Rogers, *Practicing Compassion*.

37. Richard C. Schwartz and Martha Sweezy, *Internal Family Systems Therapy*, 2d ed. (New York: Guilford Press, 2019).

38. Schwartz and Sweezy, *Internal Family Systems*, 4–5.

39. "Staff," Center for Engaged Compassion, http://www.centerforengagedcompassion .com/staff.

40. Freire, *Pedagogy of the Heart*, 29–30.

41. Flannery O'Connor, *The Complete Stories* (New York: Farrar, Straus and Giroux, 1971).

42. Paz, *The Labyrinth of Solitude*, 24.

43. Anaya, *Bless Me, Ultima*.

44. Chaim Potok, *My Name Is Asher Lev* (New York: Anchor, 2009).

45. Isabel Allende, *The House of the Spirits* (New York: Atria Books, 2015).

46. Elizabeth Conde-Frazier, *Listen to the Children: Conversations with Immigrant Families/ Escuchemos a los ninos: Conversaciones Con Familias Inmigrantes*, biling. ed. (Valley Forge, PA: Judson Press, 2011).

47. Laura I. Rendón and Mark Nepo, *Sentipensante (Sensing/Thinking) Pedagogy: Educating for Wholeness, Social Justice and Liberation* (Sterling, VA: Stylus Publishing, 2008).

48. Margaret J. Wheatley, *Who Do We Choose to Be?: Facing Reality, Claiming Leadership, Restoring Sanity* (Oakland, CA: Berrett-Koehler Publishers, 2017).

49. Rendón and Nepo, *Sentipensante (Sensing/Thinking)*, 151.
50. Diego Rivera and Gladys March, *My Art, My Life: An Autobiography* (New York: Dover Publications, 1992).
51. Hayden Herrera, *Frida: The Biography of Frida Kahlo* (London: Bloomsbury Publishing, 1989).
52. Seth Godin, *Tribes: We Need You to Lead Us* (New York: Portfolio, 2008).
53. Malcolm Gladwell, *Outliers: The Story of Success*, reprint ed. (New York: Back Bay Books, 2011).
54. Sarah Lewis, *The Rise: Creativity, the Gift of Failure, and the Search for Mastery* (New York: Simon & Schuster, 2015).
55. Dietrich Bonhoeffer, *Life Together: The Classic Exploration of Christian in Community* (Princeton, NJ: HarperOne, 2009).
56. Howard Thurman, *Deep Is the Hunger* (Richmond, IN: Friends United Press, 1978), 80.

Chapter 9. What Does Thriving Daily Look Like?

1. Brené Brown, *Rising Strong: How the Ability to Reset Transforms the Way We Live, Love, Parent, and Lead* (New York: Random House Trade Paperbacks, 2017), 255.
2. "The Purpose Challenge," The Purpose Challenge, August 5, 2017, https://purposechallenge.org/why-purpose/.
3. "Greater Good: The Science of a Meaningful Life," Greater Good, https://greatergood.berkeley.edu.
4. Austin Channing Brown, *I'm Still Here: Black Dignity in a World Made for Whiteness* (New York: Convergent Books, 2018), 181.
5. Patrick Reyes, "Wanted: Dead or Alive," TheoEd Talks, https://theoed.com/watch.
6. Ending Mass Incarceration: Faith Communities Working to Transform Justice, http://emi.odyssey-impact.org/.
7. Walter S. Gilliam et al., "Do Early Educators' Implicit Biases Regarding Sex and Race Relate to Behavior Expectations and Recommendations of Preschool Expulsions and Suspensions?" 2016, 18, https://medicine.yale.edu/childstudy/zigler/publications/Preschool%20Implicit%20Bias%20Policy%20Brief_final_9_26_276766_5379_v1.pdf.
8. Gilliam et al., "Do Early Educators'?"
9. "Criminal Justice Facts," The Sentencing Project, https://www.sentencingproject.org/criminal-justice-facts/.
10. Daniel J. Brown et al., "Human Thriving: A Conceptual Debate and Literature Review," *European Psychologist* 22, no. 3 (July 2017): 168, https://doi.org/10.1027/1016-9040/a000294.
11. Forum for Theological Exploration, "Create Conditions for Scholars of Color to Thrive: 2018 Doctoral Consultation Report," https://fteleaders.org/pages/create-conditions-for-scholars-of-color-to-thrive.
12. "Educational Attainment in the United States: 2019," U.S. Census Bureau, https://www.census.gov/data/tables/2019/demo/educational-attainment/cps-detailed-tables.html.
13. "Key Facts," California Community Colleges, https://www.cccco.edu/About-Us/Key-Facts.
14. Roxane Gay, *Hunger: A Memoir of (My) Body* (New York: Harper Perennial, 2018), 5.
15. María Del Socorro Castañeda-Liles, *Our Lady of Everyday Life: La Virgen de Guadalupe and the Catholic Imagination of Mexican Women in America* (New York: Oxford University Press, 2018).

16. Boaventura de Sousa Santos, *The End of the Cognitive Empire: The Coming of Age of Epistemologies of the South* (Durham, NC: Duke University Press, 2018), 3.

17. Santos, *The End of the Cognitive Empire*, 2.

18. Santos offers this warning as well: "People trained in the written knowledge predominant today tend to be incapable of listening to unwritten knowledges. They may hear them when they are spoken, yet still cannot in truth listen to them. That is to say, they do not understand the silences, what is implicit in what is actually being said, or what can only be said and never written down. From the point of view of written knowledge, the absence of deep listening is not a problem; rather, it is a condition to strengthen the capacity to distinguish relevant (written) from irrelevant (oral) knowledge." Santos, *The End of the Cognitive Empire*, 56.

19. Christiana Figueres and Tom Rivett-Carnac, *The Future We Choose: Surviving the Climate Crisis* (New York: Knopf, 2020), 7.

20. Figueres and Rivett-Carnac, *The Future We Choose*, 37.

21. Paulo Freire, *Pedagogy of Hope: Reliving Pedagogy of the Oppressed* (New York: Continuum, 1998).

22. "Children's Exposure to Violence," Child Trends (blog), https://www.childtrends.org/indicators/childrens-exposure-to-violence.

23. "Violence against Women," https://www.who.int/news-room/fact-sheets/detail/violence-against-women.

24. "Poverty Facts," https://www.povertyusa.org/facts.

25. Walter D. Mignolo, *The Darker Side of Western Modernity: Global Futures, Decolonial Options* (Durham, NC: Duke University Press, 2011), 176.

Selected Bibliography

Acevedo, Elizabeth. *Clap When You Land*. New York: Quill Tree Books, 2020.

———. *The Poet X*. New York: Quill Tree Books, 2020.

Alexander, Michelle. *The New Jim Crow: Mass Incarceration in the Age of Colorblindness*. New York: The New Press, 2020.

Allende, Isabel. *The House of the Spirits*. New York: Atria Books, 2015.

Alvarez, Julia. *Afterlife*. Chapel Hill, NC: Algonquin Books, 2020.

———. *How the Garcia Girls Lost Their Accents*. Chapel Hill, NC: Algonquin Books, 1991.

———. *In the Time of the Butterflies*. Reprint edition. Chapel Hill, NC: Algonquin Books, 2010.

Alves, Rubem. *Tomorrow's Child: Imagination, Creativity, and the Rebirth of Culture*. Eugene, OR: Wipf & Stock Publishers, 2011.

———. *Poet, the Warrior, the Prophet*. London: Hymns Ancient & Modern Ltd., 2002.

Anaya, Rudolfo A. *Bless Me, Ultima*. New York: Grand Central Publishing, 1999.

Anzaldúa, Gloria. *Borderlands / La Frontera: The New Mestiza*. San Francisco: Aunt Lute Books, 2007.

———. *Light in the Dark /* Luz En Lo Oscuro: *Rewriting Identity, Spirituality, Reality*. Edited by AnaLouise Keating. Durham, NC: Duke University Press, 2015.

Apple, Michael, ed. *Knowledge, Power, and Education*. New York: Routledge, 2014.

Ayres, Jennifer R. *Inhabitance: Ecological Religious Education*. Waco, TX: Baylor University Press, 2019.

Baca, Jimmy Santiago. *A Place to Stand*. New York: Grove Press, 2002.

———. *Immigrants in Our Own Land & Selected Early Poems*. New York: New Directions, 1990.

Baker, Dori Grinenko, and Joyce A. Mercer. *Lives to Offer: Accompanying Youth on Their Vocational Quests*. Cleveland: Pilgrim Press, 2007.

Baldwin, James. *The Fire Next Time*. New York: Vintage, 1992.

Bass, Diana Butler. *Grounded: Finding God in the World—A Spiritual Revolution*. Princeton, NJ: HarperOne, 2015.

Bear, Dorothy Aguilera-Black, and John W. Tippeconnic III, eds. *Voices of Resistance and Renewal: Indigenous Leadership in Education*. Norman: University of Oklahoma Press, 2015.

Berry, Wendell. *Jayber Crow*. New York: Counterpoint, 2001.

Block, Peter. *Community: The Structure of Belonging*. Oakland, CA: Berrett-Koehler Publishers, 2018.

Blount, Reginald. *Cultivating Teen Faith: Insights from the Confirmation Project*. Edited by Richard R. Osmer and Katherine M. Douglass. Grand Rapids: Wm. B. Eerdmans Publishing Co., 2018.

Boal, Augusto. *Theatre of the Oppressed*. Translated by Charles A. McBride. New York: Theatre Communications Group, 1993.

Bonhoeffer, Dietrich. *Life Together: The Classic Exploration of Christian in Community*. Princeton, NJ: HarperOne, 2009.

Bonhoeffer, Dietrich, and Eric Metaxas. *The Cost of Discipleship*. New York: Touchstone, 1995.

Boyle, Gregory. *Barking to the Choir: The Power of Radical Kinship*. New York: Simon & Schuster, 2018.

———. *Tattoos on the Heart: The Power of Boundless Compassion*. New York: Free Press, 2011.

"Breaking2." https://www.nike.com/us/en_us/c/running/breaking2.

Brokaw, Tom. *The Greatest Generation*. New York: Random House Trade Paperbacks, 2001.

Bronte, Charlotte. *Jane Eyre*. CreateSpace Independent Publishing Platform, 2015.

Brooks, David. *The Second Mountain: The Quest for a Moral Life*. New York: Random House, 2019.

———. *The Social Animal: The Hidden Sources of Love, Character, and Achievement*. New York: Random House Trade Paperbacks, 2012.

brown, adrienne maree. *Emergent Strategy: Shaping Change, Changing Worlds*. Chico, CA: AK Press, 2017.

Brown, Austin Channing. *I'm Still Here: Black Dignity in a World Made for Whiteness*. New York: Convergent Books, 2018.

Brown, Brené. *Daring Greatly: How the Courage to Be Vulnerable Transforms the Way We Live, Love, Parent, and Lead*. New York: Avery, 2015.

———. *Rising Strong: How the Ability to Reset Transforms the Way We Live, Love, Parent, and Lead*. New York: Random House Trade Paperbacks, 2017.

Brown, Daniel J., Rachel Arnold, David Fletcher, and Martyn Standage. "Human Thriving: A Conceptual Debate and Literature Review." *European Psychologist* 22, no. 3 (July 2017): 167–79. https://doi.org/10.1027/1016-9040/a000294.

Brown, Tim. *Change by Design: How Design Thinking Transforms Organizations and Inspires Innovation*. New York: Harper Business, 2009.

Bui, Thi. *The Best We Could Do: An Illustrated Memoir*. New York: Harry N. Abrams, 2018.

Burnett, Bill, and Dave Evans. *Designing Your Life: How to Build a Well-Lived, Joyful Life*. New York: Knopf, 2016.

———. *Designing Your Work Life: How to Thrive and Change and Find Happiness at Work*. New York: Knopf, 2020.

Butler, Octavia. *Bloodchild and Other Stories*. New York: Seven Stories Press, 2005.

———. *Dawn*. New York: Warner Aspect, 1997.

———. *Kindred*. Boston: Beacon Press, 1979.

———. *Parable of the Sower*. New York: Grand Central Publishing, 2019.

Cahalan, Kathleen A. *The Stories We Live: Finding God's Calling All around Us*. Grand Rapids: Wm. B. Eerdmans Publishing Co., 2017.

"California City Fights Poverty with Guaranteed Income." *Reuters*, June 6, 2018. https://www.reuters.com/article/us-california-income-idUSKCN1J015D.

Camus, Albert. *The Rebel: An Essay on Man in Revolt*. New York: Vintage, 1992.

Casas, Bartolome de Las, and Anthony Pagden. *A Short Account of the Destruction of the Indies*. Translated by Nigel Griffin. New York: Penguin Classics, 1999.

Castañeda-Liles, María Del Socorro. *Our Lady of Everyday Life: La Virgen de Guadalupe and the Catholic Imagination of Mexican Women in America*. New York: Oxford University Press, 2018.

Castillo, Ana. *Black Dove: Mamá, Mi'jo, and Me*. New York: Feminist Press at CUNY, 2016.

———. *So Far from God*. New York: W. W. Norton, 2005.

Chávez, César. "1984 Cesar Chavez Address to the Commonwealth Club of California | GVLIBRARIES.ORG." http://www.gvlibraries.org/content/1984-cesar-chavez-address-commonwealth-club-california.

Child Trends. "Children's Exposure to Violence." https://www.childtrends.org/indicators/childrens-exposure-to-violence.

Christensen, Clayton M. *The Innovator's Dilemma: When New Technologies Cause Great Firms to Fail*. Boston: Harvard Business Review Press, 2016.

Christensen, Clayton M., James Allworth, and Karen Dillon. *How Will You Measure Your Life?* New York: Harper Business, 2012.

Coelho, Paulo. *The Alchemist, 25th Anniversary: A Fable about Following Your Dream*. Anniversary edition. San Francisco: HarperOne, 2014.

Collins, Jim. *Good to Great: Why Some Companies Make the Leap and Others Don't*. New York: Harper Business, 2001.

Conde-Frazier, Elizabeth. *Listen to the Children: Conversations with Immigrant Families / Escuchemos a los niños: Conversaciones Con Familias Inmigrantes*. Bilingual edition. Valley Forge: Judson Press, 2011.

Cone, James H., and Cornel West. *Black Theology and Black Power*. Anniversary edition. Maryknoll: Orbis Books, 2019.

Costanza-Chock, Sasha. *Design Justice: Community-Led Practices to Build the Worlds We Need*. Cambridge: The MIT Press, 2020.

Craemer, Thomas. "Estimating Slavery Reparations: Present Value Comparisons of Historical Multigenerational Reparations Policies." *Social Science Quarterly* 96, no. 2 (2015): 639–55. https://doi.org/10.1111/ssqu.12151.

"Criminal Justice Facts." The Sentencing Project. https://www.sentencingproject.org/criminal-justice-facts/.

Crouch, Andy. *Playing God: Redeeming the Gift of Power*. 9.6.2013 edition. Downers Grove, IL: IVP Books, 2013.

Crow, Michael M., and Willam B. Dabars. *Designing the New American University*. Baltimore: Johns Hopkins University Press, 2015.

Cullen, Jim. *The American Dream: A Short History of an Idea That Shaped a Nation*. 9th print edition. Oxford: Oxford University Press, 2004.

Cunningham, David S., ed. *At This Time and In This Place: Vocation and Higher Education*. New York: Oxford University Press, 2015.

———, ed. *Hearing Vocation Differently: Meaning, Purpose, and Identity in the Multi-Faith Academy*. New York: Oxford University Press, 2019.

Dawson, Ben. "CDF Freedom Schools Program." *Children's Defense Fund* (blog). https://www.childrensdefense.org/programs/cdf-freedom-schools/.

Day, Dorothy. *The Long Loneliness: The Autobiography of the Legendary Catholic Social Activist.* San Francisco: HarperOne, 2009.

Diamond, Jared. *Guns, Germs, and Steel: The Fates of Human Societies.* New York: W. W. Norton, 2017.

DiAngelo, Robin. *White Fragility: Why It's So Hard for White People to Talk about Racism.* Boston: Beacon Press, 2018.

Duckworth, Angela. *Grit: The Power of Passion and Perseverance.* New York: Scribner, 2018.

Dunbar-Ortiz, Roxanne. *An Indigenous Peoples' History of the United States.* Boston: Beacon Press, 2015.

Dussel, Enrique D. *A History of the Church in Latin America: Colonialism to Liberation.* Grand Rapids: Wm. B. Eerdmans Publishing Co., 1982.

Dussel, Enrique, and Linda Martín Alcoff. *Pedagogics of Liberation: A Latin American Philosophy of Education.* Translated by David I. Backer and Cecilia Diego. Santa Barbara, CA: Punctum Books, 2019.

Edelman, Marian Wright. *The Measure of Our Success: A Letter to My Children and Yours.* Reprint edition. New York: Harper Perennial, 1993.

———. *The Sea Is So Wide and My Boat Is So Small: Charting a Course for the Next Generation.* New York: Hyperion, 2008.

"Educational Attainment in the United States: 2019." United States Census Bureau. https://www.census.gov/data/tables/2019/demo/educational-attainment/cps-detailed-tables.html.

Enders, Giulia. *Gut: The Inside Story of Our Body's Most Underrated Organ.* Vancouver: Greystone Books, 2018.

"Ending Mass Incarceration | Faith Communities Working to Transform Justice." http://emi.odyssey-impact.org/.

Escobar, Arturo. *Designs for the Pluriverse: Radical Interdependence, Autonomy, and the Making of Worlds.* Durham, NC: Duke University Press, 2018.

Esquivel, Laura. *Malinche.* Translated by Ernesto Mestre-Reed. New York: Atria Books, 2007.

"Family Separation by the Numbers." American Civil Liberties Union. https://www.aclu.org/issues/immigrants-rights/immigrants-rights-and-detention/family-separation.

Fanon, Frantz, Jean-Paul Sartre, and Homi K. Bhabha. *The Wretched of the Earth.* Translated by Richard Philcox. New York: Grove Press, 2005.

Figueres, Christiana, and Tom Rivett-Carnac. *The Future We Choose: Surviving the Climate Crisis.* New York: Knopf, 2020.

Fitzpatrick, Kathleen. *Generous Thinking: A Radical Approach to Saving the University.* Baltimore: Johns Hopkins University Press, 2019.

Fluker, Walter E. *The Ground Has Shifted: The Future of the Black Church in Post-Racial America.* New York: NYU Press, 2018.

Forum for Theological Exploration. "Create Conditions for Scholars of Color to Thrive: 2018 Doctoral Consultation Report. https://fteleaders.org/pages/create-conditions-for-scholars-of-color-to-thrive.

Foucault, Michel. *Power.* Edited by James D. Faubion. Translated by Robert Hurley. New York: The New Press, 2001.

Frankl, Viktor E. *Man's Search for Meaning.* Foreword by Harold S. Kushner. Afterword by William J. Winslade. Boston: Beacon Press, 2006.

Freire, Paulo. *Pedagogy of the Heart*. New York: Bloomsbury Academic, 2016.

———. *Pedagogy of Hope: Reliving Pedagogy of the Oppressed*. New York: Continuum, 1998.

———. *Pedagogy of the Oppressed, 30th Anniversary Edition*. Translated by Myra Bergman Ramos. New York: Continuum, 2000.

Freire, Paulo, Stanley Aronowitz, and Donaldo Macedo. *Pedagogy of Freedom: Ethics, Democracy, and Civic Courage*. Translated by Patrick Clarke. Lanham, MD: Rowman & Littlefield Publishers, 2000.

Freire, Paulo, and Henry A. Giroux. *The Politics of Education: Culture, Power and Liberation*. Translated by Donaldo Macedo. South Hadley, MA: Bergin & Garvey Publishers, 1985.

Gafney, Wilda C. *Daughters of Miriam: Women Prophets in Ancient Israel*. Minneapolis: Fortress Press, 2008.

Ganz, Marshall. *Why David Sometimes Wins: Leadership, Organization, and Strategy in the California Farm Worker Movement*. New York: Oxford University Press, 2010.

Gay, Roxane. *Hunger: A Memoir of (My) Body*. New York: Harper Perennial, 2018.

Giroux, Henry A. *Between Borders: Pedagogy and the Politics of Cultural Studies*. East Sussex, UK: Psychology Press, 1994.

———. *Fugitive Cultures: Race, Violence, and Youth*. New York: Routledge, 1996.

———. *On Critical Pedagogy*. New York: Continuum, 2011.

Gladwell, Malcolm. *Blink: The Power of Thinking without Thinking*. New York: Back Bay Books, 2007.

———. *Outliers: The Story of Success*. New York: Back Bay Books, 2011.

———. *Talking to Strangers: What We Should Know about the People We Don't Know*. New York: Little, Brown, 2019.

Glissant, Édouard. *Poetics of Relation*. Translated by Betsy Wing. Ann Arbor: University of Michigan Press, 1997.

Godin, Seth. *Tribes: We Need You to Lead Us*. New York: Portfolio, 2008.

Gramsci, Antonio, and Antonio Callari. *Prison Notebooks*. Translated by Joseph A. Buttigieg. SLP edition. Vol. 2. 3 vols. New York: Columbia University Press, 2011.

———. *Prison Notebooks*. Translated by Joseph A. Buttigieg. Vol. 3. 3 vols. New York: Columbia University Press, 2011.

Grant, Adam, and Sheryl Sandberg. *Originals: How Non-Conformists Move the World*. New York: Penguin Books, 2016.

Guerrero, Andrés G. *A Chicano Theology*. Eugene, OR: Wipf and Stock, 2008.

Hale, Jon. *The Freedom Schools: Student Activists in the Mississippi Civil Rights Movement*. New York: Columbia University Press, 2018.

Harvey, Jennifer, and Tim Wise. *Raising White Kids: Bringing Up Children in a Racially Unjust America*. Nashville: Abingdon Press, 2018.

Heifetz, Ronald. *Leadership without Easy Answers*. Cambridge, MA: Harvard University Press, 1998.

Helsel, Carolyn, and Y. Joy Harris-Smith. *The ABCs of Diversity: Helping Kids (and Ourselves!) Embrace Our Differences*. St. Louis: Chalice Press, 2020.

Hernández, Roberto D. *Coloniality of the US/Mexico Border: Power, Violence, and the Decolonial Imperative*. Phoenix: University of Arizona Press, 2018.

Herrera, Hayden. *Frida: The Biography of Frida Kahlo*. London: Bloomsbury Publishing, 1989.

Hildreth, Paul. *Knowledge Networks: Innovation through Communities of Practice.* Edited by Chris Kimble. Hershey, PA: IGI Global, 2003.

Hinojosa, Rolando. *The Valley / Estampas Del Valle.* Bilingual edition. Houston: Arte Publico Press, 2014.

———. *A Voice of My Own: Essays and Stories.* Houston: Arte Publico Press, 2011.

Hinojosa-Cisneros, Carolina. *Becoming Coztōtōtl.* McAllen, TX: FlowerSong Books, 2019.

hooks, bell. *Killing Rage.* New York: Holt Paperbacks, 1996.

———. *Teaching Community: A Pedagogy of Hope.* New York: Routledge, 2003.

———. *Teaching Critical Thinking: Practical Wisdom.* New York: Routledge, 2009.

———. *Teaching to Transgress: Education as the Practice of Freedom.* New York: Routledge, 1994.

Hurston, Zora Neale, *Barracoon: The Story of the Last "Black Cargo."* Edited by Deborah G. Plant. Foreword by Alice Walker. New York: Amistad, 2020.

Iger, Robert. *The Ride of a Lifetime: Lessons Learned from 15 Years as CEO of the Walt Disney Company.* New York: Random House Large Print, 2019.

Jones, Robert P. *The End of White Christian America.* New York: Simon & Schuster, 2017.

Kamp, David. *Sunny Days: The Children's Television Revolution That Changed America.* New York: Simon & Schuster, 2020.

Kelley, Alexandra. "Attacks on Asian Americans Skyrocket to 100 per Day during Coronavirus Pandemic." The Hill, March 31, 2020. https://thehill.com/changing -america/respect/equality/490373-attacks-on-asian-americans-at-about-100-per-day -due-to.

Kendi, Ibram X. *How to Be an Antiracist.* New York: One World, 2019.

———. *Stamped from the Beginning: The Definitive History of Racist Ideas in America.* New York: Bold Type Books, 2017.

Kincheloe, Joe L. *Critical Pedagogy Primer.* Second edition. New York: International Academic Publishers, 2008.

King, Martin Luther Jr., Vincent Harding, and Coretta Scott King. *Where Do We Go from Here: Chaos or Community?* Boston: Beacon Press, 2010.

Knapp, Jake, and John Zeratsky. *Make Time: How to Focus on What Matters Every Day.* New York: Currency, 2018.

Knapp, Jake, John Zeratsky, and Braden Kowitz. *Sprint: How to Solve Big Problems and Test New Ideas in Just Five Days.* New York: Simon & Schuster, 2016.

Kondō, Marie. *Spark Joy: An Illustrated Master Class on the Art of Organizing and Tidying Up.* Illustrated edition. Berkeley, CA: Ten Speed Press, 2016.

Kondō, Marie, and Scott Sonenshein. *Joy at Work: Organizing Your Professional Life.* New York: Little, Brown Spark, 2020.

Laura E. Pérez. "Writing with Crooked Lines." In *Fleshing the Spirit: Spirituality and Activism in Chicana, Latina, and Indigenous Women's Lives.* Edited by Elisa Facio and Irene Lara. Tucson: University of Arizona Press, 2014.

Leon, Luis D. *The Political Spirituality of Cesar Chavez: Crossing Religious Borders.* Oakland: University of California Press, 2014.

Lewis, Sarah. *The Rise: Creativity, the Gift of Failure, and the Search for Mastery.* New York: Simon & Schuster, 2015.

Lewis, Stephen, Matthew Wesley Williams, and Dori Baker. *Another Way: Living and Leading Change on Purpose.* St. Louis: Chalice Press, 2020.

Liedtka, Jeanne, and Tim Ogilvie. *Designing for Growth: A Design Thinking Tool Kit for Managers*. New York: Columbia Business School Publishing, 2011.

Liedtka, Jeanne, Randy Salzman, and Daisy Azer. *Design Thinking for the Greater Good: Innovation in the Social Sector*. New York: Columbia Business School Publishing, 2017.

Lomong, Lopez, and Mark Tabb. *Running for My Life: One Lost Boy's Journey from the Killing Fields of Sudan to the Olympic Games*. Nashville: Thomas Nelson, 2016.

Maldonado-Torres, Nelson. *Against War: Views from the Underside of Modernity*. Durham, NC: Duke University Press, 2008.

Marquez, Gabriel Garcia. *One Hundred Years of Solitude*. Translated by Gregory Rabassa. New York: Harper Perennial Modern Classics, 2006.

McLafferty, Sara, and Valerie Preston. "Who Has Long Commutes to Low-Wage Jobs? Gender, Race, and Access to Work in the New York Region." *Urban Geography* 40, no. 9 (October 21, 2019): 1270–90. https://doi.org/10.1080/02723638.2019.1577091.

Merton, Thomas. *No Man Is an Island*. San Diego: Mariner Books, 2002.

———. *The Seven Storey Mountain*. San Diego: Mariner Books, 1999.

Mignolo, Walter D. *The Darker Side of Western Modernity: Global Futures, Decolonial Options*. Durham, NC: Duke University Press, 2011.

———. *The Idea of Latin America*. Oxford: Blackwell Publishing, 2005.

———. *Local Histories / Global Designs: Coloniality, Subaltern Knowledges, and Border Thinking*. With a new preface by the author. Princeton, NJ: Princeton University Press, 2012.

Moraga, Cherríe. *Loving in the War Years: Lo Que Nunca Pasó Por Sus Labios*. Boston: South End Press, 1983.

Moraga, Cherríe L. *A Xicana Codex of Changing Consciousness: Writings, 2000–2010*. Durham, NC: Duke University Press, 2011.

Moraga, Cherríe, and Gloria Anzaldúa, eds. *This Bridge Called My Back: Writings by Radical Women of Color*. New York: New York University Press, 2015.

Morales, Yuyi. *Dreamers*. New York: Scholastic, 2020.

Morrison, Toni. *Beloved*. New York: Vintage, 2004.

Nanko-Fernandez, Carmen. *Theologizing En Espanglish: Context, Community, and Ministry*. Maryknoll, NY: Orbis Books, 2010.

Newport, Cal. *Deep Work: Rules for Focused Success in a Distracted World*. New York: Grand Central Publishing, 2016.

———. *Digital Minimalism: Choosing a Focused Life in a Noisy World*. New York: Portfolio/ Penguin, 2019.

O'Connor, Flannery. *The Complete Stories*. New York: Farrar, Straus and Giroux, 1971.

Orange, Tommy. *There There*. New York: Vintage, 2019.

Page, Scott E. *Diversity and Complexity*. Princeton, NJ: Princeton University Press, 2010.

Palmer, Parker J. *The Active Life: A Spirituality of Work, Creativity, and Caring*. San Francisco: Jossey-Bass, 1999.

———. *The Courage to Teach: Exploring the Inner Landscape of a Teacher's Life*. San Francisco: Jossey-Bass, 1997.

———. *Let Your Life Speak: Listening for the Voice of Vocation*. San Francisco: Jossey-Bass, 1999.

Parker, Priya. *The Art of Gathering: How We Meet and Why It Matters*. New York: Riverhead Books, 2018.

Paz, Octavio. *The Labyrinth of Solitude: The Other Mexico, Return to the Labyrinth of Solitude, Mexico and the United States, the Philanthropic Ogre.* New York: Grove Press, 1994.

Peña, Matt de la. *Carmela Full of Wishes.* New York: G. P. Putnam's Sons Books for Young Readers, 2018.

———. *Love.* New York: G. P. Putnam's Sons Books for Young Readers, 2018.

———. *Mexican White Boy.* New York: Ember, 2010.

Petrella, Ivan. *The Future of Liberation Theology: An Argument and Manifesto.* Burlington, VT: Ashgate, 2004.

Pink, Daniel H. *Drive: The Surprising Truth about What Motivates Us.* New York: Riverhead Books, 2011.

Placher, William C., ed. *Callings: Twenty Centuries of Christian Wisdom on Vocation.* Grand Rapids: Wm. B. Eerdmans Publishing Co., 2005.

Potok, Chaim. *My Name Is Asher Lev.* New York: Anchor, 2009.

Powell, Colin. *It Worked for Me: In Life and Leadership.* New York: Harper Perennial, 2014.

Preskill, Stephen, and Stephen D. Brookfield. *Learning as a Way of Leading: Lessons from the Struggle for Social Justice.* San Francisco: Jossey-Bass, 2008.

Putnam, Robert D. *Our Kids: The American Dream in Crisis.* New York: Simon & Schuster, 2016.

Rabb, Chris. *Invisible Capital: How Unseen Forces Shape Entrepreneurial Opportunity.* San Francisco: Berrett-Koehler Publishers, 2010.

Reich, Robert B. *The Common Good.* Vintage, 2019.

Rendón, Laura I., and Mark Nepo. *Sentipensante (Sensing/Thinking) Pedagogy: Educating for Wholeness, Social Justice and Liberation.* Sterling, VA: Stylus Publishing, 2008.

Reyes, Patrick B. *Nobody Cries When We Die: God, Community, and Surviving to Adulthood.* St. Louis: Chalice Press, 2016.

———. "Practical Theology as Knowledge of Origin and Migration: An Essay." In *Let Your Light Shine: Mobilizing for Justice with Children and Youth.* Edited by Virginia A. Lee and Reginald Blount, 121–34. New York: Friendship Press, 2019.

Ridge, John Rollin, and Diana Gabaldon. *The Life and Adventures of Joaquín Murieta: The Celebrated California Bandit.* Edited by Hsuan L. Hsu. New York: Penguin Classics, 2018.

Rivera, Diego, and Gladys March. *My Art, My Life: An Autobiography.* New York: Dover Publications, 1992.

Rodriguez, Luis J. *Always Running: La Vida Loca: Gang Days in L.A.* New York: Atria Books, 2005.

———. *It Calls You Back: An Odyssey through Love, Addiction, Revolutions, and Healing.* New York: Atria Books, 2012.

Rodriguez, Patty, and Ariana Stein. *The Solar System with Ellen—El Sistema Solar Con Ellen.* Bilingual edition. Los Angeles: Lil' Libros, 2020.

Rodriguez, Richard. *Brown: The Last Discovery of America.* New York: Penguin Books, 2003.

———. *Darling: A Spiritual Autobiography.* New York: Penguin Books, 2014.

———. *Hunger of Memory: The Education of Richard Rodriguez.* New York: Dial Press Trade Paperback, 2004.

Rogers, Frank. *Practicing Compassion.* Nashville: Fresh Air Books, 2014.

Romero, Robert Chao. *Brown Church: Five Centuries of Latina/o Social Justice, Theology, and Identity.* Downers Grove, IL: IVP Academic, 2020.

Romero, Rolando, and Amanda Nolacea Harris, eds. *Feminism, Nation and Myth: La Malinche.* Houston, TX: Arte Publico Press, 2005.

Romero, Simon. "Migrants Are Detained under a Bridge in El Paso. What Happened?" *The New York Times*, March 29, 2019, sec. U.S. https://www.nytimes.com/2019/03/29/us /el-paso-immigration-photo.html.

Rothstein, Richard. *The Color of Law: A Forgotten History of How Our Government Segregated America*. New York: Liveright, 2018.

Sachs, Jonah. *Winning the Story Wars: Why Those Who Tell (and Live) the Best Stories Will Rule the Future*. Boston: Harvard Business Review Press, 2012.

Saldívar, José David. *Trans-Americanity: Subaltern Modernities, Global Coloniality, and the Cultures of Greater Mexico*. Edited by Donald E. Pease. Durham, NC: Duke University Press, 2011.

Salinger, J. D. *The Catcher in the Rye*. Boston: Back Bay Books, 2001.

Sánchez, Erika L. *I Am Not Your Perfect Mexican Daughter*. New York: Knopf Books for Young Readers, 2017.

Sandberg, Sheryl. *Lean In for Graduates: With New Chapters by Experts, Including* Find Your First Job, Negotiate Your Salary, *and* Own Who You Are. New York: Knopf, 2014.

Santiago, Esmeralda. *Almost a Woman*. Reading, MA: Perseus Books, 1998.

Santos, Boaventura de Sousa. *The End of the Cognitive Empire: The Coming of Age of Epistemologies of the South*. Durham, NC: Duke University Press, 2018.

Schultz, Howard, and Joanne Gordon. *Onward: How Starbucks Fought for Its Life without Losing Its Soul*. New York: Rodale Books, 2012.

Schwartz, Richard C., and Martha Sweezy. *Internal Family Systems Therapy*. New York: Guilford Press, 2019.

Schwehn, Mark R., and Dorothy C. Bass, eds. *Leading Lives That Matter: What We Should Do and Who We Should Be*. Grand Rapids: Wm. B. Eerdmans Publishing Co., 2020.

Segal, Gilly, and Kimberly Jones. *I'm Not Dying with You Tonight*. Naperville, IL: Sourcebooks Fire, 2019.

Shapiro, Thomas M. *Toxic Inequality: How America's Wealth Gap Destroys Mobility, Deepens the Racial Divide, and Threatens Our Future*. New York: Basic Books, 2017.

Shetterly, Margot Lee. *Hidden Figures: The American Dream and the Untold Story of the Black Women Mathematicians Who Helped Win the Space Race*. New York: William Morrow Paperbacks, 2016.

Shor, Ira. *Empowering Education: Critical Teaching for Social Change*. Chicago: University of Chicago Press, 1992.

Siegel, Daniel J., and Tina Payne Bryson. *The Power of Showing Up: How Parental Presence Shapes Who Our Kids Become and How Their Brains Get Wired*. New York: Ballantine Books, 2020.

Simpson, Leanne Betasamosake. *As We Have Always Done: Indigenous Freedom through Radical Resistance*. 3rd ed. Minneapolis: University of Minnesota Press, 2017.

———. *This Accident of Being Lost: Songs and Stories*. Toronto, ON: Astoria, 2017.

Sims, Angela D. *Lynched: The Power of Memory in a Culture of Terror*. Waco, TX: Baylor University Press, 2017.

Smyth, John. *Critical Pedagogy for Social Justice*. New York: Continuum, 2011.

Stevenson, Bryan. *Just Mercy: A Story of Justice and Redemption*. New York: One World, 2015.

Suarez, Cyndi. *The Power Manual: How to Master Complex Power Dynamics*. Gabriola Island, BC: New Society Publishers, 2018.

Tatum, Beverly Daniel. *Why Are All the Black Kids Sitting Together in the Cafeteria? And Other Conversations about Race*. New York: Basic Books, 2017.

Thurman, Howard. *Deep Is the Hunger*. Richmond, IN: Friends United Press, 1978.

———. *For the Inward Journey: The Writings of Howard Thurman*. San Diego: Harcourt Brace Jovanovich, 1984.

Townsend, Camilla. *Fifth Sun: A New History of the Aztecs*. New York: Oxford University Press, 2019.

Treuer, David. *The Heartbeat of Wounded Knee: Native America from 1890 to the Present*. New York: Riverhead Books, 2019.

Trounstine, Jessica. *Segregation by Design: Local Politics and Inequality in American Cities*. New York: Cambridge University Press, 2018.

van der Kolk, Bessel. *The Body Keeps the Score: Brain, Mind, and Body in the Healing of Trauma*. New York: Penguin Books, 2015.

Vuong, Ocean. *On Earth We're Briefly Gorgeous*. New York: Penguin Press, 2019.

Warren, Rick. *The Purpose Driven Life: What on Earth Am I Here For?* 10th Anniversary edition. Grand Rapids: Zondervan, 2013.

Wheatley, Margaret J. *Who Do We Choose to Be? Facing Reality, Claiming Leadership, Restoring Sanity*. Oakland, CA: Berrett-Koehler Publishers, 2017.

Wiesel, Elie. *Night*. Translated by Marion Wiesel. New York: Hill and Wang, 2006.

Wink, Walter. *Engaging the Powers: Discernment and Resistance in a World of Domination*. Minneapolis: Fortress Press, 1992.

Woodson, Carter Godwin. *The Mis-Education of the Negro*. Edited by Tony Darnell. Suwanee, GA: 12th Media Services, 2017.

Yugar, Theresa A. *Sor Juana Inés de La Cruz: Feminist Reconstruction of Biography and Text*. Eugene, OR: Wipf and Stock, 2014.

Index

CPSIA information can be obtained
at www.ICGtesting.com
Printed in the USA
LVHW050717180222
711231LV00003B/6